Advance Uncorrected Proof

This copy is supplied for review purposes only, and for limited distribution. As the work is still under review by the author and the publisher, there may be corrections, deletions, or other changes before publication. **Not for resale.**

THE EYE YOU SEE WITH

The
EYE YOU
SEE WITH — 166

Selected Nonfiction

ROBERT STONE

Edited by Madison Smartt Bell

Houghton Mifflin Harcourt
Boston · New York
2020

For information about permission to reproduce selections from this book, write to trade.permissions@hmhco.com or to Permissions, Houghton Mifflin Harcourt Publishing Company, 3 Park Avenue, 19th Floor, New York, New York 10016.

hmhbooks.com

Library of Congress Cataloging-in-Publication Data
CIP data TK

Book design by Chloe Foster

Printed in the United States of America
DOC 10 9 8 7 6 5 4 3 2 1

Acknowledgments

My thanks to Lauren Wein and Pilar Garcia-Brown for helping the wheels turn smoothly, and to Janice Stone for her meticulous cataloging of the corpus of Robert Stone's nonfiction. Thanks to Anna Young for rendering order out of the chaos of the raw materials of this book. Larry Cooper was the manuscript editor for several of Stone's most important books (not to mention several of mine); to work with him on this volume was a boon. —*MSB*

Contents

THE HEART OF THIS STRANGE STORY

Introduction

A ll American novelists are embarked on a search for meaning; Robert Stone conducted his version of the quest in a
style and within a structure uniquely his own. We assume too
that our writers are products of their origins. Stone's origins
were obscure, his childhood difficult, his youth quite seriously
dangerous. A weaker, less talented and intelligent person would
not have survived those circumstances, much less prevailed in
the way that Stone did, as a great artist and as a pellucid, un-
flinching observer and analyst of the time in which he lived.

The "Homer Stone" on his birth certificate was perhaps a
convenient fiction. Born in 1937, Robert Stone was raised by
his mother, Gladys Grant, a couple of generations before single motherhood would come to be viewed as a socially acceptable, even admirable, "lifestyle choice." Gladys was an unusual
and in some ways a redoubtable person, a cosmopolitan whose
enactment of her independent spirit was many decades ahead
of her time. She also suffered from progressively worsening
mental illness, which meant that when Stone was a small boy

she lost her job as a schoolteacher and the relative stability that went with it.

With his mother hospitalized, Stone was catapulted from a reasonably comfortable New York apartment to the orphans' dormitory of St. Ann's school on Lexington Avenue. After a few years Gladys was able to bring him "home," though in fact they were sometimes homeless, in Chicago and in New York. At ten, eleven, twelve years old, Stone was a street urchin living by his wits, developing his first skills as a fiction writer by inventing stories to keep out of the clutches of Child Protective Services. In his middle teens he joined a street gang called the Saxons. New York youth gangs fought with knives rather than firearms back then. Some were killed, nevertheless, not only by steel but, increasingly, by heroin.

Expelled from his senior year at Saint Ann's high school for a range of rebellious behavior, Stone joined the US Navy at age seventeen. During the three-year cruise, he continued his education as an autodidact, reading everything he could get his hands on, from Conrad to Kerouac. He also wrote some short fiction shipboard, and at the end of his enlistment, he was on his way to becoming one of the great writers of the late twentieth century. One might have called it a Horatio Alger rags-to-riches story, except that Stone, who in no way resembled any Alger hero, would have dismissed any such idea with scornful laughter.

Though he wore a cynical carapace, Stone was not really a cynic. His satirical bent, and the considerable anger that drives his most passionate work, comes from frustrated idealism. His frustrations had both a social and spiritual dimension.

After the navy, Stone attended New York University briefly, on a scholarship, which he lost because he could not manage to be both a full-time student and a full-time employee of the *Daily News*. He married young, and children came early; Stone was wont to call his children "hostages to fortune," quoting Francis Bacon. He traveled with his wife, Janice, first to New Orleans, then to San Francisco to take up a Stegner Fellowship, awarded him on the basis of a few early stories, though he'd never been anywhere near attaining an undergraduate degree. Wallace Stegner was an influence, and much more so Ken Kesey; Stone was for a time enveloped in Kesey's charmed circle while somehow always managing to keep a certain ironic distance from it.

Experience with LSD and the early counterculture did much to reshape his mind. So too did a sojourn in Vietnam (as a journalist and observer), in the midst of the American war in that country. Stone had reached adulthood at the end of the 1950s — before the opening of the doors of perception and the winds of revolution had begun to work their seismic changes on American culture and society. He was in those transformations — often up to his neck — but never entirely of them.

His first three novels (*A Hall of Mirrors*, *Dog Soldiers*, and *A Flag for Sunrise*) were acclaimed as having captured the American zeitgeist of the periods in which they were set. The success of the third novel consolidated Stone's position not only as an artist but as a social commentator to be attended to. He was never quite the sort of public intellectual that Hemingway had been and Norman Mailer very consciously tried to be — if only because that role, for literary novelists, had been retired by the time Stone reached the stage. Still, in the five decades of articles and essays he published, before and after the end of the "American Century," he was something like that.

Stone's ambition and achievement as a novelist were both very great. He always had a hand on America's heartbeat, as its rhythms altered from one phase to the next. The making of art was his first concern. Stone was a political novelist, a philosophical and sometimes a religious one. He was always a novelist of ideas, and the pieces in this volume are particular refinements of his ideas—sometimes as conclusions abstracted from novels he had already written and sometimes as explorations for novels yet to be composed.

During the last movement of *A Flag for Sunrise*, one of the principals (adrift in an open boat) has a hallucinatory dream in which a couple of sharks tell each other a sort of joke:

"What is there?" the shark asked his companion.

"Just us," the other shark said.

Take away the bitter irony and it might be seen as the statement of a secular humanist—one who believes in nothing beyond the realm of human interaction. Or as the same character says in the same sequence, "we have nothing but each other."

Stone did espouse that point of view, but without (paradoxical as it may seem) being limited to it. Although his mother was not especially observant, Stone grew up in a Catholic world, raised and trained in considerable part by the Marist Brothers who ran Saint Ann's orphanage and also the twelve-year school that was part of the institution. Though his years living in the orphanage were thoroughly wretched, a little later Stone went through a period of intense devotion. The reaction when it came was equal and opposite in direction. He was expelled from high school, not only for showing up half drunk but (worse in the Marist view) for tempting his fellow students down the path to apostasy—as well as declaring his own. "I felt like Luther or something," he said years later. "I really thought I was a superhero."

Stone's adult attitude to such questions, never entirely fixed, shifted around between the two extremes. "I am not a believer in God," he told one interviewer "I have been a believer in God. I am obsessed with the absence of God. I believe in that phrase from Pascal that says . . . 'Everything on Earth gives a sign of the divine presence. Everywhere we look there seems to be evidence of it. And it never yields itself to our discovery. And yet it seems to be everywhere.' Or as in the Kabbalistic notions, it is as though God has separated himself forever and would have to be put together by gathering up all these items of light which is a virtually impossible task. That whatever that was, whether it was some kind of physical force, big burst, or blast, we have seen the last of it, and yet it has conditioned the way we feel and what we want for all eternity. I think we go without it, we go with this longing and with this kind of half hallucination that we are seeing it out there. We want it to be there."

Stone's is not necessarily a world without God, but one in which God is unlikely to do much for us. A part of his idealism, and its frustration, comes from the elusiveness of a deity that might set things right, a potential presence weirdly expressed by its absence.

In a draft of *A Flag for Sunrise*, an alcoholic priest (whom Stone uses to explore certain religious speculations of interest to himself) pronounces a curious echo of Stone's words above: "But it's there, He's there, just as it says on the prayer wheels. And the reason I think is this: that the Living, even in his good place where it's all resolved and the stricken made whole again —even there the Living is lonely for himself. He's been heard to complain. So, of course, it's us he's lonely for, even as we are so desperately lonely for Him. We are His and we are Him whether either of us likes it or not. We're looking for Him through an eye, children, and through the very same eye, He's looking for us." The speech is adapted from a line in the sermons of Meister Eckhart, "The eye through which I see God is the same eye through which God sees me; my eye and God's eye are one eye, one seeing, one knowing, one love," which had fascinated Stone from the moment he first discovered it.

"One love," with its curious, post hoc Rastafarian ring, appears in none of Stone's reprises of the Master Eckhart line. The fragment of the drunken priest's sermon was cut from *A Flag for Sunrise*, though a radically abbreviated version does appear in the last scene of the book: *The eye you see with is the one that sees you back*—an inscrutable, irreducible statement, and beloved by Stone for those qualities. What follows is the expression of his particular and penetrating vision.

Madison Smartt Bell

The Red Field

The Red Field

Stone's military service occurred in the peacetime navy, from 1955 to 1958; some of its routines are described in "Uncle Sam Doesn't Want You!" written in another period of peace, though decades later (1993), during the controversy over gays in the US armed services. During his three-year "kiddie cruise," which ranged from Western Europe and Africa to Antarctica, Stone saw combat only once, in circumstances that allowed him to observe it from a position of reasonable safety. His vessel was in the harbor of Port Said when, in the course of the Suez Canal conflict, French aircraft strafed and bombed the harbor, but the United States was in a noncombatant role then, and Stone's vessel was not directly fired on.

The first thing Stone saw when he came on deck was that "the sea was red . . . And not only was it red, it was swarming with people. It was swarming with Egyptians . . . A French jet would go in. You'd hear it, I don't know how many minutes later. It was going along the *corniche* of Port Said, and it was killing every living thing . . . And what it's always reminded me of was the pictures of cavalry combats where the horses' eyes are turned to one side in the middle of a cavalry charge. It reminds me of the eyes of the Egyptians who were all around us in their reed boats while the French shot them down, blew them up ... all around me was this red water and exploding reed boats and Egyptians floating face down and Port Said being absolutely blown apart. And I thought, 'This is what I always thought it was like. This is the real thing. This is the way it is.'

"And it never occurred to me that anybody was doing anything wrong. Not for a moment ... I thought to myself, 'God, I'm glad I'm here. I'm so glad that I'm here.' ... And the illumination rounds being fired against the sunset, I thought was the most beautiful thing I'd ever seen. And people were still being killed."

Eventually, "it began to penetrate our consciousness that the harbor was filled with dead people ... But the overwhelming response that I had was 'I always knew this was the way things were.' I always thought that the world was filled with evil spirits, that people's minds teemed with depravity and craziness and weirdness and murderousness, that that basically was an implicit condition, an incurable condition of mankind. I suddenly knew what was meant when Luther said, 'The world is in depravity.' I thought I always knew it was like this. It took me all night long to figure something terrible was happening. But when I figured it out, I thought, 'This is the way it is. There is no cure for this. There is only one thing you can do with this. You can transcend it. You can take it and you make it art.'"

In 1971, Stone spent several weeks in Vietnam as a reporter. He spent most of his time observing the general scene, away from active combat zones, but on one occasion he did come under fire. For the rest of his life he was so reticent on this subject that it's hard to be certain exactly when and where it took place, but aspects of the experience were assigned to his partial alter ego, the reporter John Converse in the novel *Dog Soldiers*. "The Red Field was in Cambodia, near a place called Krek." There Converse and his companions are flattened by friendly fire — specifically, "firebombed by the South Vietnamese Air Force." Converse, "clinging to earth and life," abruptly recognizes that the world is "capable of composing itself, at any time and without notice, into an instrument of agonizing death." There's nothing resembling Stone's elation at Port Said; instead, Converse is reduced to "a little stingless quiver in the earth. That was all there ever was of him, all there ever had been."

Stone reserved this experience for the transcendence of art. Soon after his return from Vietnam he wrote about the quotidian ironies of life in wartime Saigon in his piece for the *Guardian*, "There It Is," and later he wrote a broader, more penetrating analysis of the American failure there, "A Mistake a Hundred Miles Long." The corruption of idealism is one of Stone's great subjects as a novelist, and he saw the Vietnam War as possibly the most important instance of that for his generation and the one following. Most of the characters in his novels are overshadowed by direct experience of Vietnam or, in the later work, by a sort of atavistic memory of it.

The Vietnam experience obviously colors Stone's reading of Graham Greene's *The Quiet American*, but also his reading of Stephen Crane, somewhat more obliquely. When jihad turned its sights on the World Trade Center in 2001, Stone looked at the devastating outcome with the sense of déjà vu, expressed in "Out of a Clear Blue Sky"—the wreck of the *General Slocum* serving as another proof that the world is ever ready to morph into *an instrument of agonizing death.*

"To a degree, we have claimed exemption from the forces of history," he writes in "The Holy War"—another expression of déjà vu. "Now, history has come for us, presenting old, half-forgotten due bills." By the time of that writing Stone had understood for a long time that those bills always come due, and that as the old warrior indicates in "No Such Thing as Peace," the potential of the red field is necessary for peace to be meaningful. "Before death I have nothing to offer but dread reverence," Stone wrote near the end of his life. "But the practice of hope, of life against death, of edges and surviving, were what I wanted to write about."

MSB

INTRODUCTION TO
The Red Badge of Courage

Both Stephen Crane and *The Red Badge of Courage* have a quality of mystery. The process of composition is always mysterious, but here the term applies particularly.

In the winter of 1893, a twenty-two-year-old from New Jersey, a youth of literary and bohemian pretensions living at the Art Students League, announced to his friends that he proposed to write a "historical romance, a pot-boiler" about the American Civil War. Young Stephen Crane had a painter friend named Linson with whom he sometimes attempted collaboration on humor pieces that left most editors unamused. Linson owned a set of *Century Magazine*'s series "Battles and Leaders of the Civil War," which he had stacked on a divan in one corner of his studio. Over the freezing winter months, Crane, whose impoverished style of living quite threatened his health, browsed the magazines and began writing a novel while Linson painted. Sometimes, stationery being unaffordable, he wrote on butcher paper. Later Linson remembered Crane squatting among the stacked magazines and complaining about the war memoirs: "I wonder that *some* of those fellows don't tell how they felt in those scraps! They spout eternally of what they *did* but they are emotionless as rocks!"

It turned out that Crane was not good at "pot-boilers," lacking the appropriate patience, discipline, and sensibility. Perhaps for the same reasons, he was already showing very little promise as a newspaperman. In fact, by 1893 Crane had already written one highly unsuitable novel, called *Maggie: A Girl of the Streets*. Rather than make his fortune, Crane had spent every penny of his schoolboy savings to have it privately printed. Dealing with slum life in and around the Bowery, *Maggie* was not considered a respectable publication, and only its obscurity spared the young author involvement in scandal.

With the publication of this unlikely youth's unlikely second book, *The Red Badge of Courage*, American literature entered the modernist age. Like all great works, *The Red Badge of Courage* can claim the whole of literature as antecedent and remain unique. Perhaps there are earlier novels that have so combined psychological intimacy with dense external detail. Few since have done it so simply and surely and eloquently. The effect is of light, the clear light of nature illuminating an utterly realized landscape. Clarity is the essence, clarity of thought and of description.

William Dean Howells, who was one of Crane's earliest and strongest supporters, liked to say that Crane's genius had "sprung to life fully armed," like Athena. But Athena sprang from the head of a god. *The Red Badge of Courage* and its author seem to have appeared out of the seamless American ether. Stendhal had seen Marengo and Moscow in flames. Tolstoy had commanded troops in the Caucasus. Crane's most strenuous experience before the composition of *The Red Badge of Courage* seems to have been a semester catching for the Syracuse University baseball team.

Today *The Red Badge of Courage* is in the canon, as it should be, an educational rite of passage. High school students continue to receive it as an assignment, and many of its young readers discover what the rest of us may have forgotten: that its power is shattering and undiminished by time. To reread it after many years is a rich and disturbing experience.

There is a tragic irony in the fact that so many of the young have had *The Red Badge of Courage* thrust on them. As everyone remembers, it is a novel about a youth's experience of war by a young writer who himself had no such experience. Most of its first-time readers are approaching the end of their adolescence. If they are open to books, they can hardly resist identifying with its young soldier protagonist, Henry Fleming. He stands on the brink of adulthood at its most terrifying and dangerous, facing the most dreaded and celebrated of all human endeavors. So accomplished is the realism that it persuades completely. How many who have read *The Red Badge of Courage* in high school over the years—it's impossible not to wonder—from Belleau Wood to Bastogne to Phu Bai, have approached their first battle thinking of Henry and hoping to share his pilgrimage and his survival? Yet down the generations comes this surly objection, this adolescent murmur: "He wasn't there." It's a muted objection because of the book's uncanny power, but it's always present.

Modern readers, the sort of readers that Crane was in a sense creating, highly value authenticity. We've been trained to it. Crane's heir and disciple Hemingway, with his anti-intellectualism and his vanity, claimed to set great store by authenticity. But if the existence of *The Red Badge of Courage* proves anything, it's that fiction justifies itself entirely on its own terms. For reasons we imperfectly understand, Crane in Linson's studio was seized by inward visions of hallucinatory intensity which, through the strength and simplicity of his language, he was able to transmit intact to his readers. It is as good an example of the primary process of fiction as literature affords. Mysterious though it is, it represents a unitary personal vision about which we may make certain observations.

One consistently fascinating quality of the narrative is its psychological sureness. Of young Henry Fleming we read:

> He had, of course, dreamed of battles all his life — of
> vague and bloody conflicts that had thrilled him with
> their sweep and fire. In visions he had seen himself in
> many struggles. He had imagined peoples secure in the
> shadow of his eagle-eyed prowess. But awake he had re-
> garded battles as crimson blotches on the pages of the
> past. He had put them as things of the bygone with his
> thought-images of heavy crowns and high castles. There
> was a portion of the world's history which he had re-
> garded as the time of wars, but it, he thought, had been
> long gone over the horizon and had disappeared forever.
>
> From his home his youthful eyes had looked upon the
> war in his own country with distrust. It must be some
> sort of a play affair. He had long despaired of witness-
> ing a Greeklike struggle. Such would be no more, he
> had said. Men were better, or more timid. Secular and

religious education had effaced the throat-grappling instinct, or else firm finance held in check the passions.

This passage is really much more complicated than Crane makes it seem, and it does a number of things at once. While involving the reader's imagination in the character's situation, it simultaneously defines the character, telling much that we need to know about young Henry's education, inner life, and cast of mind. As the narrative proceeds, the intensity and vividness increase. Things take on a coloration that the reader only gradually recognizes as fear. The key word is "recognizes." Little by little, the reader is displaced by Henry Fleming. Before it is declared, Henry's growing fear surprises and overtakes us. Then:

> A little panic-fear grew in his mind. As his imagination went forward to a fight, he saw hideous possibilities. He contemplated the lurking menaces of the future, and failed in an effort to see himself standing stoutly in the midst of them. He recalled his visions of broken-bladed glory, but in the shadow of the impending tumult he suspected them to be impossible pictures.

In the darkness of the night before his first fight:

> He wished, without reserve, that he was at home again making the endless rounds from the house to the barn, from the barn to the fields, from the fields to the barn, from the barn to the house. He remembered that he had often cursed the brindle cow and her mates, and had

sometimes flung milking stools. But, from his present point of view, there was a halo of happiness about each of their heads, and he would have sacrificed all the brass buttons on the continent to have been enabled to return to them. He told himself that he was not formed for a soldier. And he mused seriously upon the radical differences between himself and those men who were dodging implike around the fires.

From this point on, the reader's fortunes are Henry's, not only for the rest of the book but, as it were, for life. That is why so many young soldiers—perhaps astonished to find themselves soldiers, having thought, incorrectly, that men had become better, or more timid—have so closely pondered *The Red Badge of Courage*. But even if war stopped coming back for more unlucky generations, its power would hold.

How did Crane do it? How does genius do what it does, know what it knows? One thing is certain: young Stephen Crane, there in Linson's cold studio, had a number of the elements required for a great novel. For one thing, he was prodigiously gifted. For another, he had a vision of life and of the world, complete and thoroughgoing. At the mere age of twenty-two he may not have had a right to one, but he had it, all right: *The Red Badge of Courage* is its artistic rendering.

Part of genius is timing. The disaster of Crane's premature death obscures his placement in literary history. If all had gone differently he might have sat with Robert Frost as an ancient of the arts at President Kennedy's inauguration. He was roughly contemporary with Frost, and with Joyce and Pound. He belonged to the century he never lived to see. He was that

Anglo-Saxon phenomenon, the minister's child, the preacher's kid, or "PK," as they said at Syracuse University when Crane attended. The language of overcoming, of elevated striving and moral improvement, was in his childhood's ear. His talent, together with his vision, turned that language into something wonderful.

The Reverend Jonathan Townley Crane, DD, Stephen's father, did not possess his son's gifts but was also an author. *Popular Amusements* (1869) was one of his books. *Arts of Intoxication* (1870) was another. (He was against them.) Dr. Crane followed these up with *Holiness, the Birthright of All God's Children* (1874). (He was in favor.) When Stephen was not yet nine, Jonathan Crane died prematurely, and this may have had quite a lot to do with the vision that informs *The Red Badge of Courage*.

The vision is of what Stephen Crane elsewhere called the Red Universe. It is a specter of the world as never-ending struggle, a struggle that must be endured and even embraced. In it, life is hard and unforgiving, without security, without peace. Yet in the very inferno is a great beauty that can belong to the strong. That is what *The Red Badge of Courage* is about: the earth as battleground and field of blood, terrible, infinitely desirable. At the close of the book Henry Fleming is rewarded with a vision for the courage he ultimately displays after running away. He sees things as they are in their dreadful majesty. He believes he has the courage now to accept them:

> With this conviction came a store of assurance. He felt
> a quiet manhood, nonassertive but of sturdy and strong
> blood. He knew that he would no more quail before
> his guides wherever they should point. He had been to

touch the great death, and found that, after all, it was but the great death. He was a man.

Thus life as pilgrim's progress, as a moral journey. Reading it we are reminded that Stephen Crane was also a contemporary of Nietzsche and Theodore Roosevelt. Perhaps we have learned a few things over the past hundred years. We too hope that men will become better, or more timid.

Of course it is not possible to say what formed Stephen Crane's vision of the world as war. We can speculate about the loss of his father or premonition of his own early death or prophecy of the next century itself. In his day Americans were forgetting what they had learned about war at Chancellorsville and Gettysburg. They were reaching out, growing adventurous again. They sang about the fateful lightning, but they had forgotten what it was like.

"War, when you are at it, is horrible and dull," Oliver Wendell Holmes Jr., late of the 20th Massachusetts Volunteers, told a Harvard graduating class in 1895. "It is only when time has passed that you see that its message was divine." A war with Spain was only a couple of years away, and some in his audience would be in it. For the neo-Roman republic, an imperial age was beginning. Crane himself had only a short time to live. He had inherited his father's constitution and undermined it, partly by his never-ending journeys to every available war in quest of authenticity. As a combat correspondent in the Balkans and Cuba, he bent his descriptive powers to the service of Hearst and Pulitzer. He always felt he had to justify writing *The Red Badge of Courage* without having been there.

When Stephen Crane died young in 1900, the United States

saw itself as young also, setting out on a great journey. If our young friend Henry Fleming survived the war, he would no doubt have learned in time that life resists the unitary vision. Fiction will probably always pursue it nevertheless, doubtless in vain but as gloriously as possible. And in it we can be sure that courage—peremptory, embarrassing word—will always be required.

—Introduction to the Library of America edition, 1984

THERE IT IS

Last month I went to Vietnam and stayed there for a couple of weeks. I went because I was working on a second novel which sought to deal with the condition of American life in 1970, and this condition, as is well known, is pervaded with a consciousness of the Vietnam War. Many Americans have even come to believe that the nature of our society and its impact on the history of this century is being defined in Vietnam. In any case, I felt a certain personal necessity to transform my own awareness of the country and the war from abstract outrage to people and places I could perceive, however briefly and imperfectly, from one day to the next.

The previous occupant of my Saigon hotel room apparently had a thing about squashing lizards. There must have been nearly a dozen mashed into the walls and the tiles of the floor. Since house lizards are useful insectivores, a cheerful friendly presence in every hot country on earth, it is difficult to understand why anyone should want to massacre them in this fashion. So the vision of my faceless predecessor stalking about his Sydney Greenstreet colonial hotel wasting lizards with a framed tintype of Our Lady of Lourdes (on evidence, the hunter's instrument) is a disturbing one with which to begin the day.

Breakfasting on a croissant and a bottle of soda pop, I contemplate tiny dinosaur corpses and entertain unbidden associations. The first association is a story I have been told the night before of the Great Elephant Stomp.

In the hills some time ago, the American military authorities, who are carnally perceived in the many-faced, many-armed deity known as MACV (Military Advisory Command, Vietnam), declared elephants to be enemy agents, since they were employed in logistical transport by the NVA and the Front. There ensued what might have been an episode from the *Ramayana*, in which MACV unleashed enormous deadly flying insects known as choppers to destroy his enemies the elephants. Whooping gunners descended on the herds to mow them down with 50-millimeter machine guns, and even my scandalized informant remembers the operation with something like insane exhilaration.

Outside, a man without legs sits on the pavement holding his hat; I throw 10 piasters in it and walk on. The legless man and I exchange smiles. I'm smiling about what a good guy I am. Who knows why he's smiling?

The legless man is one of the many blown-up people one sees about the city. Some of them have been blown up by MACV and his associates, some by the Front, some, it seems, by enthusiasts of obscure affiliation. Most of the year, tons of "selective ordnance"—weird explosive weaponry out of a comic strip sadist's fantasy—is being directed at the enemy or at those who will do until the enemy comes along. Now the rains have somewhat reduced the traffic in aerial "interdiction," but people are still being blown up.

At eight o'clock in the morning it is not very hot by the standard of an American summer. On Nguyen Hue there is a flower market; stalls are bright with lilies, poinciana boughs, and small oriental roses. I walk through the hot fragrant air to the stall of a mama-san to buy a pack of Winstons and some matches. The cigarettes have no revenue stamp; presumably they were once the property of the US Post Exchange, but changed ownership at the dockside or soon after.

I walk around the street vendors and parked Hondas to an arcade in the Eden Passage, where I propose to photograph myself in quadruplicate in order to file my credentials with the Ministry of Information. Several dapper passersby softly inquire if I would like to change money.

I sit looking at my reflection in the take-your-ownpicture thing; outside, three little boys about eight years old are looking at my watch. In the course of my short walk from the hotel, I have seen several lepers, a couple of crippled ARVN soldiers, and a begging cretin led by an ancient woman, but it still seems to be the lizards that worry me.

Lights flash in my eyes—the carefully nurtured outraged humanism I brought with me seems to have stalled at "Reptiles."

Who was that kill-crazy bastard? He left a little hash pipe in the writing drawer. Maybe he freaked out and went berserk. Maybe the lizards kept him awake at night. Maybe he just didn't like them.

The ministry eventually provides me with a press card, and I go to the terrace of the Continental to buy something cold with which to wash down several aspirins. My fever is coming back, the low-grade fever I've been nursing for several days along with that outraged humanism.

From the terrace my view commands the National Assembly, which was once a theater, and a heroic statue of two ARVNs* in combat stance, which, from the positioning of the principals, is known to local Americans as the National Buggery Monument.

There is a blind ARVN soldier, led about by a small boy, who sells newspapers every day on the hotel terrace, and I have been making it a point to buy my *Saigon Post* from him. Doing so, I am challenged by a correspondent.

"He can see as well as you can," says the correspondent.

I say that he looks blind enough to me.

"He's got about ten different kids," my acquaintance insists. "He rents them. He's here at the same time every day, and every day he's got a fresh ARVN uniform. You know why he's got a fresh ARVN uniform? 'Cause he's in the ARVN—and even the ARVN don't take blind people."

In the afternoon I take a taxi to Hoa Lu football stadium; it is the day of the Saigon Rock Festival. At Hoa Lu, the infield is crowded with blank-faced mildly curious Vietnamese. Tents have been erected, and some of them raise colored streamers to the wet limp wind, but the effect is closer to the Army of the Potomac by Mathew Brady than Psychedelic City.

On the bandstand an Indonesian group called Exodus is getting badly warped by the acoustics. In the shaded stands a polite crowd of middle-class Vietnamese are drinking lemon-

*ARVN: Army of the Republic of Vietnam. —*Ed.*

ade. The ladies of the corps diplomatique are present, for the festival is in fact a benefit performance for the maintenance of the widows, orphans, and surviving remnants of Lam Son 719, the ARVN's spring offensive into Laos.

In the center of the stands is a space reserved for Madame Thieu, wife of the president of the republic. Press people on the field are speculating about whether the president's lady will appear. If she does, the press believe, it will be after CBC have played their set and departed.

CBC is the best of the Vietnamese rock groups to have appeared in the course of the Aquarian Age war. Their style is essentially San Francisco 1967 with echoes of the Grateful Dead.

But rock music is as thoroughly un-Vietnamese as bobsledding or gang rape (which seems to have been another innovation stimulated by the American presence), and watching CBC, one is aware that the process through which a twenty-five-yearold Vietnamese transforms himself into a San Francisco bass player must be extremely dislocating.

Bands of GIs, many of them hopelessly out of uniform in headbands and Japanese beads, wander around checking it all out. "Wow," they're saying. "There it is." They're smoking Park Lane cigarettes, which are filtered packaged joints — 600 piasters for twenty.

"There it is" is the great American catchphrase of the war, a three-word summary of the whole situation perceived detail by detail. The GIs go around saying it all day long, since these days consist of a series of unsolicited encounters with the nature of the scene. Dope is so pervasive that the language of the war has become head shorthand. "There it is" is a phrase to be exchanged by people who are staggering through an interminable bum trip. "It" is the Whole Expedition, the Vietnamese-American encounter, the War—which is also frequently referred to as "this shit."

Two days earlier I went into a bar on Tu Do Street, a bar that had the reputation of serving heroin in beer on request. I thought it sounded pretty improbable, but I believe it now. Inside there were about twenty beautiful Vietnamese bar girls lined up behind the bar. Since the latest army policy is to keep the number of troops in Saigon down to a minimum, business is slow during the day and I was the only customer. Leaning on the chromium, facing twenty people on barstools, I felt like I was the bartender and they had the bottles on the wrong side. The girl opposite me started dealing me a hand of cards. The beer had cost about 200 piasters and I didn't much want to play cards, so I let them sit there on the wet chrome and smiled knowingly. I didn't feel very knowing, though. Pretty lame. The ladies watched me drink my cold can of Schlitz; there wasn't any heroin in it. I was standing there with a dumb expression and my pockets full of money and there was no way they could get it off me short of turning me upside down and shaking it loose. I think one of the girls started to cry. I downed the last of the beer and looked around; they were really digging my knowing smile. As I put my hand on the door, the girl who had dealt the cards turned to the girl beside her.

"Well," she said. "There it is."

In the evening I go out to dinner in company, which is what foreigners do each evening in Saigon. No one talks about anything for very long except the war. We talk about the "contradictions"—like my presence in the country, and the fact that the Saigon bar girls seem actually to like Americans in some perverse fashion.

The people I'm with are all serious war reporters who have paid their dues. They laugh a great deal. There is speculation about the number of reporters who have gotten into smack and talk of acquaintances rightly or wrongly alleged to have habits or who have kicked their habits. The question of which general currently controls which article of contraband is raised. A magazine journalist arrives with a depressed congressman, a rural Republican who refers frequently and respectfully to "the president." The journalist has been telling him things that he has not enjoyed hearing, and he doesn't like the way the conversation at the table is going. He had spent his day having the situation explained to him by official explainers, and though he is not in his element, he is not a fool. Someone asks him if he is not afraid of being brainwashed like George Romney. The congressman looks thoughtful.

"Oh," he says. "Poor George."

After dinner, instead of going back to the Royal, I go to spend the night in a house not far from Tan Son Nhut air base, which is occupied by the Committee of Responsibility. The committee are a handful of young Americans who work with concerned organizations in the United States to provide rehabilitation for Vietnamese victims of the war. Hairy and Vietnamese- speaking, they constitute an American presence of an altogether different sort from MACV, but in fact some of them first came to Vietnam in the armed services.

Among their charges, I meet a little boy named Tho, who is learning some English. He can say "hi" and "far out." He is very fond of Americans and does not altogether realize that some time ago he was shot from the back of his water buffalo by an American in a helicopter. A brigadier general is currently facing court-martial for allegedly engaging in this heady brand of blood sport. Tho is going to school now and enjoying it very much. His father is somewhere in the II Corps area, fighting for the Front.

I pass the next few days with the COR and, one afternoon downtown, run into a very knowledgeable lady reporter who asks me if I have heard about the latest explosion. I haven't. She tells me that the government tax office has been blown up. No one is certain by whom. Perhaps by the Front. Perhaps by an irate taxpayer.

The tax office went off at about ten o'clock in the evening, while Judy and her friend were in a Japanese restaurant a block away, eating what one must presume to be the best shrimp tempura outside Yokohama. Tables tottered, chopsticks flew. When the dust settled Judy went down to take a look and found the street outside the building in bad shape. The casualties were mainly people on the sidewalk outside, for the pavements of central Saigon are crowded every evening with refugees who tend their improvised food stalls and often sleep among them. Six people are dead, and it is said that three of them are children.

Sometime later it occurs to me that I might go over and check out where the thing has been done. Arriving finally before the wasted building, I find the street strung with barbed wire, the local symbol of security, and guarded by red-bereted Vietnamese marines. Nearby buildings have their windows broken, and there are still a few shards of dishware and the odd spoon lying around among the chips of concrete. The street seems to smell of Clorox. Here and there are sprinklings of dried white powder that someone says is chloride of lime, and on one wall is a brown smear that appears to be a washed-over bloodstain.

There it is. A marginal incident represented by a day-old bloodstain. I stand in the street, getting in the way of pedestrians—the thoughtful tourist trying to draw a moral. But there isn't any moral; it makes no sense at all. It reminds me of the lizards smashed on the hotel wall.

—*Guardian*, 1971

A MISTAKE TEN
THOUSAND MILES LONG

Captain Gray Rat versus The World

"There it is," they used to say in Vietnam. It was as if an evil spirit were loose, one of the demons known to the Vietnamese as *ma*, weaving in and out of visible reality, a dancing ghost. It would appear suddenly out of whirl, shimmer for an instant, and be lost. People came to recognize it. Recognizing it, they would say without excitement, "There it is," with emphasis on the last word, to let their friends know that they had seen it and to be sure their friends had seen it too.

It was without form itself, but it could assume an infinity of forms. It was as tiny as a lizard's eye and as huge as the bad, black sky. It became events. It became things themselves.

It was at the heart of every irony, however innocuous, however hideously cruel. It might appear as a droll incongruity along some nameless road or as guilty laughter over things that weren't funny. It was as palpable as a tumbling bullet. It was lacy as light, fine enough to seep right into your deepest inward places and confront you as an oddly turned thought, a grotesque insight.

It had no strength of its own because it used human strength. It had no life of its own because it used human lives with a brave prodigality. Because it used so many young lives, it could assume a youthful, frolicsome aspect. It could display its *Alice in Wonderland* side. There were comparisons to *Alice in Wonderland*. It was said that everything was Through the Looking Glass and that there was Lewis Carroll logic. Red Queen to White Rabbit. There it is.

In fact, its Lewis Carroll dimension was moral. It had all the obsessiveness of *Alice in Wonderland* and about as much justice and mercy.

Some people called it the Gray Rat, This Shit, or The Show. Some called it Mr. Gray Rat. A marine I knew called it Captain Gray Rat versus The World.

There exists a peculiar nomenclature. Among Union soldiers, the American Civil War was called the Elephant. Before Shiloh and Chancellorsville, some sergeant would inform the plowboys who had never been in the line before that they were Going to See the Elephant. That was what going into combat was called then.

The marine mentioned above was on Operation Prairie, around the Rockpile in 1967. In one fight during Operation Prairie, thirty-two marines held off steady attacks by three hundred North Vietnamese Army regulars for two days. It was called the Groucho Marx Battle. My marine friend said Operation Prairie was a Walt Disney True Life Adventure. He was badly wounded there, so badly that the first doctor who saw him decided to amputate his right hand but changed his mind at the last minute. The marine's hand was saved, and he was credited with a partial disability. He saw Captain Gray Rat versus The World as a Saturday-morning cartoon in which you got killed.

Understand how young a lot of these people were. Their youth was a factor in how they thought and spoke. For example, they would not "say" things, they would "go" them. "So the gunny goes, 'You been doggin' the bush, Smith?' So I go, 'Hell no, gunny!'" The average American infantryman in Vietnam was seven and a half years younger than his counterpart in the Second World War.

In those days it was unsettling to hear so much bitter whimsy from young Americans. Pre-Vietnam America had become a stranger to irony. These youths and their wit were brutally sophisticated. They'd all caught a glimpse of the *ma*, the war's infernal, antic spirit.

"There it is!" they would say. There it was, the thing itself, but *what* was it? Whether they knew it or not, everyone was looking for a metaphor.

A napalmed tiger was a metaphor rich in implication. It was Captain Gray Rat's answer to culture shock, and The World's revenge on Nam, mysterious Asia beguiled. The colonial hunting preserves became free-fire zones. Tigers prowling for corpses might find themselves incinerated on a hunch. Burning bright in the U Minh Forest, the tigers demonstrated the bankruptcy of innocence. Nobody and nothing was innocent, or free, or neutral.

There was a metaphorical figure known as the Fool on the Hill, a figure of legend, compounded of fear and morning mist. The Fool might be hostile: bombproof, bulletproof, Luke the Gook. More dreadfully, he might be a duly authorized friendly sniper turned freelance. Alone above a grapefruit patch, issued amphetamine to keep him alert, seduced by the relativity of things, the Fool might turn his fire anywhere. All motion was the same to him. He saw an essential gookishness deep down things, and he kept trying to kill it.

A hospital corpsman is running through a rice field carrying a small Vietnamese child. The child's been shot off the back of his water buffalo by the Fool on the Hill. Not content with shooting the child, the Fool has popped the buffalo as well. The corpsman runs with the bleeding child, making for dry ground, risking submerged punji sticks and immersion foot. He knows that the next thing the Fool will shoot may be him.

Eventually, if it were certain he was friendly, and if there were time, someone would have to go talk to the Fool and get him down and try to make him well again.

Buffaloes enraged the Fool with their basically foolish appearance. But anyone—a bored door gunner, a senior officer on his way to an inspection—might have a shot at a buffalo. Buffaloes didn't seem innocent. They chased people and they hated grunts. It was stupid to be chased by a buffalo. The animals were a useful metaphor because the human dimension was so painful and so hard to think about.

"Vengeance on a dumb brute seems blasphemous." So the Quaker Starbuck in *Moby-Dick* sought to reason with Captain Ahab.

"Talk not to me of blasphemy, man," Ahab replied; "I'd strike the sun if it insulted me." He wasn't doing it for an abstraction, like victory or for the oil. He was a moralist in an immoral world and he was going to fix it.

It's not gratuitous that *Moby-Dick* is the great American novel and Ahab, with his passion for control and his "can do" spirit, is an American hero. Ahab started out chasing the whale because it represented everything that was wrong with the world. By the end of his disastrous voyage, no one remembered where goodness resided, and the whale and the whalers went down together in a victory for no one at all.

In Laos, we used Cobra gunships against elephants on the Ho Chi Minh Trail. Descending like gigantic insects, the Cobras achieved complete surprise. They achieved complete astonishment as the first elephant exploded.

Once a young man from Missouri, an earnest German-American farm boy, slow-spoken, Catholic, and bespectacled, pondered a moral dilemma. Reasoning carefully, he decided the Vietnam War was wrong. He talked to his dad and went to Canada. In Canada he began to think he might have taken an easy way out. He came back and took the draft and went as a medic.

He was sent to I Corps, a known conchie, looking out at it all with his honest, weak blue eyes. When he told them he wouldn't carry a weapon, they made him carry everybody's weapon on the way home. They kept it up until the first ambush. When the point went down and called for a medic, they waited to see if he would go, and he went. They found out he would always go. Everybody loved him because he was without a grain of meanness, he liked to talk about important things, and he had so much heart. Time passed. When he was short, his time in country nearly elapsed, no move was made to keep him out of the line. Other people complained on his behalf; he said not a word.

At that time they were fighting for hills on the Laotian

border in I Corps. People were confused. The American command declared that it was not a war of hills. On one hill they lost fifty-six men, and a general explained that the hill "had no military value whatsoever." There seemed to be a contradiction.

In these worthless hills the enemy liked to hurt the point in order to bring the medic up. They wanted the medicine, and they would kill the medic to get it.

The man from Missouri died in a fight twenty-four hours long. When they killed him he was out of morphine, out of almost everything. He was bringing the wounded men mints as placebos. He went back to The World in a folding box, and it no longer mattered what he believed.

Strange rumors circulated about coffins. It was said that drugs were being smuggled out to The World in them. People said, "There it is." It sounded a little too right to be true, but eventually the CID arrested some individuals at Aberdeen, Maryland, and their accomplices at Bien Hoa. Millions of dollars' worth of the purest heroin was being flown in with the KIAs. It turned out to be true after all. Then it was said that the gang at Aberdeen had missed one, and an undertaker in some tank town opened his son's coffin and found a bag full of smack beside the remains. That part was just rumor.

"There it is," we said, in our great sweep for metaphors. We never determined quite what it was. No single image served.

It was us. It was them. It was the cunning of dice play. The smoke, the rain, death—the destroyer of worlds, and the girls in the boom-boom rooms.

It was a mistake ten thousand miles long, spinning out of control. Its fiery wash burned people down and processed adolescents into bags of garbage, sucked a million people out of their skin, and turned them into their own flayed ghosts.

The images we carried away are its embers. We will never forget it.

Decades ago, the historian Ralph Roeder, in his classic study *The Man of the Renaissance*, treated with a war now almost five hundred years old: the invasion of Italy by King Charles VIII of France. "Swollen by the confluence of so many causes," Roeder wrote, "it advanced like some complex, blundering, uncontrollable force which absorbed its own authors, and which assumed more and more the featureless and irresistible likeness of fate."

Resisting the French

Vietnam's resistance to the French commenced even before the latter had completed their conquest of Indochina in the second half of the nineteenth century. The situation of a small country struggling against an imperial power was one the Vietnamese understood profoundly. Having resisted China for centuries, they knew all the weaknesses of an empire at war and all the advantages accruing to the guerrilla.

Beyond the limited circle directly profiting by French authority, the desire to be rid of French rule was universal, embracing all social classes. But the strongest and most enduring faction of the independence movement was that controlled by the Communist Party of Vietnam. This was due in great measure to the fact that the most influential and resourceful fighter for Vietnamese independence was also one of the founding fathers of the Comintern, the man known to his early collaborators by the nom de guerre Nguyen Ai Quoc, and later to all the world as Ho Chi Minh.

During World War II, a weak Vichy regime governed Vietnam at the sufferance of Japan. Foreseeing an Allied victory, Ho consolidated the resistance. From jungle redoubts, his Vietminh used traditional guerrilla tactics effectively against the Japanese.

Eventually the American forces of China Command came to recognize the Vietminh as the authentic representative of the Allied war effort in Indochina. A close collaboration developed between American OSS operatives and Ho's guerrillas.

As the war turned against them, the Japanese seized direct control of Indochina, only to surrender it in defeat to the Vietminh. After over one hundred years of French rule, the whole of Vietnam had an indigenous government.

Ho Chi Minh counted on his cordial relationship with the United States to protect Vietnamese autonomy. American policy seemed to favor the Vietminh. The United States, predominant in the Asian theater of war, opposed the restoration of French rule.

At one point, beset by Chinese pressure in the north and the arrival of British troops determined to install the regrouping French, Ho requested that the United States take Vietnam under its temporary control. His request was declined, but at ceremonies in Hanoi proclaiming an independent Vietnam, Ho announced his Vietnamese Declaration of Independence, based in large part on America's.

Supported by Britain, the French returned in force. Quite soon, their armies were engaged in the most bitter of France's colonial wars. Time after time, their carefully planned "encir-clements" ended in frustration. The terrain was hellish. Sixty percent of the country was a jungle that suffocated conven-tional armies. Monsoons and the high canopy of trees made air support difficult for a large part of the year.

The enemy was skillful and ruthless—avoiding engage-ment, then striking at isolated posts or in cities thought to be secure. It was a dirty war, fought under demoralizing condi-tions. By 1954, the French were fighting their last losing battle at Dien Bien Phu.

In the interim, America's mood had changed. Her wartime anticolonialist policy had come to seem naïve and even treach-erous. China had been "lost" and grave accusations exchanged that would paralyze the country's Asian policy for a generation. Some strategists professed to detect an American in any anti-Communist war. America must bear any burden, it was said, to preserve the free world her power had created. Her power was vast, a mighty force for good.

America's attention turned toward the seahorse-shaped "lesser dragon" of Vietnam. She had forgotten that in 1945 an American intelligence officer had declared in his last report that the white man was "finished" in Southeast Asia. She had forgotten her fierce, indomitable wartime allies and their ruth-less, single-minded rejection of foreign control.

France, free of its dirty war, watched with some cynicism as America began the process of involvement in Vietnam.

The advance guard of the American Presence appeared in Saigon, and many found Vietnam charming, with its flame trees, cafés, and lovely women. At the same time, a French scholar was writing of French soldiers' agony as their road

came to an end at Dien Bien Phu. Place names along that road
—Ban Me Thuot, Dak To, An Khe, Hue—would one day be
familiar in remote American towns. The Frenchman's book
was entitled *Hell in a Very Small Place*.

Saigon

The building that symbolized Saigon to the literate world
was the Continental Palace Hotel, its high-vaulted ceilings
abloom with enormous, slowly rotating fans. The hotel and its
terrace restaurant would be forever associated with Graham
Greene's *The Quiet American*. In the spring of 1971, the terrace
by day looked much as it had in Greene's time, but the city had
changed a great deal.

The former National Theater, at the north end of Lam Son
Square, had become the National Assembly. Its gilt was peel-
ing, its gardens were ill tended, and the plaza before it was
a car park centering on a new military memorial of singular
repulsiveness.

Facing the Continental from across the square stood the Hotel Caravelle, a sleek American job in which Graham Greene
wouldn't have been caught dead. From the rooftop bar of the
Caravelle you could watch outgoing rounds from the batteries
at Tan Son Nhut and, sometimes, the bursting of parachute
flares seeking out sappers along the field perimeter.

At the Caravelle bar they didn't know an aperitif from an
apricot. Customers were expected to get drunk and spend a lot
of money doing it. The big drinks sometimes attracted Scandinavian reporters, whose left-wing views and antiwar senti-

ments would bring them into conflict with the burly civilian hard hats who worked for Morrison-Knudsen and other contractors.

Saigon as a city had never been rooted in anything more than expedience; its charms were gratuitous or purely in the mind's eye. Its principal buildings, with the exception of fin-de-siècle artifacts like the Gia Long Palace or the City Hall, tended toward art deco curves of opaque glass that at their best suggested illustrations on the old *Normandie*'s breakfast menu. The only thing Parisian about Saigon was the number and quality of its better restaurants, the decline of which it was customary to bemoan.

That year the best and most expensive restaurant in Saigon was the Guillaume Tell, in Khanh Hoi near the Ben Nghe Canal. Ramuntcho's, in the Eden Passage near Lam Son Square, was favored by the foreign press. Givral's, the famous ice cream parlor on Tu Do Street (which *The Quiet American* knew as the rue Catinat), did business a few doors from a Dairy Queen that served water buffalo hamburgers. Along the riverfront, down streets faintly reminiscent of New Orleans, was a floating restaurant that served Vietnamese food beyond compare. A few hundred yards upriver was that blackened hulk of its late competitor, the legendary My Canh, blown up prior to the Battle of Saigon in 1968.

All along Tu Do and the streets adjoining it were massage parlors and bars catering to GIs. The GIs were few by 1971; only those personnel with jobs in the capital were permitted downtown. "Skag bars" that sold heroin were off-limits and watched by the military police. Most of the joints stood nearly empty behind their protective antigrenade wire. Inside, heavily made-up Vietnamese bar girls played solitaire before rows of unoccupied stools.

Americans walking the streets of Saigon felt accusing eyes on them. The Vietnamese, soldiers and civilians alike, had always known the scorn in which their allies held them. Jostlings and minor traffic accidents involving Americans became the scenes of near riots. Insults were shouted in the faces of passing Caucasians. The mood in the capital was evidence that Hanoi had scored a measure of success in its battle to erode the South's morale.

The malaise hanging over the city shocked some returning reporters. Street crime increased, partly because dislocations and ARVN casualties had created a multitude of orphans or half-orphans whose mothers were driven into prostitution or something like it. On every corner, stolen US property was for sale. PX cameras, GI uniforms, M16s.

The smart money was beginning to shift assets. The Phu Tho racetrack, which had been a field hospital for the NVA during Tet 1968, was a racetrack again, and the horses, better fed than most of Saigon's poor, ran for heavy purses every day.

In the hours just before curfew, an element of the city never observed before drifted downtown from the inner districts. Transvestites, junkies, and hoodlums, all quite local, appeared on the sedate terrace of the Continental. Long-haired groups of juvenile delinquents waited for drunks in the darkness outside.

What sustained the spirits of Saigon's extensive demimonde was the continued presence of the Indian moneychangers. From tiny offices beyond metal doors in the buildings over the Eden Passage, they traded in currency, offering as much as 500

Vietnamese piasters to the dollar. One morning, it was said, there would be a portent of the beginning of the end. Saigon would awaken and the Indians would be gone.

War in the Village

In Saigon, toward the end of every workweek, MACV would wonder about the villages. The villages were where the people were, and there was a theory current that the war would be lost or won among them.

MACV was a collective entity—Military Assistance Command, Vietnam, the organization in charge of the American military in Vietnam—but it had a name like a man's. I used to think of it as a man—a hairy-handed war chief out of the Celtic annals. Mac V of the Fiery Fist, Mac V of the Hundred Thousands.

One might picture Mac V of an evening, bending an ear toward the twilight forest, listening to whispers and murmurs. He was never certain what it was he heard.

In Washington they wanted everything on graphs. Mac V would have his wizards give them graphs. The graphs purported to reflect the allegiances of Vietnam's innumerable villages, the state of their hearts and minds. The graphs were on green printouts in black ink. Imagine Mac V, his broad brow furrowed, studying his copy of the graphs. His stout honest heart felt a queer foreboding, an unfamiliar sense of uncertainty. The printouts were called Hamlet Evaluation Reports.

The Asian village was a timeless social tool, an instrument

of survival. It was a person's appointed place under heaven, his God-given place. Its ideal was harmony, continuity, peacefulness. Since the world was sometimes inharmonious, chaotic, and threatening, under pressure it could transform itself into a weapon.

The village was the traditional weapon of the weak against the strong—half hidden, resilient, yielding before pressure, then snapping back like a stake on a trip wire. Out of the village came such grim surprises as the tiger trap, the punji stick, the deadfall.

In theory, Mac V had crossed the ocean to help defend the villages of Vietnam, but the theory was unsound. In many of the villages, an abiding love of the land and the children of the land, their countrymen, inclined the villagers' sympathies toward Mac V's enemies, the NLF guerrillas. The NLF surely was not above coercion; it excelled at coercion. But in contrast to the Americans, the NLF guerrillas were children of the land and therefore children of the people.

More often than not, young Americans entering the rural "villes" with their monosyllabic bebop names walked into a furnace of treachery and casually concealed hate. Exhausted, frightened, bereaved, the Americans stared into blank faces.

The Vietnamese villager never saw some reminder of his lost son or brother among what to him were crazy-looking, oversized blond men or the crazy-looking, oversized black ones. The Americans never got a sense of home from the frowning grannies or the frightened women whose unseeing eyes seemed to bid them despair and die. And though it might be thought that kids were the same everywhere, there were ugly stories about murderous children. Sophisticates on both sides smiled in mutual recognition. The villagers were seeing foreign devils. The Americans were seeing gooks.

The so-called Vietcong was turning out to be something very like the peasantry itself in arms.

In Malaya, the British had used fortified villages defended by loyal inhabitants. Mac V employed the tactic in Vietnam, although the circumstances were different. Thousands of peasants were removed from the soil of their ancestors, assembled, enclosed in wire. Mountain tribesmen and delta peasants were recruited as auxiliaries. Sustained efforts were made to separate friend from foe.

Mac V sighed. He was not without scruples. His trumpets gave forth an uncertain sound. Still, wars were to be won. Precautions had been taken, and it was not time to talk of precautions anymore. The other side destroyed its enemies in the villages without mercy. In World War II, the Allies had bombed the Dutch, the French, the Danes to get at Hitler. They had incinerated numberless Germans of every age and station. Mac V turned his fury on the villages.

Clouds of fire and steel descended on the countryside of Vietnam. It was demonstrated to recalcitrant peasants that their esteemed townships were little piles of junk. Before their unbelieving eyes, their villages, anchors of their very identity, were transformed into litter.

If they tried to flee as fish, Mac V of the Hosts turned the water into boiling oil. If they pretended to be trees, Mac V became a wind of fire. Confounded, they wept and died.

When it was done, Mac V put his ear to the forest. What he heard was not the sound of victory. He realized that most of the villages had been lost before the war began.

In Washington, they wanted only graphs. In Saigon, reporters joked that noodle restaurants were wrapping chicken in the Hamlet Evaluation Reports.

Strategy of Attrition

The big battles before Tet may have been the last battles fought by American soldiers of the old style. The America they came from is not the same. Gone is the unambiguous, unembarrassed patriotism that sent so many of them to Vietnam. The senior officers and many of the senior noncoms had seen something of what the youngsters referred to as Double-U Double-U Deuce. More had been in Korea. The average infantryman in those days had gone in believing that you owed a service to your country, and even though Double-U Double-U Deuce was an old black-and-white movie to him, he believed that being out there fighting, surviving, and dying in those twentyshades-of-nightmare-green places was the discharging of a natural debt.

They were the young men who had always turned out when assured the nation needed them, yet another generation of American fighting men, succeeding their fathers and older brothers as those in turn had succeeded theirs. They were the inheritors of a long tradition of righteousness and victory.

Their adolescent swagger concealed both conviction and self-doubt. Conviction was their birthright, after all. They were quite certain they were in Vietnam to assist the common people in a struggle against hated foreign invaders from the

North. They had been told this and they believed it. They had confidence in the men who led their country and its armed forces, but secretly their confidence in themselves was quite often a little shaky.

Their overall superior in Saigon was a Southerner, a former Eagle Scout from a family with a long military tradition. When asked if he could do a job, his instinct was to affirm vigorously that he could. That was the American way. Americans were winners.

General Westmoreland was not a sophisticated man, and he appears not to have realized how gravely the cards were stacked against him. His approach reflected a military philosophy, unique to the United States, which held that war was somehow a nonpolitical event. This philosophy had its roots in a salutary tradition excluding the armed forces from political involvement. The results of this tradition did not always serve the national interest. In World War II, to Churchill's consternation and Stalin's bemusement, American troops made no attempt to reach Berlin before the Russians, or to establish a Western military presence in central Europe. Eisenhower, acting on General Marshall's orders, declared that political considerations would not be allowed to influence military operations. Such a statement was utterly nonsensical to the war leaders of Europe, but most American soldiers accepted its soundness.

That the leading soldiers of a country born in insurrection should subscribe to such a doctrine is ironic, but Westmoreland, like his predecessors, did so. In the case of Vietnam, he could not have been more mistaken.

The enemy fought for precisely defined goals. Westmoreland served an administration whose war aims were so bound to political restrictions, foreign and domestic, that they could never be clarified beyond a generalized desire for good news. What state of affairs was he expected to bring about in Vietnam? Did he ever ask? The techno-maniacs and politicians to whom he reported never took the political risk of telling him. Sometimes they seemed to behave as though the Vietnam War was his idea and had nothing to do with them.

His declared tactics of search and destroy—finding and eliminating the enemy's main force—turned to rubble in his hands. He failed to gain the initiative at the outset and would never, in his years in Vietnam, succeed in attaining it. The strategy he employed would one day be described by some military historians as no strategy at all. Eventually, on the highest levels, everybody was faking it.

Out in the boondocks they were not faking it. At Dak To and Bong Son, in the A Shau and Ia Drang valleys, they were giving everything they had against a barely seen enemy deploying what may have been the best army of its time. They understood that they were not universally welcomed as liberators and that the enemy might be any Vietnamese, that the distinction between civilian and hostile combatants was obscure. They found themselves going short of food and water for fifty hours at a time because the choppers couldn't find a path through enemy fire, taking objectives at grave cost and abandoning them because there was no line of battle. They were ceasing to be what they had been, surprising themselves with their own endurance and sometimes with their own brutality. They were beginning to trust no one but each other.

The Other Side

In Vietnam, one's choice of words when referring to the enemy defined one's attitude toward the war. This was true of the servicemen and also of the civilians there, the press corps, the AID people, the contractors, social workers, and spooks.

The lowest term for the NLF, so low that it indicated a baseness of character on the user's part, was "the Cong." This was the term favored by the *New York Daily News*. It was employed by rightwing American civil servants and by certain visiting politicians who came over to be photographed in the act of "fact-finding." They would use the degrading term in conversation with the troops they wanted to be photographed among, imagining that it made them one of the guys. A politician who referred to "The Cong" was sure to find facts supportive of a continuing effort. The term "The Cong" was also used archly by those well out of the line.

"Vietcong," originally a derogatory reference in Vietnamese, was more or less neutral; its users often incorrectly applied it to include NVA regulars. "Charlie" was in general use, but it presumed an actual acquaintance with the enemy and sounded fatuous from anyone who had never heard an AK-47. "Victor Charlie" was straight phonetic alphabet, less familiar and preferred. Civilians and others who wanted to sound serious referred to "Victor Charles." Black soldiers, to whom "Charlie" was somebody else back home, often spoke of plain "Charles."

In the line, where the general feeling held that a gook was a gook, the term "gook" was applied to all Vietnamese, hostile, friendly, or stoically indifferent. Superstitious short-timers and admiring soldiers spoke of "Sir Charles" or even "Charles, sir" and applied it to all enemy combatants. Quakers, third-country nationals, and left-wing journalists referred to "The Front," meaning the Communistled National Liberation Front.

It was declared a great mystery that Vietnamese in the VC and NVA fought so furiously and well while our ARVN allies so often performed poorly. The answer, as everyone well knew, was motivation and leadership.

The sacrifices expected of a VC or NVA soldier were awe-inspiring. That they were, in general, performed was more so. Their leadership was not conservative of their lives; the acceptable casualty rate in the NVA was higher than that in the Japanese army during World War II. General Giap's statement has often been quoted: "Every minute hundreds of thousands of people die on this earth. The life and death of a hundred, a thousand, tens of thousands of human beings, even our compatriots, means little."

Over here we try not to think like that. The general sounds to our ears like a wartime movie villain, confirming the old saw about Asians and the value of life.

Yet his troops behaved as though they agreed with him. Living in unlivable jungle, often without medicine or hope of rescue if injured, without fires to cook or warm themselves from the night's chill, without word of their families, they went out to scatter their lives like pebbles.

"Can it be just *dulce et decorum est*?" someone once asked during a bull session in some safe place.

"What else can it be?" someone else answered by asking.

Dulce et decorum est pro patria mori.

Sweet and righteous it is to die for the fatherland.

A modern poet has called that motto an "old lie." Many Americans once believed it, or at least it did not seem to them altogether impossible.

Some of the unsophisticated among the first troops we sent to Vietnam believed it. It quickly became a sick joke, or would have if anyone had had the nerve to recite it on the line.

But to the other side it was a religion. Their soldiers didn't die for the dialectic or for the thesis on State and Revolution. They lived in an ordered world long lost to us, for good or ill. They believed what they were told, and they believed their lives belonged to the land and to the people. Their naïve faith made them the hardest and most determined enemy America ever faced.

Khe Sanh

Who won what at Khe Sanh remains obscure. Both sides claim it as a victory. It was a remote battlefield, either strategically vital or nowhere at all. Its value depended on the strategic perspective, the personal interest, or the public relations position of the evaluator.

Were the marines sent there to hold the "western anchor" of South Vietnam's defenses and close the Ho Chi Minh Trail? Or were they there as bait to draw the Communists into a conventional battle in which their army might be destroyed by superior fire and air power? Or were the NVA divisions themselves the bait, there to lure American forces into an unoccupied corner of the country while the Tet offensive struck at the centers of population? Were the NVA forces repulsed in their determined attempt to inflict a major defeat on the United States? Or was their effort a feint to distract MACV's attention from plans for the more strategically important assaults?

For the strategists in Saigon, Honolulu, and Washington, Khe Sanh became a state of mind. Lyndon Johnson, master of persuasion and hyperbole, dreaded the reaction of the press and the Congress to a setback there. Above all, he dreaded the reaction of the public, whose love and admiration he required.

Dreadful analogies suggested themselves. The words "Dien Bien Phu" were uttered. The public read those words and heard them on television. "Dien Bien Phu," horrible words, dust on the tongue, mud, defeat, capitulation. Incomprehensible words, the name of a place to buy opium and of a foreign army's destruction, became a symbol of the land war in Asia that America had been cautioned against since MacArthur's day. Its shadow fell across time and distance to dishearten the country's war leaders.

Sleepless and haggard, Johnson paced the White House situation room. A sand reproduction of Khe Sanh had been built for his benefit. He read and tried to interpret every incoming dispatch. He was squandering the last of his optimism, energy, and determination. As the siege wore on and the reports of the Tet offensive kept coming, Johnson's writers struggled for the right words of explanation. Seen from Washington or even Saigon, the situation was complex.

For the six thousand US Marines and three hundred ARVN Rangers inside the Khe Sanh perimeter the situation was elemental. Ranged against them were up to four divisions of North Vietnam's regular army, equipped with heavy guns and even tanks. For seventy-seven days, between the end of January and early April 1968, the men at Khe Sanh endured a sustained attack that ceased to be an event with cause, beginning, and foreseeable end, but became a condition of life to which the only alternative was death.

They never got a glimpse of the Big Picture. There were only small pictures, moments of fire, pain, and sudden death. Only those who were there can really know what it was like.

One who was there was the great war photographer David Duncan, who shared the marines' ordeal and took the pictures. Combat troops often asked journalists why the writers were in the line. Duncan answered most eloquently in words he wrote after covering the war in Korea and used again at Khe Sanh to explain his business.

"I wanted to show what war does to a man," Duncan wrote. "I wanted to show the comradeship that binds men together when they are fighting a common peril. I wanted to show the way men live, and die, when they know death is among them, and yet they still find the strength to crawl forward armed only with bayonets to stop the advance of men they have never seen, with whom they have no immediate quarrel, men who will kill them on sight if given first chance. I wanted to show the agony, the suffering, the terrible confusion, the heroism which is everyday currency among those men who actually pull the triggers of rifles aimed at other men known as 'the enemy.' I wanted to tell a story of war, as war has always been for men. Only their weapons, the terrain, the causes have changed."

Nearly five hundred marines died defending Khe Sanh, and perhaps ten thousand North Vietnamese soldiers assaulting the place were killed or wounded. But the war, in its perversity, had a way of denying the most valiant the fruits of their valor. Once the fighting was over, the dead of both sides buried, and the wounded removed to where they might be healed, Khe Sanh had no attraction for either side. General Westmoreland ordered the base dismantled.

Tet!

Vietnamese tradition held that the turning of the lunar year should bring auspicious signs and gladness of heart; thus it had become customary for both sides to observe a truce during the holiday celebrations. In 1968, a thirty-six-hour cease-fire had been agreed upon, to commence at midnight on January 30.

Centuries before, Vietnam had won a great victory in her running war with the Chinese by attacking their Hanoi garrison at the height of the Tet observances. In 1968, the Communist-led forces in Vietnam chose to create their own auspicious signs by repeating history.

A little after midnight on January 30, they assaulted the Nha Trang perimeter. All day long, from Quang Tri to Ca Mau, in a barrage of rockets and mortars, they attacked provincial capitals and divisional headquarters. No target was too formidable. They attacked Bien Hoa, Cam Ranh Bay, and even Tan Son Nhut. Vietcong and NVA soldiers were fighting in the streets of Hue, Da Nang, and Saigon itself.

In a sense, the Tet battles of 1968 saw both sides fall victim to their own propaganda. When NVA divisions began converging around the combat base at Khe Sanh in early January, President Johnson worried about a "second Dien Bien Phu."

MACV welcomed the prospect. According to his body-count scorekeeping, the enemy was on the ropes. Dien Bien Phu would be refought, and he would win it. He threw the bulk of his combat maneuverables into I Corps to engage NVA regulars. By the morning of January 31, "the Front" was outside his back window, F-100s were flying tactical air support over the streets of Saigon, and there were firefights in progress on the US embassy lawn. The ARVN had gone on holiday routine.

But all was not going according to plan for the attackers. They found no "general uprising" to welcome their "general offensive." Confident of victory and conscious of history, Communist guerrillas fought their way into every city in the country and foundered there, fish out of water. Whether they acted as a matter of policy or out of frustration at their compatriots' lack of ardor, some of the worst atrocities charged to their account occurred during the twenty-six days they held power in sections of Hue. Afterward, more than three thousand bodies were found in mass graves around the city. Some had been buried alive.

After the fact, MACV would take comfort from the enormous numbers of enemy dead. His spokesmen would call the Tet offensive a "last-ditch struggle" and compare it to the German winter offensive of 1944. But something was wrong. It became apparent that the enemy had taken MACV by surprise. His spokesmen said contradictory things about the enemy's intentions. His own intentions were unclear. He seemed not to be in control. He was fighting the enemy's war in the enemy's good time. If the enemy chose to fight on MACV's front porch, the enemy had the capability. If the enemy chose western Quang Tri Province, MACV would hasten to meet him there.

With Tet, Vietnam finally got America's attention. Millions of Americans watched the battle for Saigon on the evening news, and many who were not personally involved took notice for the first time. In the winter dusk of America as 1968 proceeded, dreadful sights were broadcast. The cameras recorded burnings, executions, even the sight of American soldiers falling in battle. MACV was powerless to control news media that no longer trusted him. He had sincerely believed there would be nothing to hide.

Lyndon Johnson tried to explain it away, and his own credibility suffered. On February 27, the avuncular Walter Cronkite, a public surrogate, pondered the question of whether "the bloody experience of Vietnam is to end in stalemate." The decade that had opened in the winter sunshine of Kennedy's inaugural was flickering out in a confusion of shadows and unwholesome light.

War at Home

In the autumn of 1961, I was working as a house painter in a cavernous apartment on Central Park West. Over some hipster station on my radio, a man with an impenetrable foreign accent was engaged in a diatribe against American policy in Southeast Asia. I let him ramble on until I had second-coated a corner lintel, then I climbed down my ladder and turned the dial in search of something with a better beat. I didn't want to hear it.

Not many years later, on the street separating Oakland, California, from Berkeley, I saw the Oakland cops open their ranks to let some Hells Angels get at the marchers in a demon-

stration against the Vietnam War, while the Berkeley police
—responsible public servants with degrees in law enforcement
—tried to fight off the bikers. A couple of years after that, the
conflict between authority and protest had grown so intense
that the Berkeley police were discharging bird shot into demonstrators' faces, friends of mine were in jail or being chased
by the FBI, and I got beaten up in High Spire, Pennsylvania,
for having a beard.

And finally I was there, hiding at midday among the rubber
trees and sliding diphthongs, trying to read myself into a paperback copy of *Nicholas and Alexandra* and out of Binh Duong
Province and the Republic of Vietnam.

It seemed as though it would never go away. Now there are
college students who don't know the first thing about it, and a
lot of people who wish they didn't either.

During the same years that President Kennedy was trying
to find his way through the rococo politics of Vietnam, a new
generation of the expanded American middle class was coming of age. There may be some principle by which powerful
industrialized systems generate romantic revivals; in any case,
America had something very like one during the late fifties and
early sixties. The generation coming up seemed to have no
tolerance for the long-accepted scandals and the dirty secrets
America had always lived with. Reinhold Niebuhr, a Cold War
theologian and a pessimist, had preached an imperfect world
in which one measure of a nation's strength was its ability to
reconcile itself to inevitable injustices. The middle-class young
of the sixties felt it was their responsibility to change the world
and to reconcile American rhetoric with American reality. Born
to relative security in a powerful country, they felt firm ground

beneath their feet, and they thought they saw very clearly what should be changed. They were witnessing the dismantling of institutionalized racism; some of them had taken part in that process.

John Kennedy was shot down before their eyes. When Lyndon Johnson mistook his election for more than a mandate and began leading the country into a foreign war, they would not follow him. When he lied, a new generation of journalists and teachers was ready to expose his stratagems. Their opposition became more obstreperous and more offensive. They were ready to listen to radical counsels that had been suppressed in the fifties. They were ready to develop a radicalism of their own. A mass bohemia came into being, despising those outside it and becoming despised in turn.

If the administration was going to win its war in Vietnam, it needed to do so quickly and unambiguously. Lacking clear objectives, it was bound to fail. Johnson's good intentions and social idealism disappeared in a chorus of shouted obscenities. Because of the war, America would never love or honor him in the way that he required. The road to hell is paved with good intentions.

The part of America that was not young or middle class — those who had always known you got nothing for nothing, you got what you could, you were lucky to get what you worked for — turned coldly nihilistic. It was hard to tell which they hated more, the war or its opponents. The Selective Service was in effect raiding the towns and the ghettos. Little flags were whipping on the wind in mean cemeteries, from the New England mill towns to the Southern Pacific tracks.

Where love and peace failed, grief, bitterness, and disillusionment prevailed. The youthful rapture ended, and Nixon seemed to be president after all. Nixon, who did not care much for causes, eventually brought the boys home.

Withdrawal

At the Five O'Clock Follies, as the press called the daily MACV briefing, officers continued to refer to American and ARVN troops as the "Allies." The term made reporters wince, because it seemed so transparently a forlorn attempt to invoke the sense of relentless moral and military victory that accompanied World War II's closing days. Beyond their attempts at homespun agitprop, MACV's spokesmen had little to report by May 1971. Like tragedians in a bad melodrama, they tried hard not to be laughed at; they had learned what the laugh lines were and avoided them.

The Big Story was Vietnamization, which was to enter its second phase during the coming summer. Operation Lam Son 719, ARVN's solo incursion into Laos earlier that spring, had been a substantial test of Vietnamization, America's plans to turn the fighting over to the South Vietnamese.

When that operation was over, President Nixon addressed America in a televised speech, in which he declared, "Tonight I can report that Vietnamization has succeeded." His words reflected MACV's official judgment, but the enduring image of Lam Son 719 was a photograph of a South Vietnamese soldier clinging to the skid of a medevac chopper during ARVN's frantic withdrawal. Everything had gone wrong. Bad weather had grounded air support and prevented preparatory attacks.

Bad intelligence had resulted in the ARVN raiders facing superior numbers, superior artillery, and a large, well-coordinated tank force. ARVNs had even been bombed mistakenly by the United States Navy while forming up.

In Saigon, MACV took the long view. His statistics led him to conclude that "the NVA had taken another beating." Issues of *Time*, *Newsweek*, and other publications reporting the extent of the debacle were banned by Thieu's government.

The Corsican proprietor of my hotel professed to believe that America would change sides to win. The United States was in the war for oil, he believed. It would abandon Thieu and cut a deal with Hanoi—that, he insisted, was what the Paris peace talks were about.

Rumors of American accommodation with the enemy spread, and some Vietnamese hastened to make accommodations of their own. We heard that one of the Vietcong cadres in Saigon had absconded with a fortune in "tax" money. All over the country, government authorities approached their Communist opposite numbers, and arrangements for peaceful coexistence were worked out.

Meanwhile, the US military was going through a crisis. Fraggings of officers and noncoms by their troops and refusals of combat seemed to be increasing, but it was hard to tell how frequently they occurred. If the Public Affairs people knew, they weren't letting on. A group of young lawyers was dispatched from Harvard Law School to defend court-martial defendants —the antiwar movement was showing its colors in Saigon.

According to some, the seeds of a large-scale mutiny were sprouting in line units. Others claimed this was a gross exaggeration. But it was plain that soldiers called upon to risk their lives in a war they knew held no prospect of victory were angry and frustrated, reflecting attitudes at home. The doctrine of Black Power had arrived in Vietnam, and race relations in the rear echelons ranged from tense to deadly. MACV got his soldiers back to The World as fast as he dared.

The spring of 1971 seemed the beginning of the end, and so — as things turned out — it was. Reporters began to speculate privately on what the inevitable Communist victory would mean for South Vietnam. There was a story in neighboring Cambodia; few knew much about what was happening there. Those who had known were dead.

Demoralization in Saigon was visible; the city was febrile with early symptoms of terminal defeat. Many thousands of poor refugees from American bombs and NVA mortars had jammed into the capital, hopelessly overstraining its capacity to house or employ them. As Vietnamization proceeded, individual Americans began to ponder the circumstances of their own private withdrawal.

The Easter Offensive

When South Vietnamese elections came due in the autumn of 1971, the American Presence in Saigon rounded up the usual suspects and decided to stay with Nguyen Van Thieu. The customary CIA funds were disbursed to Thieu's faction. The customary victory of democracy was proclaimed.

It was entirely a matter of the lesser evil. Thieu was unsatisfactory in so many ways that the advantages of his continuance in office were largely negative. Under his leadership, the

ARVN remained an instrument of patronage in which only political reliability was rewarded. It was highly unlikely, allowing for the luxuries of hindsight, that such a man leading such a government and army could succeed against a highly motivated force of practical fanatics. Vietnamization had been nearly discredited during Lam Son 719, but it was the only formula available. American officials and advisers, who on one level knew the state of things perfectly well, spoke optimistically as from a schizoid trance. Hanoi, having rebuilt its plants, its army, and its defenses, and equipped by Communist superpowers competing for its allegiance, set out to show what it could do.

On March 30, 1972, the NVA struck on three fronts. One force came over the DMZ, a second into the central highlands, and a third into the Iron Triangle above Saigon. The suffering and devastation this Easter offensive inflicted on the South Vietnamese people may have been the most ghastly of the entire war. With sizable cities under siege, the roads were clogged with refugees whose fear of living in the line of fire or under the Communists emboldened them to flee across an inferno. The very air was deadly. Families carrying their possessions made their way through massed NVA artillery, which was firing up to seven thousand shells a day into the heavily populated city of An Loc. Exploding American bombs and naval gunfire from ships in the Tonkin Gulf added to the casualties along the road from Quang Tri. Route 1, between Quang Tri and Hue, came to be called the Highway of Terror, as it had long before been called the Street Without Joy.

The ARVN was leaderless. When facing insurgents in earlier times, it had been trained in conventional warfare. Then, under General Creighton Abrams, the American advisers had shifted emphasis to counterinsurgency, but by 1971 the enemy was employing tank units and heavy guns.

In the end, American advisers made the difference on the three fronts. Supported in large measure by American air power, the ARVN regained the shapeless, bloodstained wreckage that had been An Loc and Quang Tri. As in the past, Hanoi's offensive faded away, leaving "victors" who were decimated by casualties, exhausted, and more demoralized than ever.

President Nixon, facing protests in the United States and risking a diplomatic strategy that had invested his personal prestige in "detente" with the Communist superpowers, ordered North Vietnam bombed "as it had never been bombed before."

But Hanoi had made its point. The day was coming when Nguyen Van Thieu's Vietnam would be virtually on its own. Only US air power stood between the regime and its mortal enemies. Vietnamization, essentially, had failed.

Rumors—and that is all they were—of secret accommodation between North Vietnam and America had first circulated after Tet, 1968. With every crisis they surfaced again, and after the Easter offensive they were heard everywhere and almost everywhere believed: Americans had allowed North Vietnamese troops into the cities; the Vietnamese had avoided killing Americans and had killed ARVNs instead. The talk was always of what the Communists would do and, above all, of what the Americans would do.

Mac V, in his windowless office piled high with surveys, evaluations, and reports, went out and saw that the war was lost. Saigon, a city now more dense with refugees than ever, turned back to its old pursuits in a combination of complacency and despair. As ever, the rumor mills ground on. The Americans were the arbiters of fate. There was no limit to American duplicity, the people of Saigon felt, as there was no limit to American power.

The End

During the winter rains of 1975, Phuoc Binh, a provincial capital north of Saigon, fell to NVA regulars. Their heavy guns pulverized the city. Eight thousand strong, they stormed the ARVN perimeter.

Ho Chi Minh was dead, and Ngo Dinh Diem, and Vietnamese in numbers beyond estimation—nailed by the bombs, smoked by the Spooky gunships,* buried by NVA 85s. They had died holding each other's hands and donkey-riding their wounded out. Or carrying their teapots—the women were always carrying teapots—and carrying their children, and the children carrying children. The soil and the dead were commingled. The morning mists were filled with humble ghosts.

John Kennedy was dead. Lyndon Johnson was dead. Mac V had faded away. More than fifty thousand Americans were dead and their futures lost to us.

When the dry season came, the NVA chief of staff, General Van Tien Dung, felt the earth firm beneath his feet. Like many others, he would write a book about the war later on. It would be a book entitled, without irony, *Our Great Spring Victory*. In his book General Dung recalls the jungle in dry weather, the

*The Douglas AC-47 Spooky, a fixed-wing gunship. —*Ed.*

clearings "whose dry leaves covered the ground like a yellow carpet." The dry earth would be good for tanks, General Dung thought.

In Saigon, President Thieu's family was speculating in real estate. No one could believe it. Real estate was such a bad bet. There were no more American advisers and no more B-52s.

In March, General Dung's forces feinted toward Pleiku, panicked its garrison, then shifted direction to cut the highway to Ban Me Thuot. Ban Me Thuot fell on the tenth of March. President Thieu decided on a strategic withdrawal, the better to re-form and fight on a solid southern front. He ordered his commander in II Corps to evacuate Pleiku. The commanding general, overcome with terror, fled with his staff, leaving his army. And then it all fell apart.

Thieu ordered Hue held to the last man, then changed his orders and called for retreat. The troops in Hue, officials and their families, and ordinary people, who had learned a fear from which they would never be free, recalled the terror visited on the city during Tet, 1968. As the soldiers and their families fled Pleiku and Hue, the NVA fired shell after shell into their ranks. Hysterical thousands, crazy with fear, crazy with thirst and hunger, poured into Da Nang. Many carried dead or dying children.

What followed has often been recounted and need not be again. More horrors ensued—more, it might be thought, than such a small country could contain.

Late in April, just before the fall, President Thieu and his family left with their money. In Saigon, other families committed suicide, policemen shot themselves on street corners, Catholic soldiers emptied their rifles into each other, striving for grace. The Americans managed to get their own out, but Vietnamese who deserted the Vietcong, loyal Nungs guarding the abandoned apartment houses, native CIA operatives and lists containing their names were mostly left behind for the North's security services to deal with.

A tank pulled up in front of the presidential palace and an NVA colonel, the correspondent of the Red Army newspaper, accepted surrender from a corps of old men whose day was done.

Incredibly, there seemed to be no more Americans. We had gone home, out of their history at last, to sing our own songs and tell our own stories. The country of Vietnam fell into the hands of its inhabitants.

During the evacuation, two young US Marines were killed by enemy rocket fire on the tarmac of Tan Son Nhut. They were the last known Americans killed in Vietnam.

Some called their deaths unnecessary. There had been another miscalculation up the line. Operation Talon Vise, the final extrication of the American mission, had been delayed to the point of near disaster.

But by that time fairly few Americans were in the mood for outrage or name-calling or affixing blame. There had been so many miscalculations, just as there had been unheralded acts of valor that lent meaning to obscure deaths and the lives behind them. There had been so much outrage and so much suffering. It had been so bitter and so never-ending. It had torn apart America and destroyed Vietnam.

Who can speak of unnecessary deaths in such a war, or in any war?

—*Images of War (The Vietnam Experience)*, 1986

THE QUIET AMERICAN

The title of Graham Greene's 1955 Vietnam novel, as others have pointed out, is a joke. The eponymous character is not quiet. Like all the Americans who appear in its deft, succinct story, Alden Pyle is a prattling fool. Pyle (Greene was good with names and their associations) goes on to illustrate the joke's unspoken punch line: the only quiet American is a dead American.

Graham Greene was born the son of the headmaster at Berkhamsted School. His family was of the professional middle class, the backbone of the British Empire in its last years. If not a ruling class, it was certainly an administrative cadre and a self-conscious elite. That class had been horribly decimated in the World War, and was particularly sensitive to the erosion of British influence throughout the world. Those born to it imposed upon themselves a great measure of responsibility and accepted a tradition of individual sacrifice, for which they were compensated by the nation's confidence and a degree of moral privilege that really had no foreign equivalent. In peace and war, they set the standard.

Graham Greene was a Balliol man at Oxford, one of those whom Herbert Asquith said were provided there with "a tranquil consciousness of effortless superiority." Greene, given to restlessness and tormenting rages, had a consciousness never tranquil, but his sense of superiority was lifelong in Asquith's sense. At the beginning of his career, he knew, he wrote, that he must venture into a wider world, "dive below the polite level to something nearer common life." The descriptions of ordinary people in his early work have an aura of discovery, a measure of distaste, and an assumption that his readers will share his attitudes and stand ready to learn something about how the other half lives. When the characters in *Brighton Rock* listen to "cheap American music," the American reader can imagine the too gentle ear resisting Duke Ellington.

It was Greene's fortune, as a member of the British Empire's administrative class, to witness the rise of American influence in the world. The sense of imperial mission left him sentimental and proprietary about what we still call today the Third World. Americans had a way of showing up under palm and pine, from the deliciously opium-laced dream streets of the Far East to the heart of London itself, flattening the ambiance with their uninflected, irrepressible observations. From the sensitive traveler's point of view, it was a case of literally not knowing one's place.

The American presence seems to have taken Greene somewhat by surprise; often the anger he directs at his own country and its governance seems to be a reproach for allowing it, all at once, to happen. In sum, Greene was a better English patriot than he was a Jungian, a Catholic, or a socialist, or, as George Orwell once suggested, "our first Catholic Fellow Traveler."

Greene received the classic university education of his day, which was inclined toward unitary systems, toward logical positivism, ideology in the form of socialist political structure, and the insights of psychoanalysis. He was treated by a spiritualist-Jungian as a youth; some of his brightest admired companions at school were Marxists. Another structuralist concept appealed to him for a variety of reasons. He was courting a Catholic woman. And Catholicism's mixture of spiritual elitism with intellectual and social humiliation, the religion of Campion, Tichbourne, and the betrayer-martyrs, seemed a natural refuge for his spirit.

All in all, he was never a rebel in the sense of denying the fundamentals of his upbringing and education. Contrary to the declarations of the American founders he despised, he seems never to have found a form of tyranny over the mind of man that did not project some appeal to him. When he speculated specifically on human progress, a far-off hope, he looked toward holistic solutions and elites. He hated the false tempters, as he saw them—cruel, corrupt Mexican anticlericals in *The Lawless Roads*, the American merchant-globalists whose hypocrisy he parodies in the Ambassador's speech in *Our Man in Havana*.

When he published *The Quiet American*, Graham Greene was one of the few major writers in English with an ideological standpoint, presumably to be construed from his professed Catholicism. In fact, for most of his Anglophone Catholic readers, tyrannized by an intellectually and spiritually arid Church, Greene seemed to exist by dispensation in some heterodox and libertine level of the Church permitted to him alone. A "Foreign Legion" of the Church, he sometimes called his personal practice of religion, and it sounded very glamorous to bookish parochial school adolescents who spent Saturday evenings in confession being harassed about hell and necking. Greene, along with some of the other publicly Catholic novelists of the time, was among the modernist authors whose work was assigned reading. I believe our clerical instructors were themselves puzzled as to why the reading of Greene's paradoxical, worldly, and despairing works should be encouraged. But he was approved, "one of ours," a confessed Catholic who commanded respect in the larger world.

The Quiet American, in its bitterness, came as an unpleasant surprise to most American Catholics. In fact, it was in keeping with the attitudes Greene had represented from the very beginning of his career. Abroad, there were many of the left, including Catholics, who joined in what turned out to be, to us, a discomfiting general rejoicing at the sight of a master of moral nuance blasting the moralizing hyperpower, disdaining its wealth and careless certainty. Besides gratifying the Communists, Greene had written what many had been thinking for a few years but refrained, for various reasons, from uttering publicly. This story of a few minor players in a still remote, exotic, and deliciously described, collapsing colony of Old Europe came as refreshment to the souls of many.

When A. J. Liebling, in his hostile New Yorker review of The Quiet American, complained about a British writer accusing "his best friends" of murder, Greene scoffed at the phrase. In fact, Liebling was mistaken in his assumptions about Greene's attitude. He might have been guided by some reflection on the book's title.

In 1956, according to Newsweek, the Soviet journal Pravda

dedicated five columns of type to *The Quiet American. Pravda* is quoted as calling it "the most important event" of recent British literary history. The Soviet journal's cultural staff, which spent so much of its day pretending enthusiasm, must have turned to *The Quiet American* with genuine gratitude. Here from an acknowledged master came a book of depth and complexity that recognized the Communist role in "humanity's" cause and represented America's anti-Communist effort in Asia as not only naive but murderous.

Sympathy for the socialist side in the Cold War was not at that time easily forthcoming from the world of English-speaking fiction, attached as most of it was to character and milieu, the small canvas. In the period between the publication of *To Have and Have Not* and *For Whom the Bell Tolls*, the Communist Party had affected to claim the American Ernest Hemingway as a friend of the toiler; Hemingway, in his greed for praise, was even moved to write a play, *The Fifth Column*, featuring a Hemingwayesque American NKVD agent. That particular romance, embarrassingly rooted in mutual exploitation, did not last. Now Greene, no proletarian but a Catholic moralist by reputation, had written against the American colossus and its international role.

In *The Quiet American* the foolishness of Americans—what more polite Europeans referred to as their lack of background —their overconfiding chatter and Hollywood sensibility, is offered as an insight into the origins of American policy in Asia.

"One is impressed by Greene's nostalgia," wrote Anthony Burgess, "for the Rider Haggard, Conan Doyle, John Buchan hero pursuing the cause of British decency in some fever-ridden outpost."

If we were to examine *The Quiet American* in the light of Anthony Burgess's remarks, the "fever-ridden outpost" is Saigon before the withdrawal of the French, during the fighting that ended in their stand and defeat at Dien Bien Phu in 1954. Though he denies it, the cause of "decency" is in the shaky hands of the British journalist Thomas Fowler, a drinker and opium smoker living adulterously with Phuong, his Vietnamese mistress.

Despite his weakness for clouding the fallen world around him, Fowler's perception is his dynamic. He is a conscientious working journalist, his private desperation notwithstanding. He knows his story and, not being unduly attached to his life, is ready to put it on the line in that story's earnest pursuit. Yet, until the events of the novel unfold, he sees himself as outside the battle. Fowler is the narrator, and the only sentient presence, the only multidimensional character, in the novel.

The two other principals, Phuong and the American Alden Pyle, are present as metaphors and as soldiers of the plot, which is lively and Conradian, actually more well made and adroit than in anything by Greene's master. Phuong, Fowler's mistress, has a pretty little head which she fills with proto-tabloid celebrity gossip and interesting facts about the British royals. Childishly, she has transferred her affections to Pyle, the representative of a stronger foreign presence and one able to provide for her more generously.

There is less to her than to her conniving sister Miss Hei, who schemes through Phuong to attach the family to a useful foreigner. Miss Hei appears very briefly, but her character and interests are well defined. Phuong is a device; she might be described as the love interest.

Alden Pyle, Fowler's rival for Phuong, is just one of the novel's Americans. All of these are innocent, Pyle most of all. To be innocent is to be bumptious and stupid, rude, provincial, inconsiderate; well intentioned but at the same time conscienceless and murderous. Pyle is a CIA agent new to the country, and the third corner of the novel's triangle. Pyle knows only what he has read in books at Harvard, but he has murderous plans or orders to back a Third Force, which will be anti-French, anti-Communist, and pro-American.

If Phuong stands for the eternally complacent East, like the water buffalo who appears on the road to Tan Yin, indifferent to the foreign empire builders who come and go, Pyle, equipped with apparently fatuous books he has read at Harvard, stands for what Greene has chosen to define here as American innocence.

"I never met a man who had better motives for all the trouble he caused," says Fowler of Pyle.

Since what Greene insistently calls American "innocence" seems to be the absence of any kind of inner life, many of Greene's American readers, who imagine for themselves a certain interior existence, dislike it. On the other hand, as though to vindicate Greene's distinctly comic vision, other Americans embrace it, professing to recognize in it a dead-on portrayal of the people they must endure as compatriots day after day. Without question, it rang carillons of recognition and delight in Britain, Europe, and Latin America, implying things that many people, not only those on the left, recognized.

Various Americans, irritated at seeing their metaphorical selves, have questioned Pyle's credibility as an American, the verisimilitude of his character and speech. It is certainly true that while Washington, DC, was chockablock with Harvard-trained international studies majors, agents who smuggled plastique into cities in which plastique abounded would have tended to find their way into the CIA from the military rather than from Harvard Yard.

Pyle and all the American characters in *The Quiet American* speak with a straight man's timing. That is, they do not understand or respond to the witticisms offered at their expense. For them, words cast no shadows; they are deaf to irony: Pyle, Granger, all of them, stand mute before Fowler's very cinematic wisecracks. Pyle and the others refuse to be drawn, like Margaret Dumont subjected to Groucho Marx. They persistently offer their puppyish friendship ("Do you mind if I call you Tom?") in the face of Fowler's insults.

The novel has several areas of focus. One is the existential dilemma of Fowler: alienated, still half in love with his wife back in England, and consciously feeling himself her betrayer. Moreover, he is jealous of Pyle's having replaced him in the beautiful Phuong's attentions. There seems more pain and loss, more complexity, in Fowler's break with the offstage wife he claims not to love than in his attachment to Phuong. This is offered as a physical obsession but does not play as one, mainly because Phuong is a metaphorical figure and left undercharacterized.

The other characters in *The Quiet American* are the colorful denizens of a Conradian, pre-Americanized Asia—literate castaways, serene priests, a Portuguese half-caste—noble professional soldiers of the French Empire. The many and varied power interests at play are shown in action, each side trying to use the other, on the lookout for weakness, guile, or the main chance. In the realm of the personal, Fowler, Pyle, and Phuong are a love triangle, three little people like those whose fortunes, said Humphrey Bogart's Rick over in Casablanca, "don't amount to a hill of beans in this crazy world."

It should not surprise readers that Graham Greene spent years as a film critic, that he was the author of a number of first-class film scripts, including *The Third Man*, and that movies were among the influences that colored his work. For years he watched Hollywood films, and he was ready to praise what he thought were the good ones. But despite his professional eye, he was as ready as the next moviegoer to let films infiltrate his imagination of the world. This conceiving of things colors experience and is the wellspring of any writer's work.

It would be simpleminded to say that Greene based or took his conception of all things American from films. But the degree to which his strategies as a novelist were influenced by films, the measure of weighty insight he drew from some pretty flimsy American movies, is considerable. So is the visceral anger that seems to be controlled only with effort.

In his excellent biography, Norman Sherry quotes from Greene's review of a Hollywood adaptation of an Erich Maria Remarque novel, *The Road Back*.

> It's an awful film, one bit Mother's Day, celebrated by American youth, plump, adolescent faces with breaking sissy voices. Voices which began to break in the trenches —remembering the kid sister or watching a companion die … We've lived through a lot in that time, but not through war, revolution, starvation—but through "Can you turn me a little so I can see you go down the road?"

and the young tears ... "There's one more battle to be fought. I must find myself." And always all the time, the breaking voices, the unformed unlined faces and the well-fed bodies of American youth, clean-limbed prize-cattle mooing into the microphone. They call it an all-star cast and that always means that there isn't a single player of any distinction to be picked out of the herd.

It might be funny if it wasn't horrifying. This is America seeing the world in its own image ... what it really emphasizes is the eternal adolescence of the American mind, to which ... morality means keeping Mother's Day and looking after the kid sister's purity.

There is a certain irony in Greene choosing *The Road Back* as an exemplar of Americans' adolescent view of the world. Adapted from a German novel, Remarque's sequel to *All Quiet on the Western Front*, its principal screenwriter is, of all people, the British playwright R. C. Sherriff, author of *Journey's End*, which persists in most people's memory for the heartrending farewells declaimed by its doomed and dying public-school boy officers. Sherriff's lines for *Journey's End* sound very much like the lines he supplied to Hollywood in *The Road Back*. The picture was directed by James Whale, a British war veteran who also gave us *Showboat* and *Frankenstein*.

In fact, with its British screenwriters and director, its music by Dimitri Tiomkin, etc., *The Road Back*, like most Hollywood productions of the time, was the minor product of an industry recruited from five continents, a cosmopolitan gathering of Budapest café Communists, White Russian hairdressers, Nevada cowboys, Old Etonians, and Brooklyn Trotskyists.

Norman Sherry goes on to say: "Greene's belief in the 'eternal adolescence' of Americans must have remained dormant in his mind for twenty years, for surely the quiet American, Pyle, has this specific characteristic in the novel of the same name. Greene's strong and bitter dislike of certain aspects of American life and culture . . . must have stemmed from seeing countless American movies"

It cannot have helped that Greene later found himself in a ruinous lawsuit with Shirley Temple, a coupling at law as absurd as any comedian might require. Ms. Temple and her studio bosses claimed that in reviewing *Wee Willie Winkie*, he had accused them of slyly trading on her sexual appeal. The verdict against him put his magazine, *Night and Day*, out of business.

The review of *The Road Back* contains (or fails to contain) an impressive measure of contempt for the persons of the hapless Yanks on-screen. Mockery of inflated images in a film is a critic's job, but Greene's eager insults seem sadistic in their physicality. They suggest malice toward a victim caught in some obscene posture, the mercilessness of the tormented schoolboy Greene had once been.

At Berkhamsted School, where his father was headmaster, young Graham Greene was tortured almost to suicide by a classmate whose name he remembered all his life. Another boy, one whom he had deeply trusted, laughingly betrayed him. His rendering of all the American characters as pathetic straight men, helpless before irony, blinking in the pure light of the British characters' ordinary, instinctive decency and wholesome common sense, has a darkly familiar tone. It suggests the delight of the long-ago, storybook public-school bully at recognizing an elaborately vulnerable mark. Greene knew that satisfaction from the victim's point of view—not as a literary conceit but from life. He understood the reverse angle as well. His awareness and fascination with the tormentor was something close to admiration, he tells us in one autobiographical work, *A Sort of Life*. This admiration, detected by the sadistic classmate, would have made Greene an attractive object.

His biographer, Norman Sherry, writes that Greene "treats betrayal obsessively, its source, its nature, its prevalence in the world as a malady, its necessity as the unstated part of every man."

In the latter part of the novel, Pyle, wretched rash intruding fool, turns murderous in his feckless ignorant scheming, and Fowler decides he must intervene. Fowler's jealousy over Phuong is a complicating motive, necessary to illustrate the impossibility of a purely disinterested act in this fallen world. Essentially, when Fowler acts it is because, a wise French captain tells him in an opium den, "one has to take sides. If one is to remain human."

Someone once asked Greene if Fowler had set Pyle up falsely purely out of jealousy over Phuong. Perhaps he was reacting to Fowler's transparent satisfaction in the act, disclaimed by the character, but indulged by the author.

Along with his insight into a fallen world, Greene maintained a lifelong capacity for rage. It is expressed in his virtuoso torrents of sarcasm and loathing—and even in a fondness for practical jokes. There is no question that this capacity for hatred enriched his prose. Fowler (sounding very much like Greene the film critic) insists that Pyle's trouble is his innocence. Indeed, innocence is a problem for all the Americans in the novel, and more of a problem for those who have to deal with them.

"What's the good? He'll always be innocent, you can't blame the innocent, they are always guiltless. All you can do is control or eliminate them. Innocence is a kind of insanity."

The judgment is downright Brechtian in its ferocity.

Greene made four trips to Vietnam, usually staying for some weeks at the Continental Hotel in the center of town, hanging out at the outdoor tables there, at the exclusive Cercle Sportif or at Givral's confectionery shop on the rue Catinat. He went into the field, flew a few reconnaissance missions with the French air force, and certainly journeyed the eighty miles of French-built road to Tan Yin. His description of Pyle and Fowler's journey to the Cao Dai Cathedral there and their harrying nocturnal return to Saigon is an episode to rank with Greene's best.

Greene once told the American writer Michael Mewshaw and his wife, Linda, that one source for his plot in *The Quiet American* was the wife of an American diplomat with whom he was sleeping. He was fond of cuckolding acquaintances and boasted of his conquests. He consorted with Americans in Saigon. His biographer describes his relationship with them as openly friendly. An American, according to Norman Sherry, took him to his first opium den there.

So to the question of how true to life is the plot, even if Pyle is a cinematic buffoon. In the small sense, false. The bombing described in *The Quiet American*, in which plastique explosives were set off in downtown Saigon, apparently involved the Cao Dai sect. American historians deny the CIA was involved, and even in the novel a motive is undetectable. But in the larger sense, the Vietnamese who gave their lives to fulfill the ambitions and "tough-mindedness" of American schemers—the McNamaras, the Bundys, the Rostows, and the Colbys—are such that no man can number. I do not believe the word "innocent," even in Greene's elusive definition, can be applied to them.

Was there, though, a model for Pyle? Among his American acquaintances in Vietnam did Greene happen on some misguided American evildoer? It can hardly be said that such people did not exist, although I do not believe they resembled Pyle or spoke like him. Did the figure of Pyle emerge from the angry stories told to Greene by the French?

A couple of Americans have been put forth as originals for Pyle. One was Colonel Edward Lansdale, a former advertising executive who became a patron of Ngo Dinh Diem, providing him principally with various Madison Avenue techniques. His agents failed to pollute the fuel of the Hanoi bus system before being caught. However, Lansdale arrived in Vietnam a month after *The Quiet American* was completed, and Greene has denied using him.

Another American who became something of a legend in Vietnam, and of whom Greene may have heard, was the OSS Colonel A. Peter Dewey. Dewey was an American agent in Japanese-occupied Vietnam and had occasion to cooperate with the Communist Vietminh in a resistance movement. He was a young man of left-wing views and he apparently shared Franklin Roosevelt's expressed disdain for French Indochina. When the British Indian Army arrived in 1945 and armed its Japanese prisoners "to maintain order" while the French colonial authority was restored, Dewey protested vigorously. He was killed after a quarrel with General Gracey of the Indian Army.* To the French he had represented an American intrigue to seize Vietnam, which had sided with Vichy in 1940, in the course of a postwar settlement.

In truth, he had expressed sympathy for the Communists in Vietnam. Dewey's last report to Washington was "the White Man is finished here." Nothing about a third force, nothing about winning hearts and minds or importing explosives. He was an angry American, as angry as Greene. The posting and arming of hated Japanese troops and the reinvented prestige of the formerly Vichy colonial power made Dewey as angry as the sight of Americans drunk at the Continental made Graham Greene. Who knows what would have happened if they had met? Would Colonel Dewey have come out like Pyle? Unfortunately he might, if he had been written, so to speak, in advance. The real Dewey's death also remains mysterious. If he had been more innocent, he might have remained unpunished.

It is possible, as has often been done in America, to dismiss the characterization of Pyle. Assertions of American complicity with the bombers of Saigon in January 1952 do not really hold up. How is it, then, that every experienced American commentator on Vietnam to one degree or another admires

---

*Dewey was fatally shot in a Viet Minh ambush in Saigon on September 26, perhaps in a case of mistaken identity. Dewey, who believed that the Viet Minh were not targeting Americans at this time, had wanted to fly the American flag from his jeep, but General Gracey prohibited that, following a protocol that only general officers were allowed to fly such flags from their vehicles. —*Ed.*

The Quiet American? Fifty years after it was written, more than thirty years after the Vietnam War, it remains one of the great novels of the anticolonial struggle and the Cold War. During the Vietnam War, American journalists presented it to each other on arrival in-country.

For one thing, it is a model of the realist novel in the post-Conradian mode. Its story unfolds with a wonderful expertness and with the greatest economy. Its descriptive passages, its sense of Vietnam and Saigon, are richly pleasurable.

The condemnation of human sacrifices to America's materialistic, ignorant anticommunism is in keeping with Greene's Jansenist Catholicism. Fowler's sudden enthusiasm for "humanity" is not, and may strike some readers as cant. But *The Quiet American's* metaphorical power is undeniable; it carries a weight of truth that America and American readers will have to live with. Greene witnessed the beginning of a terrible mistake, a deadly mistake, the mistake of a great power armed to the teeth attempting to inflict its will in a part of the world to whose language and gestures it was tone-deaf.

Indeed, the real Alden Pyles were the smart, articulate, Vietnamese-speaking American agents sowing their youthful wild oats upcountry later in the war. There were many young men in "special programs" blinded by vanity, youthful machismo, and egotism some may have mistaken for idealism, bent on proving themselves in a treacherous war. It is not true that they never learned cunning. They were corrupted by the power war gave them, and they brought dreadful misfortune on others and on themselves.

How large a "big picture" must one insist on? The Korean War and the demands of NATO produced the atmosphere and the American policies that inspired *The Quiet American*. How-ever, there were fights going on in various other parts of the world, and Greene's sentimentalizing of the Communists, his invocation of humanity, was a shot for the wrong side. We may speak now of a wrong side, at least in that late-century strug-gle. Nevertheless, history has reduced those American over-achievers to the dimension of fools like Pyle in its ruthless rec-ollection. Because time loves language, as Auden said, because novels like this own their time and place, they are remembered in the caricature of a man who hated them.

It is also true — and those of us who read this masterly novel must take it under consideration — that as this edition of *The Quiet American* goes to press, highly educated young men have again set out to remake the world, to visit war on people of whom they know little.* How can we deny the truth *The Quiet American* contains?

—Introduction to the Penguin edition, 2004

---

*Stone refers to the United States invasion of Iraq, which began in 2003. —*Ed.*

UNCLE SAM
DOESN'T WANT YOU!

In 1956 I was eighteen years old and a seaman first class in the United States Navy. I had joined during the summer of 1955, at seventeen, and been sent to the navy's radio school at Norfolk, Virginia. Later that year I was assigned to the class of ship known as an AKA, or attack transport. In those grainy old wire photos of the Normandy invasion or Okinawa, AKAs are always visible offshore. They have the classic single stack and superstructure outline of cargo ships but with large A-frames fore and aft. Amphibious landing craft are stacked and secured over their cargo hatches. The ship that features in Thomas Heggen's novel *Mister Roberts* was an AK, a noncombatant cousin of the AKA.

Heggen's novel catches something of the spirit of the "Gator Navy," as the amphibious force is called, in the period during and after the Second World War. Then as now, its ships were specialized, their form grimly followed function, and they were as plain as dumpsters. The navy did not generally dress them up in pennants for display. During the 1950s, in the Sixth

Fleet's own Mediterranean, while the cruisers and supercarriers basked in the sunshine of Rapallo or Villefranche, the amphib gator ships were elsewhere: Bari, Patras, Izmir. Much time was spent practicing amphibious assaults on beaches in Turkey, Crete, or Sardinia.

Like hotels, colleges, and prisons, ships have their particular informing atmosphere. And despite the navy's mode of slate-gray uniformity, each vessel had qualities that could be isolated and analyzed, largely in terms of the human factor. To lifers, career petty officers, the first question about a ship was often "Is she a good feeder?" Eating was the principal pleasure available at sea. Good cooks were prized.

The personnel clerk who typed the orders transferring me from radio school to my new ship was a fellow New Yorker. We fell into conversation, and he told me I was going to a problem ship.

"They're always falling off ladders," he said.

During the 1950s, discipline in the US Navy was tight and fairly effective. Nevertheless, a ship was essentially its crew. Certain ships were dominated, prison-style, by cliques of sailors—sometimes men from the same tough town—who enforced a code of their own belowdecks. It has to be said that this was not universal, but everyone heard the stories. Such a ship's officers might be only vaguely aware of the system that prevailed in the enlisted quarters. Masters-at-arms and senior petty officers either looked the other way or, like crooked cops, made some political accommodation with the de facto leadership. Certain captains naïvely approved, seeing a form of rough democracy, crude peer pressure that furthered cohesion.

Taking up my new billet, I was assigned to bunking space

of the deck division because there were no bunks presently available in the radio gang's sleeping quarters. At that time, men assigned to each of the ship's divisions bunked in the same compartment. The sleeping arrangements then consisted of "racks," four or five high from the deck, sheets of canvas stretched within metal rectangles and secured to the bulkhead by lengths of chain.

One day during our first week at sea I went below to arrange my gear in the deck division's compartment and encountered Flem (not, as they say, his real name), a third-class boatswain's mate, who was goldbricking belowdecks while better men worked topside. He ran a little tailoring and pressing shop in a tiny locker off one of the passageways. Seeing me settle in, Flem assumed I was a new seaman in his notoriously tyrannized deck division, thus his inferior in rank and with my fortunes at his disposal. He was a small, freckled man, round, neckless, and thick-featured. With his slack smile and shifty eyes he looked like a lying witness at a country murder trial.

When Flem introduced himself he made no offer of shaking hands, itself a considerable insult. He told me a few things I already knew about how tough life was aboard that particular AKA and how much tougher he could make it. He told me I looked like "tender gear" to him. "Tender gear" was a common navy expression, dating back to the good old days. It was applied to sailors of youthful appearance, when imagined as passive partners in prison-style, "facultative" homosexuality or as the victims of rape. (The phrase was one of the many homoerotic terms current in the navy. Like them, it could be used insultingly, ambiguously, or good-naturedly, as in, "Carruthers, I'm so horny, you look like tender gear to me." A man's reputation for wit, something useful and valued, could ride on the quality of the rejoinder.)

But Flem wasn't my buddy, and he wasn't kidding. He wasn't starry-eyed with affection either. That night I thought it prudent to take a spare bunk chain to bed with me. Sometime during the dead of night he woke me up with a lot of prods and heavy breathing. So we ended up fighting up and down the faintly lit compartment. A few men were awake and silent or laughing; I was new, nobody much cared. In those days I was always blundering into fights, only to be reminded that it wasn't like the movies, to be amazed by the strength and determination of my opponent. Although beery drunk, Flem had the energy of an insect and, apparently, great single-mindedness.

But I was younger, stronger, and sober, my reputation on a new ship was at stake, and I had the chain. I was also considerably embittered. The youthful appearance that aroused lust in Flem seemed to make any woman I had the temerity to approach dismiss me as a Sea Scout. Flem went into the head to wash the blood off himself, cursed me out from a distance, and crept back to the tailor shop where he lived. The next day his face was swollen and covered with welts, as though he had landed on his chin in poison ivy. The worse Flem looked, the better for me, since every enlisted man aboard soon knew the story.

A few days later we were off Gibraltar, and I went past his shop and he said something to me I couldn't hear. I doubled back, lest it be thought he could mock me with impunity.

"How's that?"

He stood stood beside the presser, looking down at a blue jumper on the pad.

"You cried just like a cooze," he said, still not looking at me. I had an immediate anxiety that he was speaking for effect, trying to make anyone within earshot believe things had turned out differently. But there was no one around, so I went on my way. Appearances were everything.

I didn't want to think I had cried during our engagement, but it occurred to me that I might well have. I didn't care for the picture the reflection summoned forth, me whacking Flem repeatedly with a bunk chain, weeping away "like a cooze."

I was surprised by the memory of my difficulties with Flem sometime last year when I was about to engage in a public discussion on the subject of sexual harassment. I had originally approached the issue as an examination of conscience, looking back on my relations with women over the years.

Flem and I were not romancing the wilder shores of love; we were acting out an old dirty sea story that must go back to the Phoenicians and has more to do with power, cruelty, strength, and weakness than with any kind of attraction. I'm sure Flem felt about the same fondness for me that he felt for his favorite farm animal back home. Flem today, if he's alive, retired in his trailer among the palmettos, is unlikely to regard himself as "gay." I think it very likely he thoroughly opposes the notion of gays being able to serve in the military.

A second bit of reminiscence about my time in service. About two and a half years after the business of Flem, I was serving aboard a different ship, also an AKA. By this time I was a petty officer myself, feeling very experienced and salty. The ship had just returned to the States from a long voyage that had kept it at sea for many weeks at a time and away from the United States for the better part of a year. Evenings at sea or on duty nights in port when we could not go ashore, a group of us, junior petty officers, took to gathering on the ship's fantail or in the shipfitter shop. We were would-be intellectuals of about college age, on average twenty-one or twenty-two. We met to smoke and talk and hang out. We liked progressive jazz and thought the *Playboy* Philosophy was pretty hot stuff.

It was 1958, the year *On the Road* was published. We were all short-timers, a few months shy of our discharges; the Road seemed to be waiting for us. Moreover, we found in the navy an inexhaustible fund of humor and buffoonery. Everything about it, from the hats we shared with Donald Duck to the grotesque locutions of the Uniform Code of Military Justice, struck us as risible. Without question, we got on some people's nerves. We were presently to learn the nature of the nerves we got on.

One evening while I was in New York on leave and on my way to the Central Plaza for an evening of jazz with my date, I was arrested by a couple of plainclothes New York cops on a charge of being absent without leave. I was not in fact AWOL. Nevertheless, I was turned over to the New York military police headquarters in Hell's Kitchen, where I spent several hours leaning against a wall on my fingertips, trying to persuade an MP sergeant to call my ship in Norfolk. Eventually the sergeant did, the ship's duty officer confirmed my leave status, and I was released.

My false arrest had been part of the shockwave from a purge touched off by some incident in the naval district. Foolish inquisitions and malicious informing were being promiscuously encouraged. Someone had told the executive officer about our gang of malingerers in the shipfitter shop. It seemed that we were planning to found a motorcycle gang, to be named the

Weird Beards, in the Bethlehem Steel yards in Staten Island. The gang would engage in unlawful activities and actions prejudicial to good order. Its members would carry arms and be dangerous. They would worship Satan, harass Christians, use marijuana, and, conveniently, be homosexual.

This was all amusing in every regard save one: the navy in those days was obsessed with in-service gangs and homosexuality and tended, on not much evidence and without much formality, to lock down alleged violators in the bowels of Portsmouth Naval Prison for years and years. The report (based, needless to say, on some fantasy spun in the shipfitter shop) seemed to speak most urgently to those obsessions.

The executive officer panicked and ordered the immediate arrest of everyone mentioned in the report. He must have imagined us already on the highway, darkening the horizon, mincing into Harley shops, torching roadside chapels. Some people came back in chains.

We discovered that lockers had been broken into, letters removed, possessions rifled through and, of course, occasionally stolen unofficially. I happened to own a paperback called *Immortal Poems of the English Language*, which I subsequently spotted on the desk of the master-at-arms in the ship's brig. Evidence, for sure. The MAA handed it back to me as though he were afraid there was semen on it.

In the aftermath, when the whole thing fell apart, the exec apparently felt silly. He would even show up in the shipfitter shop to be pals, making us all stand to attention and upset our coffee. When I applied to college, being under twenty-one, I needed a signature on my application from a "parent or guardian." I was directed to the exec, who signed it and gave me a

nice letter to go with it, not a word about homosexual motorcycle gangs or anything like that.

"Of course," he said, chuckling, "I'm not really your
guardian."

"No, sir," I said.

Had I the naïveté to report Flem during the first incident, I
would have seen many a sour face and disgusted expression of
which I, not Flem, would have been the object. I would have
branded myself a pussy, a snitch, and quite possibly a homosexual. A man was expected to cope. Not quite conversely, if
Flem had been able to coerce me into accommodation, shipboard opinion would have despised me, not him. A lingering
tradition would have excused him, not legally but morally. The
navy preferred not to know about the potential for forcible
sodomy, but could work itself into a moralizing dudgeon over
rumors of subversion, with poetry as evidence. And as surely as
today's charges of kindergarten child abuse tend to incorporate
accusations of witchcraft, subversive notions in the navy were
profoundly associated with homosexuality.

Whether or not the preceding sad story has a moral, it reflects
the shabby and sordid way the armed forces have approached
homosexuality in the ranks over the years. This is the subject
of Randy Shilts's long book, *Conduct Unbecoming: Lesbians and
Gays in the Military, Vietnam to the Persian Gulf.* Shilts's business
here is advocacy, and he writes in favor of the right of gays and
lesbians to serve in the US armed forces. His arguments seem
to grow more reasoned and less strident as the book proceeds,
and he has a good reporter's instinct for the core of a story. He
begins, somewhat irrelevantly, by invoking the Sacred Band of

Thebes and George Washington's silk tights, but the cumulative effect of *Conduct Unbecoming* is a clear indictment of the morally confused and weak-minded policy that has prevailed so far.

If there is a single reference point against which the whole of *Conduct Unbecoming* may be viewed, it is the report he cites, one officially entitled, "Report of the Board Appointed to Prepare and Submit Recommendations to the Secretary of the Navy for the Revision of Policies, Procedures and Directives Dealing with Homosexuals." This classified document, known less ponderously as the Crittenden Report, might well surprise today's congressional zealots for a one hundred percent he-man heterosexual military. Shilts quotes from and summarizes it at length.

"There is no correlation between homosexuality and either ability or attainments. Whether or not public opinion holds homosexuality to be synonymous with degeneracy, the fact remains that a policy which long remained contrary to public opinion could not but have an adverse effect on the Navy," the board wrote. Elsewhere the panel concluded: "A nice balance must be maintained in changes of policy to ensure that public sensibilities are not offended in any attempt to promote a forward-looking program in recognition of the advances in the knowledge of homosexual behavior and treatment, nor can there be any intimation that homosexual conduct is condoned. It is not considered to be in the best interests of the Military Departments to liberalize standards ahead of the civilian climate; thus in so far as practicable it is recommended that the Navy keep abreast of developments but not attempt to take a position of leadership."

Drawing on testimony from a variety of experts, the report generally refutes every truism behind the ban on homosexuals: There are "many known instances of individuals who have served honorably and well, despite being exclusively homosexual." The notion that gays were security risks was "without sound basis in fact . . . No intelligence agency, as far as can be learned, adduced any factual data to support this conclusion." In fact, "there is some information to indicate that homosexuals are quite good security risks."

It goes on to recommend that discovered homosexuals no longer be less than honorably discharged. It refers to the concentration of homosexuals in certain specialties—the medical services, the women's branch—as known facts of life, and it ends by suggesting that the navy "keep abreast of social attitudes toward homosexuality."

This extraordinary document was prepared not, as might be thought, in preparation for a Clinton presidency but during the second Eisenhower administration, in 1957. Like all those bottles of ketchup we heard about but never saw, a crucial part of this wisdom was apparently tucked away somewhere in one of the navy's subtropical depots and forgotten. The absurd homosexual purges, which continue to the present day, very often have more to do with perception than with discipline. They concern the way the services see themselves as being seen, rather than the way in which they really see themselves or the way they actually are. Years later, the military would indignantly deny the very existence of the Crittenden Report, and only persistent application of the Freedom of Information Act retrieved it from the caves of the Pentagon.

There are many personal stories in *Conduct Unbecoming*,

maybe a few more than the reader can keep track of. One of the saddest occurs over and over again, the pattern repeating itself as names and precise circumstances change: A young person, often a teenager, joins the service. In the course of enlistment that person discovers himself or herself to be gay. Service conditions provide the opportunity for an affair, not infrequently the first. Discovery follows, and arrest, and then terrorizing interrogations by the squalid keyhole cops of the military investigative services. There are the usual threats of disgrace; the prisoner's parents will be told, her hometown neighbors, his high school coach, the boyfriend or girlfriend back home, and so on. And as often as not, it seems, even after the victim destroys the remains of his or her own self-respect by naming names, the threats are made good. Then, Crittenden notwithstanding, the subject is usually released into civilian life with a bad discharge, humiliated, sometimes traumatized for life.

This comes about, Shilts demonstrates, as a result of a routine procedure — the turning over of suspects to the military investigative services, whose livelihood has always been charges of homosexual behavior. Like the medieval church remanding heretics to the secular arm, commanding officers have dispatched accused personnel to the mercies of these agencies, of which the civilian-manned Naval Investigative Service is the most notorious. Shilts records an observation current in the fleet: "Call the NIS and tell them you've got a dead body and the agents may show up in the next week or so. Call and say you've got a dead body and you think the murderer was homosexual and the agents will be there in thirty seconds."

The stories Shilts marshals about the NIS are harrowing. Most harrowing of all is its attempt to blame the explosion in the USS *Iowa* gun turret on a fabricated gay relationship, in support of which it ruthlessly doctored circumstantial evidence and posthumously blackened the name of a sailor killed in the explosion.

The navy could have done with a better, wiser, and more humane investigative service, because its ships were not without problems. In recounting the case of a 1980 lesbian purge aboard the USS *Norton Sound* that was instigated by the complaint of a female sailor, Shilts describes post–Vietnam War conditions at their nadir: a ship utterly out of control, undisciplined, and rife with dope dealing, loansharking, violence, and tension between every identifiable group—racial, sexual, or otherwise. Anyone who has ever served aboard a US Navy ship will know the sort of floating hell such a vessel can be. The USS *Belleau Wood*, an amphibious ship whose admittedly gay crew member Allen Schindler was murdered last year, seems to have supported similar conditions.

Until the mid-1970s, the military succeeded in living with the kinds of contradictions that only a prestigious bureaucracy, with good public relations, can resolve. It was well aware that its ranks contained homosexuals, whose presence it often tolerated out of expedience. From time to time it would arrest and sacrifice one, *pour encourager les autres*, a process of culling meant to demonstrate that the armed services were still part of Middle America.

During the Vietnam War, the numbers of homosexuals the military was shocked to detect in its ranks mysteriously diminished. Shilts asserts that during that war, draft boards were instructed to demand "proof" from inductees who claimed to be homosexual, proof that not only would be embarrassing but would make anyone who supplied it criminally liable in almost all of the United States. In other words, like society in general, the services dealt with homosexuality in an inconsistent, arbitrary way, entirely on its own terms.

But the world was changing, and after the Vietnam War the military was no longer so prestigious, nor were its public relations so effective. A wave of activism was washing away old arrangements. In March 1975, a career air force sergeant with twelve years' service, Leonard Matlovitch Jr., wrote a letter to the secretary of the air force via his commanding officer. Matlovitch had an outstanding record; he was the kind of senior noncom who makes the services work, a wounded veteran of Vietnam, a wearer of the Bronze Star. One can only imagine the foreboding that ascended the chain of command with this document.

"After some years of uncertainty," Matlovitch wrote, "I have arrived at the conclusion that my sexual preferences are homosexual as opposed to heterosexual. I have also concluded that my sexual preferences will in no way interfere with my Air Force duties, as my preferences are now open. It is therefore requested that those provisions in AFM39-12 relating to the discharge of homosexuals be waived in my case."

The US military had been overtaken by what might be called the American Factor. The most moralizing and legalistic country on earth, the land where everybody is responsible for everything, although nobody is responsible for anything, was about to quarrel with itself. With its customary moral valor, the military looked wildly about for a moment, then sided with what appeared to be the respectable element. Its instincts were conservative, and it wanted nothing more than to appear respectable. The air force initiated discharge proceedings against Matlovitch, invoking AFM39-12, the very ordinance he had challenged. But as of March 6, 1975, the days of arbitrary punishment and arbitrary tolerance were numbered.

Any story whose subject is social change in America will consist in large part of legal detail, and *Conduct Unbecoming* is no exception. The book sets forth scores of cases and describes scores of proceedings and procedures, from discharge hearings to sessions of the Supreme Court. The case of Leonard Matlovitch is one of many. Yet it runs like an informing thread through the period under discussion, and there are few accounts in the book more poignant. Shilts sentimentalizes Matlovitch to some degree, but the sergeant's naïve idealism and his unhappy fortunes are actually the stuff of drama. In 1980, discouraged by Reagan's election, he accepted a substantial cash settlement from the air force, failed to prosper in civilian life, and died of AIDS in 1988.

Shilts also describes a case with a happier outcome, that of Perry Watkins, an African American who told his Tacoma draft board in May 1968 that he was gay. It being 1968, his draft board told him otherwise; there were no gay blacks of military age in Tacoma in the year of the Tet offensive. Watkins went into the army and liked the life. His female impersonations became the hit routine of every army entertainment, and each time he was presented with a form demanding after his sexual preference, he declared himself gay. So it went for sixteen years of army service, until finally, during the Reagan years, his status was challenged and he was discharged. Watkins sued. In 1990, the US Court of Appeals ordered his reinstatement, and the administration appealed. Finally, in November of the same year, twenty-three years after his surreal visit to the Tacoma draft board, the Supreme Court found for Watkins, and ordered him all pay and allowances.*

Media accounts of gays in the military have tended to focus on homosexual men. In reality the impact has always been greater on the female side, in terms of both numbers and ambiance. On the whole, a greater proportion of lesbians than male homosexuals have sought military careers. As Shilts makes plain, many have served in the military with particular success. His narrative follows the paradoxical fortunes of a number of lesbians who, while turning in above-average professional performances, have run afoul of the military's social instincts. In some cases, trouble developed as a result of tensions between lesbians and male personnel; sometimes there were complaints from nongay women who felt intimidated by lesbians. But the most famous case recounted here is that of Miriam Ben-Shalom, a lesbian who openly revealed her sexual preference upon graduation from drill sergeant's school and was discharged from the army reserve in 1971 as a result. After decades of litigation, Ben-Shalom's administrative discharge was upheld by the Supreme Court in 1990.

By then there were many cases in the courts, and the legal situation continued to seesaw. At one point in the Matlovitch proceedings, Judge Gerhard Gesell of the federal district court in Washington called on the military to take "a more discrimi-

---

*The Ninth Circuit Court of Appeals awarded Watkins a retroactive promotion, $135,000 in back pay, full retirement benefits, and an honorable discharge. In 1990, the Bush administration appealed the ruling to the Supreme Court, which declined to review the case. — Ed.

nating and informed approach" to the issue, but found against Matlovitch on technicalities. The judge added: "It seems to the court a tragedy that we must confront—as I fear we will have to unless some change takes place—an effort at reform through persistent, insistent and often ill-advised litigation."

But persistent litigation is the American way. By the nineties the services had tried to tighten the court-worthiness of their regulations. The armed forces had seen their first in-services AIDS case at Letterman Army Hospital in San Francisco in July 1982, a factor that would alter both the arguments and the underlying reality. But it was plain by the election of 1992 that the services' traditional and irrational methods of dealing with homosexuality had worn away. President Clinton's compromises may be less than the total vindication some activists have called for, but no amount of resistance will bring back the old system.

Various foreign military establishments have their methods of dealing with gay personnel, and Shilts approvingly cites some of the more reasonable. But foreign examples are not necessarily useful. The United States has the largest and most active gay rights movement in the world, one completely committed to the right of gays to serve. Gay rights organizations in most other countries—even countries with civil rights laws that protect gays—are not as prominent. In Europe most gay rights organizations are ipso facto antimilitary and inhabit a different world than their armed services. Military service is not one of their priorities.

Charles Moskos, a sociologist at the University of Chicago, who testified before the Senate Armed Services Committee, has pointed out the flaws in basing assumptions on foreign examples. "More gays in the military have come out of the closet in the American military," Moskos writes, "where homosexuality is proscribed than in those countries (e.g., Israel, Germany, Scandinavia) where it is technically allowed." In those forces where gays are unrestricted, most gay members nevertheless remain in the closet. A distinction must be made, Moskos says, "between de facto and de jure treatment of gays."

Regarding Israel, often cited for its tolerance, Moskos says flatly, "No open gay holds a command position in a combat area anywhere in the IDF." The situation in France, which nominally admits gays to its service, is suggested by the diffident language employed by two French military sociologists: "In the military [homosexuality] is shrouded in a kind of silence that does not express embarrassment but a complete lack of interest. The clue may be that most homosexuals are screened or self-selected out."

The situation in Britain, whose forces are governed by restrictions more or less equivalent to those of the United States, seems to be the reverse of the French position: legal prohibition but discreet selective tolerance, at Her Majesty's Pleasure. "The practice is to not act unless they call attention to themselves. Indeed, if their orientation becomes known but they are not openly engaged in homosexual behavior, they might be counseled and warned against misconduct, rather than discharged."* Last spring, the RAF discharged Sergeant Simon

---

*David R. Segal, Paul A. Gade, and Edgar M. Johnson, "Social Science Research on Homosexuals in the Military," in *Gays and Lesbians in the Military: Issues, Concerns, and Contrasts.* —Ed.

Ingram after he openly declared himself gay. "I'm even going to have a proper leaving party," Ingram told a reporter. "But the system doesn't change, my career is in ruins and nobody has explained to me why I'm losing my job."

It would be a mistake to assume that there are no problems for gays in services that technically do not discriminate. Plainly, many foreign military establishments function by way of arrangement, in which the de jure regulations cover some form of de facto accommodation. This may well prove the case in Australia and Canada, which recently responded to gay rights pressure by ending discrimination in their services.

What all this suggests is simply that every country's military is a reflection of its society. Our continuously divided society has always sought to accommodate different social elements according to the strict letter of the law. We are not good at creating "understandings" because so many of us understand completely different things. No other country has anything like the polarization between progressive and conservative forces that exists in the United States. No other country has either our strong gay rights movement or our military religious right. The religious right is not without influence in that section of society from which the military is recruited. As Pat Buchanan is fond of saying, "The wars are fought by Catholics and Baptists." Certainly no other country has witnessed anything like the endless hours of testimony, defiance, rhetoric, moralizing, and accusation that have piled American court records on this one subject to the height of the Tower of Babel.

Plainly Bill Clinton was naïve to think that he could lift the restrictions against gays in the military with the stroke of a pen. A sample of the arguments being drawn up by military experts opposed to ending the gay ban can be seen in the spring issue of *Parameters*, the US Army War College quarterly. An article there, by Major R. D. Adair and Captain Joseph C. Myers, is titled "Admission of Gays to the Military: A Singularly Intolerant Act."

Adair and Myers attack even the "don't ask, don't tell" proposal, calling it "remarkably hopeful" and also legally unenforceable. "[The policy] begs an obvious question: Is the lifestyle or sexual orientation or whatever term might be used in an Executive Order or Act of Congress legitimate or not? If it is, then why delimit anyone's rights that flow from that lifestyle?" The article goes on to ask about homosexual marriages in the service. Would gay spouses be able to use PX facilities? Would they be assigned government quarters? "Would officers' and non-commissioned officers' spouses' clubs open themselves to the significant other of homosexual members?" They pursue the issue into the sphere of affirmative action: "Within a very short period after the new policy's implementation we could well see tacit floors, quotas and other affirmative action devices to assure that homosexual personnel get their 'fair share' of benefits."

Adair and Myers offer these prospects as a reduction to absurdity. In fact, they are questions that the military may well have to answer in the real world. The handwriting is on the wall. Political pressure from the White House and the Congress, legal mandates from the courts, will compel the military to cope with the question of how to incorporate openly gay people into its ranks.

If the proponents of gay rights cannot get everything they require for their constituency, neither can Major Adair and

Captain Myers have the world back as it was. Some kind of mutual accommodation will be required, unlikely as the prospect may seem.

One of the defiant letters from gays cited in *Conduct Unbecoming* is from an enraged hospital corpsman, protesting antigay discrimination aboard his ship. "I will no longer live a second, secret life," the corpsman writes, "because the Navy has seen fit to adhere to an ante-diluvian, Judeo-Christian posture that no longer and never was congruent with social realism [*sic*]."

But to what extent can the Catholics and Baptists (not to mention Jews) be called upon to abandon their "Judeo-Christian posture"? And to what extent can gays be asked to abandon their gay identity? The US military lacks a grand heraldic or aristocratic tradition. Our army is and always was a "people's army" to a greater degree than that of any other major power. Our informing military totem is the minuteman, the plow jockey turned soldier. The military establishment is common ground; it does in fact belong to all Americans, just as Shilts claims it does.

In this country, we are not good at subtle arrangements. We tend to get everything in writing, which would seem to make difficult any accommodation between two deeply self-righteous points of view. It may be that we will need to exercise considerably more flexibility in terms of the letter of the law. Problems, if they arise, will have to be worked out on the local level, company by company, vessel by vessel. Conditions like the ones that prevailed aboard the *Norton Sound* cannot be permitted, because no accommodation can survive in such an atmosphere. It will be necessary to enlist the consent of all parties to abide by certain guidelines, just as in the past sailors signed the ship's articles as an earnest of their intention to be governed by the necessities of a vessel at sea.

This, of course, is what Major Adair and Captain Myers would call "remarkably hopeful"; it's easier said than done. In smaller units, where people know each other, provision can be made for everyone's attitude. In the impersonal atmosphere of large installations and supercarriers, it's very difficult to maintain such things as consent and mutual understanding. But the simple fact is that our forces are not like other countries' forces; they serve a litigious, volatile country that worships Possibility, and they will have to work it out somehow. It will call for strict discipline, high morale, and some assistance from that Power whom Bismarck once claimed has a special providence for fools and the United States.

In the late summer of 1991, while the navy was preparing to grapple with the latest strategies of gay liberation in the wake of the Persian Gulf War, some of its wholesomely heterosexual young aviators—and a few older ones—were preparing for Tailhook '91. If the name sounds faintly risqué, nothing in the Tailhook Association's summary of its September "symposium" suggests anything other than huffy-puffy right-mindedness: "By the time the event ended with a farewell brunch on a Sunday morning, the Tailhook Association knew to a certainty that the Naval Aviation Symposium had realized its full potential. With a varied, objective assessment of the first victory in a full-scale war in half a century, America's fleet aviators departed with enhanced pride in their profession and in themselves."

At the end of the summary, the author's boundless self-satisfaction leads him to echo the immortal Voltaire: "If the United

States Navy did not already have access to a Tailhook Association, there would be every good reason to create one."

Not a word about "butt-biting." Nothing about "ball-walking." No reference to the unfortunate mooning episode in which the mooners managed to moon right through the window, sending broken glass and very nearly some of their number down on the Las Vegas Hilton's swimming pool. And not a whisper about the ninety separate "indecent assaults" that the revelers chalked up, giving the sleuths of the Naval Investigative Service an unaccustomed exercise on the straight side of the street.

The assaults were mainly endured by women who ran a "gauntlet" of scores of drunken young men who happened to be naval and Marine Corps aviators. A couple of visiting British pilots seem to have participated as well. In the gauntlet, the women were lured into a narrowing corridor, surrounded, and then generally felt up, pinched on the breasts and buttocks, and otherwise groped and insulted. In the light of day, a few women claimed they enjoyed it. Others "blew it off" and dismissed the drunken aviators as "jerks." But a great many were thoroughly terrified and seriously feared for their safety. The gauntlet was repeated over the several nights of the symposium, growing in relative violence. Its victims included navy wives, strippers, hired bartenders, and local college students lured to the event by handbills. It also included many young female naval officers.

Besides the gauntlet and "ball-walking" (a naval jollity in which a drunken man parades with his trousers so adjusted that his testicles are exposed), symposium activities included, according to the Department of Defense investigators, "streaking," "mooning," "leg shaving," and "chicken-fighting." Chicken-fighting is an aquatic contest more consensual than the gauntlet, in which two young women in a swimming pool, mounted on the shoulders of naval aviators, attempt to remove each other's bathing suits.

No less than thirty-five admirals attended the high jinks in Las Vegas, though no one seems to have been in charge. The presence of the secretary of the navy appears not to have sobered the mood. Not until Lieutenant Paula Coughlin, an admiral's aide, complained to her boss did the incidents begin to become an issue.

Coughlin's boss, Admiral John W. Snyder Jr., was the commanding officer of the Patuxent River Naval Air Test Center, an extremely desirable and influential posting. Unfortunately for his career, he took no action on Coughlin's complaint. When she saw that she was getting no satisfaction from the admiral, Coughlin made her beef official. This involved the NIS, whose investigators, so zealous in the pursuit of gays, found themselves stymied by a conspiracy of silence. Their investigation produced few names. They also seemed to have overlooked the presence at Tailhook '91 of Navy Secretary H. Lawrence Garrett III.

Finally, to preempt what she believed was a covert campaign to destroy her reputation, Coughlin went to the press, that ruthless but imperfect agent of redress. The ensuing carnage was terrible. Garrett was revealed as being in Las Vegas in '91 and ordered by the White House to resign. Admiral Snyder was transferred to a far less prestigious billet: "The kind of thing," an officer said, "where they leave a pistol on the table and everybody leaves the room." An assistant chief of naval operations being groomed for a position among the Joint Chiefs of Staff was made to retire at a reduced rank. The Defense Department was compelled to commence a more thorough investigation, one that still continues.

The Tailhook Association, a curious organization that facilitates contacts between naval officers and civilian contractors, saw its semi-official sponsorship by the navy withdrawn. Its conventions were a true feminist's nightmare, a macho revel of the actual military-industrial complex itself, slack-jawed, booze-swilling, and sexually predatory. The pilots who took part in Tailhook '91 were mainly young males, aged twenty-one to twenty-six. What happened was partly the result of alcohol and partly a function of that atavistic anti-femaleness that seems to lurk in the hearts of surprisingly many men.

There was a note of possible cheer for social progress here, however. At the press conference announcing the release of the Defense Department's report on Tailhook, Admiral Frank B. Kelso, the chief of naval operations, declared: "Tailhook brought to light the fact that we had an institutional problem with women . . . It was a watershed event that brought about social change."

And two of the officers who had their buttocks pinched and fondled were men.

—*New York Review of Books*, 1993

OUT OF A CLEAR BLUE SKY

If the arts and their practitioners approach the September 11 catastrophe, respect requires that they begin by confronting death. But death does not bear confrontation; it does the confronting; and with its ineffable, impenetrable mystery it stops us cold. For all our elegies and mortuary verse, we know nothing about how to treat it, whether to deny it or to flatter it as glorious. Only the wisest art elevates death from the necessary vulgar rituals humankind requires. It's only that we can't understand — how could we?

When I try to consider the impact of the death of thousands, I find myself reminded of the great slaughter of my parents' youth that had such an impact on my New York. In 1904 the excursion steamer *General Slocum* sank in the Hell Gate. It was carrying picnickers from St. Mark's Lutheran Church's parish school on the Lower East Side, in the neighborhood called Kleindeutschland — Little Germany. Hundreds of children and many of their mothers either burned on the steamer or jumped into the swirling East River currents and drowned. In Kleindeutschland workmen came home to their tenements to find they had no families left. At that, historians will tell you the neighborhood died; the childless Germans turned away and left their church buildings to other denominations. The yellow brick jugendstil façades with the vitalist German mottos remain: *Einigkeit Macht Stark. Für Lincoln und die Union.* 5th New York Regiment of Volunteers, Pomeranian.

Kleindeutschland never recovered from the *Slocum* disaster. In German churches the next Sunday, the reverend pastors strained for a message from their Lutheran God: "Get up, go on. Seek grace, question not. Adore the will of your creator." It was not enough for Kleindeutschland. Misfortune makes people ashamed. A few people bond, but most people never want to see each other again. So the Germans left, and their city within the city was forever gone. They left, everyone says — it's part of the story — quietly. Working people, their commemorative art was churchy and sentimental.

If we think of art and catastrophe, some perverse lines of archetype send us to Orson Welles's *War of the Worlds* radio program. Witnessing the World Trade Center attacks, or even seeing them on the edited television footage of that day, had something of the unimaginable vision in it. A scene not wholly unfamiliar imposing itself forever on the mind's eye, suggesting theatrics, and the theatrical element containing some absurdity for reprieve: that it was the second coming of Orson Welles, that it was a hoax. Strangers cannot appear out of a clear blue sky for the purpose of killing us, to wreak such destruction, except in fiction.

So we have death as a subject, and then mass death, the death of whole communities, the irony, the comfort, the bitterness of its having been invoked in our entertainments as practical jokes. Another aspect of this event was the killing. The jihadis spoke more about the killings than about anything—killing the "sacrifices," killing quickly, killing with a smile, killing the body and dispatching the soul to hell, through their burning buildings to eternal fire in the next world. Killing is never far from religion. Violent death. Martyrdom. Because God welcomes all who give up their lives in his name. Because he will not be mocked. He wants his friends to kill his enemies. His beloved go forth to battle and leave heaps of slain.

Heaps of slain are also to be seen in those biblical movies where the temple and colossi of the pagans implode, trapping long-legged extras and shaven priests of Baal. Those epics derive from the renderings in early-nineteenth-century narrative paintings that depict the sacking of Rome. There, suddenly, we have a classical perspective, the first putting to the torch of the second Babylon, the transatlantic Rome. Yet the Romans looking into themselves saw rectitude and virtue. Their empire prized diversity and tolerated a wide variety of religions. The Romans prized relativism, so that Tacitus could write rather ignorant, unconstrained praise of the warlike Teutons, contrasting his effete, self-indulgent fellow Romans, for their own good, with these fearless noble fellows. The noble fellows themselves had little time for relativism; they were most single-minded. And thousands of years later, Nazi schoolmasters, with no more use for relativism, would use Tacitus to demonstrate the universal and timeless qualities of belligerent German polity.

Where will all this take us artists and our métier?

In the earlier part of the last century we had an art besotted with primitivism and with vitalism, art insisting on some cleansing violent wind, a wind that killed, to sweep away comfortable, ignoble, philistine cities of the Western world. It came. And now in this world of war, are we going to live out primitivism again? The women sang of Saul's thousands and David's ten thousands. The first poets sang of battle, singing swords, the wind at the feathered harp of a thousand arrows. The vitalists required shed blood of art, required eros with thanatos, struggle. Heroes forward. We already have our heroes; they have theirs. Do we find our way back again to it all?

Henry Fleming, the hero of *The Red Badge of Courage*, has, before he enters the Civil War, "long despaired of witnessing a Greek-like struggle. Such would be no more, he had said. Men were better, or, more timid. Secular and religious education had effaced the throat-grappling instinct."

But as it happens, this is not the case. Henry goes to battle. He runs. But then, an elected child of grace, he gains courage and its red badge. "He felt a quiet manhood, nonassertive but of sturdy and strong blood . . . He had been to touch the great death, and found that, after all, it was but the great death. He was a man."

Modernism began in this worship of strife. There was no reason think we were better or more timid. Again it appears that Husak* is right and Marx wrong: consciousness conditions reality, and not the other way around. Shall we be asked to celebrate physical courage as a visible manifestation of grace? In the harder creeds, the more single-minded ones, there is no moral courage without its physical side. Will we be put to

---

*Gustáv Husák, general secretary of the Czechoslovakian Communist Party from 1969 to 1989. —*Ed.*

this hard question, if we are Rome again, holding out until the
naïve faith and simple confidence of the barbarians fail so that
we get back to celebrating the exquisite pains of renunciation,
for example, instead of the joys of battle?

—Not previously published, circa 2001

NO SUCH THING AS PEACE

In its December 14, 1981, issue, *Newsweek* magazine published a fifteen-thousand-word report on the experiences of fifty officers and enlisted men of C Company, 2nd Battalion, 28th Infantry Regiment of the 1st Infantry Division—the Big Red One. Charlie Company was an outfit that spent an inordinate amount of its time in harm's way. *Newsweek*'s article dealt not only with the events that befell these men during their tours of combat, but also with what seemed to be the war's subsequent effects on their lives as civilians. The dead were also recalled, in the recollections of their comrades and the emotions of their survivors.

The article served as a basis for a CBS documentary presented the same month that Charlie Company's people were assembled in Florida at the network's expense for a televised reunion some twelve years after their Vietnam service. Now Newsweek Books and William Morrow and Company have presented the article in expanded form as *Charlie Company*, under the principal coauthorship of Peter Goldman and Tony Fuller.

No reader of Michael Herr's *Dispatches* will ever address a book dealing with the Vietnam War without the compulsion to celebrate once again that uncanny masterpiece of conjury. Like a shaman, an inspired medium, Herr somehow absorbed the properties of the war and transmuted them into language. It is his book that will forever come closest to providing that answer eternally required of the chronicler: What was it like?

Though *Charlie Company* doubtless owes something to *Dispatches*, it does not function on the same level of inspiration, nor does it aspire to do so. Nevertheless, it is a very fine book, balanced and wise in its attitudes, admirable above all in its avoidance of hype and hyperbole. The work's restraint, its lack of pretentiousness, and its professionalism provide *Charlie Company*'s readers with an experience more profound than if the book had self-consciously sought the usual tame quarry — the military mind and the rascality of patriots. Since it refrains, in large measure, from moralizing, it compels the best sort of moral reflection, the sort not preshrunk and trivialized by specialists in the field.

The sixty-five men profiled in *Charlie Company* were for the most part draftees. They were infantry soldiers in a war that differed significantly from most of America's previous wars — not in being some kind of genocidal ax murder perpetrated by fiends, but in being an absolute nonstarter attempted in impossible conditions. If the overall political objective of the war was the containment of China's ambitions in Southeast Asia, this objective had been obviated by the time that most American personnel and matériel were committed. Strategic objectives, to the extent that such might be pursued within the political restrictions surrounding the conduct of the war and the geographic limitations on its operations, seem to come down to little more than disruption of the enemy's logistics. To the further confusion of our can-do-spirited honchos, the North Vietnamese were about the most gifted and original logistics specialists since Bismarck's General Staff. They seem also to have been favored with some political gifts.

Traditionally, the defining role of the infantry has been to seize and hold ground. In a war marked by such obscure objectives as the one in Vietnam, fought among xenophobic nationalists who were subject to merciless reprisals for collaboration with the foreign foe and against an enemy who did his best to obscure the distinction between civilians and combatants, the problems of serving as an infantryman are apparent. Even the grim satisfactions of conventional war — the occupation of the opponent's turf, the prospect of his ultimate ruin — were denied the men of Charlie Company, whose remote masters were compelled to fall back on that singularly repulsive measure of relative success, the body count. For the conduct of this war, American forces employed troopers who were, on average, six and a half years younger than the young men who fought and won in World War II.

These youths, as so many of them have been called, were obedient to our laws. They were ordinary boys from Ottumwa and Janesville and Brooklyn — black, white, brown. Virtually to a man, they went in to serve their country, to do the right thing, and before very long a lot of the world and some of their own countrymen would call them criminal murderers, sadists, Nazis. It is very hard, sad reading, *Charlie Company*, because there is so much suffering in it, so much pain and death and anger, because so many of these men were so heartbreakingly young when they fought, and because they are ours, our brothers and sons, our people, ourselves, so to speak—us. Only the most deluded poseur or the slimiest hypocrite could declare himself in principle the moral superior of these men.

A record of this sort brings forth from within its readers all manner of associative recollection, some appropriate, some not. When I'd finished *Charlie Company*, my thoughts turned for some reason to a boozy afternoon I spent years ago in the bar of the Asia Hotel in Bangkok—gateway, as it was then, to the world. A Thai whom I took to be some sort of political policeman approached and began to inquire into my attitudes about the war, then in progress a few hundred miles to our right as we faced the bottles. I don't know what attracted his official attention; I wasn't looking any weirder than the usual suspects at the Asia Bar. Doubtless I savored of both subversion and 'Nam, those fragrances of the sixties to which so many of us were exposed.

In any case, I treated the fellow to a little homily on the disadvantages of warfare to the people who have the bad luck to encounter it. When the Thai had examined my passport, subjected me to a menacing sneer, and gone his way, I found myself in conversation with a compatriot, lately arrived, as was I, from the A-O, the area of operations. My fellow drinker had observed the Siamese debriefing; he was a big man, not tanned but sallow, with a jungle pallor. His bare arms were tattooed, and on the basis of my own experience in the amphibious forces I would have taken him for a SEAL, a naval commando. SEALs were feared; they were mighty men of battle.

My own situation was quite different. Years a civilian, I had spent most of my last weeks in Saigon learning considerably more than I wanted to know about the illegal drug trade there. Until recently, the last shot I had heard fired in anger was one released in 1956 by a French carrier-based aircraft over Alexandria, where, as a very young sailor, I was assisting in the evacuation of American nationals from that city during its siege by combined French, British, and Israeli forces following Mr. Nasser's seizure of the Suez Canal. I had seen dead then, and colored tracer rounds. One of my clearest recollections, for some reason, was the spectacle of a donkey riddled with machine-gun bullets, hurtling through the air and exploding like one of those blood bags that contemporary film audiences find so entertaining. When I had finished my business in Saigon, I seemed to feel, for reasons that now strike me as idiotic, that honor required my reparation to a point in-country where ordnance of some sort might be discharged in my general direction.

Off I went, to a place whose name I've forgotten; I think it was about thirty kilometers northwest of Saigon. A grunt who briefly traveled with me expressed the hope that since I professed a moral responsibility to be shot at (or at least near), I might find it in me to get my ass killed outright. This was the fate he found suitable for the sort of people who were in Vietnam when they didn't have to be.

Anyway, there we were in the Asia Hotel—me, the SEAL, and the martial tourist. We talked about The War—what else? —and I said my piece. I was pretty drunk, I'd just delivered my frame to the A-O, I felt entitled to an opinion, even in conversation with the commando. The giant let me run on in my secular-humanist fashion. Then he explained to me the necessity of wars. "You gotta have 'em," he said. "Absolutely got to."

I asked him what he meant by that, and you can be sure I was wondering what manner of jerk-around, militaristic homespun I'd be served up by way of an answer.

"'Cause without 'em," the SEAL told me, "there's no such thing as peace."

At first I thought it was a bad joke. Then, a little later on, it seemed only trivial, a banal pseudo-insight. Two hours later I was still at the bar, and I was still trying to figure out what the SEAL's comment amounted to, whether it made the slightest sense or not. Eleven years have passed since that afternoon, and I'm still working on the boatswain's mate's conundrum. I couldn't tell you how many times I've picked up the newspaper or flipped on the television to tune in to some ghastly circumstance of mutual human obliteration and had that drawled declaration come to mind.

Now, the SEAL's observation may be the most meretricious piece of barroom sophistry ever spoken, but the point is that I can't say for sure. The fact that I can't tells a great many things about me. It says that although the nature of things is my very stock in trade, I can't fundamentally understand the essence of the human condition, its purpose or its lack of one. I cannot understand and cannot measure the capacity of mankind for liberating itself from its own pathology, from the tyrannies of its own history.

Somehow I find myself trying to graft that SEAL's statement onto the personal histories of the soldiers recounted in *Charlie Company*. It doesn't work, really. I know—on the level of common sense—that the only lesson to be learned from this excellent book is the cruelty and unwisdom of committing young soldiers to wars they should not fight and cannot win.

Yet I want somehow to learn more from it. My desire for a further and more complex answer is not to be taken as criticism of *Charlie Company*. I've already commended the book for straight dealing, for its avoidance of deep-think. The very lucidity of the reports contained is what whets my appetite for large resolutions.

I wish my resolutions were available, but of course they aren't—not to the authors of *Charlie Company*, not to the grunts whose stories are therein contained, not to me, not to the survivors of the early dead.

I suspect my old Ancient of War said a true thing back there in Bangkok. We have to hope that if we cannot take his message as comfort or consolation, we can take it as a place to start, a position to commence whatever remains to us of our history.

—*Esquire*, 1983

THE HOLY WAR

Put yourself in the mind's eye of the conspirator, whoever he is. It's likely he first saw the city from the air, looked out and saw the twin towers mirroring each other's dizzying rise. Maybe he stood at the window of some safe house in Queens or Jersey and looked at them. Thrusting so immodestly more than a thousand feet in the air, they mocked his passionate intensity, he no doubt thought.

The World Trade Center towers don't have much poetry in them. It might be harder psychologically to bomb one of the old cathedrals of commerce, like the Empire State or the Chrysler Building. These seem to contain some transcendent urge to aspire beyond Mammon belonging essentially to a bygone era; they no longer challenge the world. The Michelin Guide to New York describes them for the bargain-hunting foreign tourists of the nineties in virtually archeological terms.

The World Trade Center towers were built for an age that for a number of reasons will probably never come to pass. They represent an ultimate reduction of the American Dream: America as home of unadorned Economic Man — practical, rational, powerful, even brutal. They can be seen as the external expression of an aspect of America our true-believing enemies have learned to hate and fear.

Now, as our influence contracts, the world returns to its old romances. In Europe, "Blood and soil" is back. In what used to be called the Third World, religion flourishes. In our radical interpretation of democracy, our rejection of elites, our well-nigh demagogic respect for the opinions of the unlearned, we are essentially alone.

Nobody loves you when you're down and out. Our country has been so long identified with its wealth and power that a sense seems to grow abroad that the United States will eventually somehow disappear, as though we were no more than our own compulsive communicating, a media phenomenon, a pop artifact going out of style.

Although every president since Roosevelt has denied it, we did set out, years ago, to be the world's policeman. The image was of Uncle Sam, rolling up his sleeves and wading in to do the right thing. The unheralded corollary was that we might do well by doing it. After all, the original Uncle Sam was a defense contractor.

On the international scene these days, our trumpets have sounded slightly sour and uncertain. Our pro bono military operations have been conducted with noticeable diffidence. And it has been noticed, in friendly and unfriendly quarters. Cops make enemies. The best cops are good diplomats, which we have not always been. The impression of weakness, even relative weakness, always invites predation.

Malcolm X, exercising his customary cruel wit, called the assassination of President John Kennedy a case of the "chickens coming home to roost." His allusion was to the murder of President Diem of South Vietnam, in which some felt the United States had colluded. The world is so much smaller now than even during Malcolm's lifetime. The poor are poorer and more restless. Entire populations are on the move. The migration of the world's poor in the late twentieth century has been compared to the "barbarian" migrations of the fifth century AD. Borders are porous; in jet planes and on rafts, desperate people cross oceans.

Literally and figuratively, our cities have no walls. We have lived for a long time like ancient Rome, relying on our far-flung power for defense. To a degree, we have claimed exemption from the forces of history. Now history has come for us, presenting old, half-forgotten due bills. In striking at symbols, terrorists destroy the real lives of American working people, traumatize actual American children.

In the face of this, we will learn to cope as other nations have; we are good at coping. Eventually, few Americans will remember the country as it was before X-ray machines appeared at airports and at the vestibules of public buildings, before the minimum-wage security guards were deployed at every other corporate door.

When I imagined the conspirators' "passionate intensity," I was thinking of "The Second Coming" by Yeats, the chilling, prophetic dream of "mere anarchy" loosed on the world. "The best lack all conviction," Yeats wrote, "while the worst are filled with passionate intensity." A dozen or so individuals, as human as we, fly planes full of doomed, terrified people into the Pentagon and the World Trade Center, a teeming city in the air.

Are they moral monsters? Are they really the worst, driven by sheer evil?

Though we are being judged, despite our grief and loss, we cannot really judge. We are steeped in relativism, as confined by our narratives as the murderers are confined by theirs. History is a story we have accepted; our lives are the stories we tell ourselves about the experience of life.

In the Middle East, where gods were born, where narratives were sacred and the books in which they were inscribed considered sacramental, the ancient narratives are glorified again. After the 1967 war, for example, Jewish settlers awaiting the Messiah founded settlements among their ancestral stones, risking their lives and the lives of their families, ready to kill and to die in the name of a sacred narrative soon to be vindicated.

So in the Muslim world, the sacred historical destiny of Islam is reasserted. The will of God is to be done on earth. One narrative contained in the Koran speaks of the people of Ad. "Their sin is arrogance," the book says. The people of Ad rely on their power and their material wealth to prevail in the world. "They," says the Holy Koran, "will be brought low."

The dreadful sights of September 11 took on a surreal edge. All the horrors—planes hitting towers out of a cloudless sky, all the rest—seemed somehow unreal. I don't think it was their utter unfamiliarity that caused our vertiginous denial, made us refuse to believe what we were seeing. I think it was déjà vu and a weird recognition that these images had been half seen before. Rendered by movies, imagined, described in novels. The unreality we experienced was of something fictive.

We saw, in the shocking elemental collision that our conscious minds denied, the violent assault of one narrative system upon another. People deeply enclosed in their sanctified world view were carrying out what they experienced as a sacred command to annihilate the Other.

The expressions from Washington are nothing surprising —assurances of "resolve" and retribution. But in various ways our internal narrative, our social and political foundations, circumscribe our capacity for revenge as they limited our capacity for a surer defense. The internal narrative of our enemies, their absolute ruthless devotion to an invisible world, makes them strong. Our system too is a state of mind. We need to find in it the elements that will serve our actual survival.

The power of narrative is shattering, overwhelming. We are the stories we believe; we are who we believe we are. All the reasoning of the world cannot set us free of our mythic systems. We live and die by them.

During the Cold War, we lived in fear of nuclear holocaust. Now we know that if a nuclear device ever goes off in an American city, it will not likely come launched from some Siberian silo. More probably it will have been assembled by a few people, perhaps in the guise of immigrants, in that safe house with a view of lower Manhattan. These days people are dying again for their national or religious identity. The new breed of terrorists may be those whose cause we have offended perhaps by simply being what we are.

—*Rolling Stone*, 2001

Disruption

If not for what he terms the "disruption" of the 1960s, Robert Stone might have lived out his life as a good Catholic boy gone just a little wrong—if only in the sense of straying from the faith. The hardships of his semi-orphaned childhood stood to be redeemed by the standard proffers of social betterment to working-class Americans at the end of the fifties: the stability of military service, plus somewhat limited educational opportunity, followed by skilled or semi-skilled employment. Stone might have committed permanently to one of the métiers he briefly tried, and finished as a newspaperman, or an art gallery publicist, or a copywriter for a furniture store.

Instead, his Stegner Fellowship took him to California in 1962—into the orbit of Ken Kesey, who was then serving as Lord of Misrule for the early phases of the psychedelic revolution—as Stone recounts in "The Boys' Octet" and "The Man Who Turned On the Here." The world turned from black and white to Technicolor, while Stone and his prankish companions were transformed into "the stuff of dreams."

Stone emerged from that experience as a fully fledged literary artist. His years spent living in London in the seventies gave him a cosmopolitan cast. Restless to the bone, he traveled constantly, combining journalistic assignments with research for his novels—from New York Harbor ("Changing Tides") to Cuba ("Havana Then and Now") to Israel ("Jerusalem Has No Past"). Having sailed around the world on the surface of the sea, he also needed to go to the bottom of it, for "Under the Tongue of the Ocean." His engagement with American life and American politics led him to cover national political conventions ("Keeping the Future at Bay" and "The Morning After") and to debunk the War on Drugs in "A Higher Horror of the Whiteness." Many of his international excursions were sponsored by the US Agency for International Development, and these allowed him to evolve a new perspective on America within a global context, a part of which is expressed in "East-West Relations" and "Does America Still Exist?"

These essays are an anthology of Stone's performance as a public intellectual. From the 1960s into the twenty-first century, culture changed with bewildering speed, and Stone's occasional writing tracked those changes, with the same perspicacity that his novels do. Context for it all is set by his 1984 meditation on Orwell—international in scope but also a particularly American take. "Forty years later, forty years of anarchy and poverty embracing a world larger than Orwell's superstates, we live with fears he could not have invented for us."

Stone contrasts Orwell's dystopia with the idealized "World of Tomorrow" presented by the 1939 World's Fair in New York City—no doubt dazzling to the little boy he was then—but as Stone's essay points out, that vision of Tomorrow never happened. Other things occurred instead: World War II, the postwar atomic age, Vietnam, and the psychedelic and political revolutions of the sixties, with their sequels rolling forward into the present day.

Those decades, when Stone was in his prime, are rife with failures and betrayals, to which Stone often reacts with anger, some bitterness, and an ironic, sometimes satirical edge that derives, like Orwell's own, from frustrated idealism—a sense the two writers share that things are never as they should be, nor as they might have been. In "Does America Still Exist?" Stone draws this conclusion: "We have never been the people or the nation we pretended to be . . . God doesn't manifest himself in history; men do. Nor is this God's country but ours, and thus the responsibility for its ordering. If we choose to awake and see ourselves in our own baseness, we might well be a more agreeable nation and the world might be a safer place. On the other hand, the opposite might be true. Should we abandon the Dream, perhaps we'd breathe easier . . . There'd be no more cant about a New Order of Ages. Yet nothing is free, not even disillusionment."

Despite such attitudes—"nothing is free" is one of his most deeply held beliefs—Stone would describe himself as living in hope, somewhat paradoxically for a writer ending this essay thus: "And it is just possible, as a result, that we might find our place in history as the betrayers of the noblest vision of civil order and probity that this imperfect world, and the cautious optimism of Western man, will ever be capable of producing." Between the lines is an opposite view: Stone's world just might evolve into a better place, though chances are it won't. As Stone puts it in his "Nineteen Eighty-Four," "The quality of hope itself seemed to change."

MSB

NINETEEN EIGHTY-FOUR

Incredibly, for one my age, the time has elapsed. Sometimes, with our constant edging toward the brink and our eternally simmering brushfire wars, it seemed as though we would never make it—but we have. It's 1984, the quintessentially futuristic year.

The political storms that broke over the publication of George Orwell's book in 1949 have settled to a degree, although I've met old lefties in New York and San Francisco who can still summon up rage against him as a slanderer and traitor. Of course, such folk are rare.

I've also met young lefties in the same places who've never read a word of Orwell. They can tell you that they themselves have heard at second hand—that he was an old-time right-winger, one of the architects of the Cold War. *Nineteen Eighty-Four*, they know, was the last spiteful utterance of a dying despairing reactionary. The guy who wrote the well-known children's book *Animal Farm* meant to discredit revolution, whereas *Fanshen* is the sort of book you'd want to read to know all about revolutions. Savants in the affinity group will have heard that he once wrote a fanatically anti-Communist book about Spain, *Homage to Catalonia*. The dude took money from the CIA, it's a well-documented fact.

If you know the sort of people I'm talking about, you'll know that just about everything they've ever heard and found agreeable qualifies as a well-documented fact.

Indeed, years before, at the time of *Nineteen Eighty-Four*'s New York publication, the American Communist Party's reaction had been rather short on professional courtesy and grace. "There is a hideous ingenuity in the perversions of a dying capitalism," lyricized the party's *Masses and Mainstream*, "and it will keep probing for new depths of rottenness which the maggots will find brilliant and morally invigorating."

George Orwell, born Eric Blair in British India. His last work remains for the orthodox remnant of the Old Left a stumbling block, for the struggling New Left, a scandal. An utterance of prophecy about what, at last, has become our present: 1984.

Orwell undoubtedly took satisfaction in the shower of vitriol with which the party press greeted his most famous novel. The hostility of our contemporary leftist intellectuals would neither distress nor surprise him, for he was a most acute critic of the middle-class left-wing intelligentsia, and he tended to find them unlovable. But what would he make of the fact that we in the non-Communist West, perhaps most particularly in America, have subsumed him into the ideology of capitalism, employed his gaunt image as a talisman in the continuing struggles we wage to maintain the influence of institutions of which he was so frequently and mordantly critical?

It's a well-documented fact, if you'll pardon the expression, that when *Time* and *Life* and the *Wall Street Journal* greeted

Nineteen Eighty-Four on its publication as rightist, antisocialist scripture that deduced the rights of man and the democratic system from the business ethic and unregulated commerce, he was not pleased. Toward the end of his life, in an essay called "Why I Write," he spelled out his allegiance: "Every line of serious work that I have written since 1936 has been written, directly or indirectly, against totalitarianism and for democratic socialism as I understand it."

Still, he was drafted into service—in the United States and wherever the Cold War was being fought—as one of conservativism's men at arms. His works, *Nineteen Eighty-Four* above all, although aimed at the tyranny of Moscow and the fatuities of tiny-souled fellow travelers, had dealt the left in general a heavy blow. He was loved by many he would have despised. Not many of his new admirers can have read that passage in *Homage to Catalonia*, effectively as anti-Communist as anything of his, in which he describes the experience of revolutionary Barcelona in December 1936 that impelled him to join an anarcho-syndicalist militia. In the service of revolutionary Spain, fighting the Phalangists who were to become quite popular with these later admirers, he received a nearly mortal wound. It was the sight of what he considered free Barcelona that made him turn soldier in a war he had come, like the self-serving Hemingway and others, to watch.

"I believed," he wrote," . . . that this was truly a workers' State and that the entire bourgeoisie had either fled, been killed, or voluntarily come over to the workers' side." This, he believed, was "a state of affairs worth fighting for."

One of his biographers, Alex Zwerdling, wrote of his relationship with the left that his "criticism was always designed as internal; it was precisely Orwell's unquestioning fidelity to the ideals of the movement that, in his mind, justified his uncompromising criticism of some of its theories, tactics, and leaders."

Time has served to make much of this a bit clearer. What we have in Orwell, with all his faults, is an honest man who demanded honesty of the causes he served so unselfishly, who hated cruelty and cant. Orwell, as one of his biographers has observed, was his work; the moral presence of the individual is present in his writings in a way that's rare even in the most passionately engaged writers. The fact is that some of those we think of, or once thought of, as passionately engaged writers have had their commitment exposed as posturing, whereas Orwell felt his very life on the line for the things he believed in. His life and work have left us a standard against which we would do well to measure our actions and our values. On the occasion of this desperately interesting year, I propose to do two things. One, against all criers-out to the contrary, I shall claim for George Orwell a certain affinity with what I believe is best about the United States. Second, I will say one or two things about America's sense of itself and its reality in the year of Orwell's prophecy.

In doing these things I will endeavor not to trivialize Orwell's concerns and profess to spot a totalitarian impulse in bureaucrats who propose attaching photographs to driver's licenses. Nor will I, in claiming an affinity between Orwell and the aspect of America to which I owe allegiance, attempt to claim for her his affection or approval. I don't really think he would find the place at present congenial. In fact, Orwell seems never to have been particularly interested in the United States.

But a country never exists entirely in its present; history is a kind of time machine in which the past is always somehow at hand, and we cannot understand the United States of 1984 without a look toward the foundations. There's a sense in which we, as individuals, are defined by our own sense of who we are—in a pinch we're liable to act according to that sense. This is far more true of nations.

Nations exist not only as geographic entities and political divisions but also as living stories. The national mythology is always there; its relationship to reality may be dubious, but no one can understand a country who does not understand its self-image, its story about itself.

The United States, I think, sees itself as the culmination of the Anglo-Saxon reforming spirit, of Whiggery and the struggle against the Stuarts—in other words, of Puritanism. She is, for good or ill, an heir of English Puritanism, and it is on this basis that I make my claim for Orwell's affinity with us. Orwell was an English Puritan to the marrow of his bones, and whatever we make of him, or he of us, there are attitudes held in common.

In a brilliant essay on Orwell that serves as the introduction to the American edition of *Homage to Catalonia*, Lionel Trilling speculates on Orwell's response to a suggestion by the German philosopher Karl Jaspers. Jaspers, at one point in his work, invites us to consider the necessary "decision to renounce the absolute claims of the European humanistic spirit, to think of it as a stage of development rather than the living content of faith." Trilling is quick to point out that having witnessed at first hand some results of such exercises in moral relativity, Orwell would have seen the necessity as survival rather than "development." Indeed, in the hindsight of 1984, Jasper's references to development at the expense of humanistic values carry the faint echo of Teutonic heavy breathing in a bad forties film. Trilling goes on to point out that unlike some of the ideologues who helped create the states that inspired *Nineteen Eighty-Four,* Orwell "does not dream of a new kind of man, he is content with the old kind, and what moves him is the desire that this old kind of man should have freedom, bacon, and proper work." This mode of thought gives him much in common with the pragmatism that has characterized American moral thinkers from Jefferson to James to Niebuhr; it grows from the same homely plant. What is defined here in Trilling's insight is the secularized remnant of that emphasis on what Cromwell called the Inward Man — on rectitude, on conscience, and on common sense that English-speaking Protestantism so valued, which were such prominent qualities in the thoroughly unchurched Orwell and represent the best of post-Christian America. The qualities embodied in this attitude are not metaphysical or superhuman; they kept neither Cromwell nor England nor America from acts of brutality and injustice. But they have their honorable uses, and they represent a common ground between the spirit of George Orwell and the best of America.

I once had a character in a novel I wrote claim that there were two Americas, the self-promoting, superconfident one with a Way of Life, and the secret one. We should all resist the first one, I think; not because it's so vulgar and we're so finely honed, but because it's a place that has betrayed its own ideals too often. Its most famous citizen was and remains Uncle Sam, the celebrated chiseling factor and war profiteer, followed by

Al Capone and those smiley men in golf shoes who provide our current governance.

The other, the Secret America, binds my allegiance because as a native I have to pick one or the other. What the average civilized person chooses to think of her is very much a matter of taste. Secret America, as my character called it, is a spooky neurotic place, truly Puritan, tortured, perfectionist. This is the place that sees herself as striking at the vineyards where the grapes of wrath are stored. Her prophet is not Walt Whitman but Melville, whose *Moby-Dick* is the most uncanny act of incantatory prophecy known to fiction. Unlike *Nineteen Eighty-Four*, it's nearly unreadable, talking in tongues and uttering visions. It defines the future of the West and Western man and his impact on what is not Western and not man, the sacking of nature for industry, of the rape of virgin earth in the name of progress and the guilt incurred. "Man," says Melville's Ahab, "I would strike the sun if it wronged me!" Western man as the Hindu triad: Creator, Preserver, Destroyer.

Save the whales, indeed!

In Hadley, Massachusetts, which is deep in Secret America, near Bondsville and Longwood and Rock Springs, is buried the last surviving regicide of the English Civil War. In Secret America slaughtered Indians dance back the slaughtered buffalo. Under her too bright sky Emily Dickinson faced Jonathan Edwards's God with a passion she mistook for love.

This is not the past. The is the secret nation, 1984.

During the Second World War, the Walt Disney people put out one of those comic books for which our nation became famous, which included a particularly poignant section entitled "Mickey Mouse in the Post-War World." In this little cartoon feature we were not, as some may suppose, plotting a program of cultural imperialism or the Disney cartel, but attempting to cleave to a beloved conceit, one of which the stark reality of war had deprived us. The conceit was "Tomorrow."

Remember Tomorrow? It was a part of that fragile, almost pretend optimism to which the world grew so attached in the years just before the Second World War. There was, of course, a level on which everyone knew better; we were whistling in the dark.

We had Tomorrow well before Mickey Mouse. If you want to see what it looked like, you can find it illustrated in any number of magazines and Sunday supplements of the time — the whole popular press in the prewar years positively reeked of Tomorrowness.

In Tomorrow, great cloverleaves of monorail carried sleek vehicles — part tram, part space shuttle — past an infinity of gleaming Art Deco towers. Here and there, carrying on amid all this surreal splendor, were tiny, vaguely unisex figures in tights or tunics — the people of Tomorrow. Sometimes the people of Tomorrow went in couples, sometimes they were in family groups. Mainly content, placid, downright emotionless — there wasn't going to be anything to get upset about Tomorrow. It was all going to be quietly agreeable. The illustrated people also looked mildly busy, as if they were on their way to perform some vital but not especially demanding or exerting task. Everything was so much neater and cleaner than in the boring, uneasy-making present that if you were old enough to appreciate the bitterness of it all, you cursed yourself for being born too soon, into the primitive, nasty, and misshapen world around you.

I myself never really saw Tomorrow; it was over before I was

old enough to appreciate it. I remember only its wartime resi-
due, which was called "the Post-War World," Mickey Mouse's
bright future. However, I did glimpse the bright ruins of its
climax and apotheosis, the New York World's Fair of 1939.

The fair's sponsors chose this unfortunate year because it
marked the 150th anniversary of George Washington's inauguration, but by all the evidence it was not particularly patriotic in theme and most certainly not nostalgic. Rather, it was
earnestly internationalist, and its official theme was actually (in
capital letters) THE WORLD OF TOMORROW. The fair's logo
and symbol was an enormous piece of walk-in sculpture called
the Trylon and Perisphere, which towered about 728 feet over
the central mall. It was the world of Wallace Harrison, who designed another little corner of TOMORROW, Rockefeller Center in New York. The Trylon and Perisphere stood for years
in Flushing Meadow until it was removed in the mid-forties
and broken up for war materials. In its heyday at the fair it was
explained to visitors as "an expression of the shape of things to
come."

Sixty-three nations* participated in the fair, which made it
the most broadly representative international exposition ever
mounted until that time. How pathetic it was, this desperate
stirring of doomed hope, a ludicrous, pious, foolish, and utterly unanswered prayer. During 1940, the second year of its
run, one after another of the participating nations closed their
pavilions and went home to war, many to worse than war—
to physical destruction, ruthless occupation, death camps. For
some, their participation in the World of Tomorrow would be

---

*Actually, fifty-two nations and eleven colonies. —*Ed.*

their last manifestation. They were to pass out of history, out of existence.

The 1939 fair was the last international gathering of the prenuclear age. We in America were left with Mickey Mouse's Post-War World. This had a number of Tomorrow's artifacts, but since it was basically a wartime conceit, it seemed to incorporate a confused ideology, as though to rival the enemy's. It was full of uncertainties and contradictions, a sterner place. Little shards of Tomorrow kept turning up in magazines, usually in advertisements for goods that were presently unavailable but which we must be sure to buy in the coming Post-War World.

But Tomorrow really ended with the last months of 1939, and the Post-War World came to a close with the first Post-War war; we found ourselves in the atomic age. Disney and Mickey Mouse never officially gave up on futurism, but their heart and soul went into something called Yesterday, which was just as bland and antiseptic as Tomorrow and made the children of the present feel even more unlucky, since they had no chance at all at it.

In 1948, compounded of the immediate past—Stalinism, fascism, the Battle of the Ebro, Tomorrow, the Post-War World, and the atomic age—George Orwell gave his era that nightmare image of the future which would haunt its consciousness above all other visions. All the 1930s Art Deco sleekness was revealed for what it had been—the hope of a world fed for generations on hope and visions of progress, trying to recover from the terrible disillusionment it had suffered in the First World War. Neither Tomorrow nor "the new man" would be the goal, but survival. The twentieth century, sold to its inheritors as an age of wonders, was going to serve as a collection agency for the nineteenth. We would pay off. We would get to act out all the theories.

Born in 1903 under the old order, in the last decade of "the sunlit lawns," Orwell served it in his youth, ironically, as a colonial policeman. His manhood and middle age coincided with the growth of totalitarianism, which was inspired in large measure by the theorists of the nineteenth century and brought into reality by the demagogues and generalissimos of the twentieth. He lived to fight it, physically in Spain during the civil war in that country, and spiritually in his writings, the best known of which were a direct attack on the totalitarianism he saw threatening the future.

Orwell was the sort of radical who makes enemies on both sides of epic struggles. In Cold War terms, the anti-Soviet forces feel secure in his approval because of the way in which both *Animal Farm* and *Nineteen Eighty-Four* satirize a state recognizable as the Soviet Union. We should remember that it was service in a Western police force that helped develop Orwell's libertarianism. He "disliked," he says on the dust jacket of the American edition of *Burmese Days*, "putting people in prison for doing the same things which he should have done in the circumstances." His feeling for the left was further encouraged by a spectacle he witnessed on the trip home to England, a demonstration in Marseilles against the execution of the anarchists Sacco and Vanzetti in America, where they were charged with murder.

"I had reduced everything to the simple theory that the oppressed are always right and the oppressors are always wrong: a mistaken theory, but the natural result of being one of the oppressors yourself," he was to write in *The Road to Wigan Pier.*

Yet it was a left-wing government, on whose behalf he was fighting, that threatened him with imprisonment and even execution in Spain, and the British government he scorned that effected his rescue.

Orwell's originality and intelligence, above all his thoroughgoing honesty, always got him in trouble. A writer and man more predictable and dull, and less infernally scrupulous, would have had a better time of it.

He was, as someone has remarked, a "conserving radical"; he tended to see modern-style tyranny not as the continuation of age-old oppression but as innovation, and in this he may offer his greatest insight. The English writers he most resembles are William Hazlitt and William Cobbett, both "conserving radicals" and both, usefully for my purposes, people with connections to the United States. Hazlitt spent his childhood here. Cobbett, an ex-Redcoat, was a newspaper editor in Philadelphia, and after his return fled back to the States in 1818, when threatened with arrest. (He would go home yet again.)

If we want to get to the heart of Orwell's concerns in *Nineteen Eighty-Four*, we might do well to turn to the statement he made through his publishers in the year of its publication, when he thought the book was being misinterpreted and misrepresented, particularly in the United States. Here, in part, is what he wrote:

> It has been suggested by some of the reviewers of *1984* that it is the author's view that this, or something like this, is what will happen inside the next forty years in the Western world. This is not correct. I think that, allowing for this book being after all a parody, something

like *1984* could happen. This is the direction in which the world is going at the present time, and the trend lies deep in the political, social and economic foundations of the contemporary world situation.

Specifically the danger lies in the structure imposed on Socialist and on Liberal capitalist communities by the necessity to prepare for total war with the U.S.S.R. and the new weapons of which of course the atomic bomb is the most powerful and the most publicized. But danger lies also in the acceptance of the totalitarian outlook by intellectuals of all colors.

The moral to be drawn from this dangerous nightmare situation is a simple one: *Don't let it happen. It depends on you.*

This is not the whole of Orwell's press statement, but it covers the principal concerns. In America he seems to have seen war fever and its attendant nationalism, "one hundred percent Americanism," as the chief threat, together with the managerialism predicted and espoused by the sociologist James Burnham. He went somewhat out of his way to bring in the dangers of totalitarian America; he had deeply shocked even his old friends on the British left who saw him as abandoning all hope of human betterment through socialism. His publisher Fredric Warburg wrote that the book was worth "a cool million votes to the Conservative Party." With the publication of *Nineteen Eighty-Four* Orwell had undone illusions a century old. The words of the title subsumed the future. Tomorrow and the Post-War World were swept aside. The quality of hope itself seemed to change.

Early in the century, just before and just after the First World War, the United States had its chance to become what has since been referred to as a superpower. Twice impelled by powerful isolationist elements, it effectively declined, at the same time reaping some commercial advantages. "The business of America is business," said an American president of the twenties, not exactly the war cry of a conquering race.

Orwell had given up on the Communist world when, in writing *Nineteen Eighty-Four*, he spoke of "the necessity to prepare for total war." He meant a war between the Soviet Union and the West. Not inevitable, perhaps, but which needed preparing for. Part of his fear was that the preparations, which unfortunately we still have with us, would undermine the free institutions that had evolved over the centuries in the West. He singled out several specific threats in his statement about the book; totalitarianism in America was one. Now that forty years have passed, we can examine to what degree his fears have come to be realized.

In *Nineteen Eighty-Four*, Orwell imagined the functions of oppression in Oceania as divided between four ministries: "the Ministry of Truth, which concerned itself with news, entertainment, education, and the fine arts; the Ministry of Peace, which concerned itself with war; the Ministry of Love, which maintained law and order; and the Ministry of Plenty, which was responsible for economic affairs. Their names, in Newspeak: Minitrue, Minipax, Miniluv, and Miniplenty."

The hard fact is that Orwell's predictions were both insightful and meaningless. Because the plain truth is that no matter how ingeniously we twist it, America in 1984 resembles Orwell's

1984 no more than it resembles Tomorrow or Mickey's Post-War World. Minitrue, if that's what we want to call the news, entertainment, and the fine arts, is more Mickey Mouse than Orwell, but that's as it should be. Television counts for much more in news, which is partly to be regretted but not quite death-in-life either. American television news is definitely more Mickey Mouse than Orwell; it's tedious with its long commercials and ethnically balanced, photogenic anchor people, but it doesn't blare lies and propaganda round the clock for the edification of zombies. Well, a little propaganda for the odd zombie, but no more than the next country's, and when a war was broadcast over it in color, the result was not bloodthirstiness on the home front but a movement to end the war. Administrations, even the present one, which handles it fairly skillfully, regard network television as an enemy. Print journalism is the same jumble of secondhand, sort-of-not-quite-the-way-it-happened chaos it was in 1948. No icy totalitarian hand has been laid on there. Britain and America have a handful of good newspapers and magazines. Bad British papers tend toward vulgarity, bad American ones toward inexpressible boringness. In literature, my business, as far as I can tell you get to write what you like. The attempts to remove certain novels from certain school libraries represented not at all official censorship but rather a working-class revolt against pedagogy, started by a group of fundamentalist parents who had, through their children's reading assignments, taken their very first look at the American contemporary novel. This may be boobery, but it's not Orwell.

The Orwellian wars were public relations operations, fought for the diversion of the masses, in which the allies and enemies changed regularly. The war establishment in the United States is a servant of the administration. The weapons it commands might be said to be Orwellian in their awesome power. Whenever instruments of such destructive capacity are concentrated, there is a suggestion of tyranny, of the totalitarian. This is where we come closest to Orwell's world, in the confrontation of mightily armed blocs claiming a monopoly on virtue and purely defensive intent. But then this is the part that Orwell drew from life. It has not changed between 1948 and 1984; the difficulty is that it has not.

We have no Miniluv here, but we have the Law, and the Law is an ass. I doubt that any country in the world has so many interlocking, overlapping jurisdictions, or such incredible legalism. This is partly the result of a proliferation of lawyers, about twenty times proportionally the number that Japan gets by with. The American legal system is bound more by the letter than by the spirit, which is not exactly totalitarian but somewhat weird. Plea bargaining and a complex criminal justice system tend to produce a system that pleases no one. Crime as an issue is highly politicized, and highly visible.

There has always been a thoroughgoing resentment of any kind of authority in the United States, which would make it somewhat un-Orwellian in spirit. Our police vary in efficiency and attitude, and technically, at least, are bound by a great many restrictions unheard of in more civilized places. And are, as elsewhere, generally unloved. In terms of corruption they probably stand somewhere about the midpoint among Western police forces, with some geographical variations. They see themselves as fighting a war unsupported by the public. American cities, with a few exceptions, constitute a phenomenon

Orwell could not have foreseen. Here the middle class, which created the city as an institution, has tended to abandon it. The city has become therefore a desolate and dangerous place.

From time to time projects are mounted to reclaim the downtown cities as places of wholesome amusement and entertainment. Sometimes, as in Baltimore, Boston, and few other places, there's some limited success. At other times, as with the Pruitt-Igoe houses in St. Louis some years ago, whole residential projects become so decrepit and crime-ridden they have to be evacuated and demolished. The destruction of Pruitt-Igoe in the seventies was a science-fiction touch to terrify all futurists.

This was and remains a land of plenty. It is always possible to produce the statistics in terms of agriculture, timber, steel, and so on. America has always had poverty, though not starvation, and has never succeeded in totally doing away with a permanently deprived underclass, whose future, as technology changes, becomes all the more uncertain.

Since the New Deal legislation of the thirties, America has acquired the system of social welfare one expects to find in Western countries. But it has always been a place that thought in terms of make or break, the place to go to strike it rich, the land of "making it." A stigma attaches to poverty here, which serves to make its experience more bitter than in other, poorer places.

Orwell's nightmare was compounded of trends that were part of the reality of 1948. *Nineteen Eighty-Four* really has more to do with the failure of Spanish democracy, the purges of Moscow and Prague, the privation and disillusionment of postimperial Britain, the disappearance of socialism, and the beginning of the Cold War in America than it had to do with 1984. While there are insights into the nature of totalitarianism in Orwell's work that will always be true, it remains, like all great satires, essentially timeless. The West has survived the arbitrary forty years of Orwell's prophecy with its imperfect institutions intact; they were stronger than he feared, and our commitment to them was greater.

We may never produce a greater political novel than *Nineteen Eighty-Four;* it has done its work for us. Forty years later, forty years of anarchy and poverty embracing a world larger than Orwell's superstates, we live with fears he could not have invented for us. And also, as did he, with hope.

—Not previously published, circa 1984

DISRUPTION

The word that I associate with the sixties is "disruption." There was, for example, technical disruption, just as there had been around the invention of the printing press. The computer, which had started the decade sitting in a corner looking like your mom's refrigerator, climbed down off itself and became freakishly empowered tiny chips of silicon that would end up littering the surface of the very moon.

Other technical disruptions followed. In Dusseldorf Mr. Moog had been working on his synthesizer, and we would get to hear it a lot. And I remember as a toddler in the early forties being led into a newspaper office full of typewriters, smoke, profanity, and fedoras. The newspaper office of 1960 looked very much the same. But the newspaper office of 1970 looked very different. I think newspapermen stopped wearing hats and smoking cigarettes because they couldn't be balanced on word processors.

The word "happening" gathered an uncanny sensory force. This was an era that kept insistently defining itself as a process, demanding to be experienced self-consciously as an event in time. Any decade that would look back at itself through sex, drugs, and rock 'n' roll was bound to be following its own moves hyperconsciously. Never did a decade cry out so brazenly to be witnessed by its inhabitants, its victims, its personnel. And as disruption continued, everything got stranger. Beckett's haunting line from *Endgame* seemed weirdly relevant: "Something is taking its course."

What was taking its course was ineffable but peculiar. Certainly strange things were happening. Sometimes they simply happened, but we were doing some of them. We lived on East Fourth Street between First and Second. A few blocks away a follower of Ayn Rand opened an espresso café. We knew him as a follower of Ayn Rand by the dollar sign that hung outside his window. He had a sideline selling hallucinogenic peyote cacti, ordered from Smith's Cactus Ranch in Texas. One evening a friend of mine, myself, and my fiancée — three of us — rode a motorcycle off the street and into the café, jumping the curb, over the sidewalk, through the door, passing among the tables alive with deluded merriment, into the sad autumnal garden. Months later Baron, the Randite proprietor, mysteriously died. Dealers are very often called "Baron," for some reason. Before the sixties, though, one saw few individuals like Baron, the fiscally conservative Peyote Man.

My fiancée, now my wife, had two jobs. Early in the evening, dressed like a crewperson on the starship *Enterprise*, she worked as a guidette in the RCA Building, selling tickets to the roof, across from the Rainbow Room. Cute as a button in her form-fitting spaceperson suit. Later at night she worked in a café in black skirt and sandals — gear for listening to Allen Ginsberg, Gregory Corso, and friends read poetry. She would serve coffee, sometimes with whipped cream, while the customers listened. *I saw the best minds of my generation* — all that. Kerouac read there too. He was there the night she took off so she could get married to me. Her sister filled in, and Jack explained the dharma to this child of fifteen.

Disruption quickly creates ironies. Jack Kerouac is associated with the sixties because it was then so many young people fell in love with his mystified nomad life as rendered in *On the Road.* This was a book published in 1957 that celebrated the lost American highways of the forties and fifties just as they were going under, replaced by the Cold War interstates of the Eisenhower era.

On a freezing cold winter night early in the sixties, we stood in a frigid doorway holding some weed. We had weed but no papers. What to do? Removing my gloves, exposing my fingers to the cold, I ripped the filter off a Kool or some other mentholated cigarette, took out the poison tobacco, and jammed the weed into the white paper. A fat, ugly joint. The mentholated scent suited the South Pole–like weather. We each did a toke of mentho-weed. It was messy and wasteful.

But at that moment we heard John Coltrane on his soprano sax play the opening bars of "My Favorite Things." Oh my God, how wonderful it was! Coltrane was playing live at the Jazz Gallery on St. Marks Place. McCoy Tyner might have been with him, I don't know. But Coltrane! It left me having to explain that despite my reverence for the Dead and the Doors, the one piece of music I flipped over in the 1960s came from *The Sound of Music.*

And in California all through the sixties you saw and smelled the disruption and felt it under your feet along with shocks from the seismic fault. The parks were redolent of marijuana and patchouli oil. But the young who had not come to party had come to be dispatched to war. The cops were helmeted and the streets were angry. America had entered one of its spells of disruptive idealism. More than a hundred years before, the associates of Emerson and Margaret Fuller had complained about their friends, men with beards and barefoot.

On starry nights high over the Santa Clara Valley, exhausted, enraptured, in love, toward dawn — "girl we couldn't get much higher" — we, the young, would look out toward the bay and think it was all one big party and all about us. We'd hardly notice that among the blossoms most of the fruit trees were gone. How could we have believed that all this magic we were living, and the world of which it was made, was not our own?

Well, the world in truth belonged to Fairchild Semiconductor and the Stanford Research Institute. We were the stuff of dreams.

—*Vanity Fair,* 2013

THE MAN WHO
TURNED ON THE HERE Kesey

I will stand on your eyes,
your ears, your nerves and your brain
and the world will move in any tempo I choose.

—Marshall McLuhan, paraphrasing
the modern Archimedes

One cloudy day last October, a muscular young man wearing a cowboy hat and carrying a guitar walked up to the US Customs and Immigration station at Brownsville, Texas, and looked uncertainly about him. He was obviously somebody's hard-times cowboy, and they had not treated him right South of the Border. "How long you been in Mexico?" asked the customs man. "Too damn long," the cowboy said.

He was Singin' Jimmy Angland, he explained, and he had been down there to play a little old country music gig and damn if the Mexes hadn't laid him out and cleaned him. Hell no, he didn't have no papers. He didn't have no money neither. Why, he didn't have nothin'. 'Cept (*pat, pat*) his geetar. Yep, the women and the margaritas and the streets of Matamoros had laid Old Singin' Jimmy low and all he wanted out of fortune was into God's country and then home to good old Boise.

Boise, yessir, that's where he was born. Boise, Idaho.

Thus, her maternity stirred, the republic reclaimed a bruised offspring, and Ken Kesey, "freshest, most talented novelist of his generation," creator of a New Aesthetic, diabolist, dope fiend, and corrupter of youth, passed the brown bank of the Rio Grande to his native soil.

He had not been in Mexico overnight to play country music. He had been there since the previous January, and he had gone there concealed in a truck after being arrested for the second time on charges of possession of narcotics.

Kesey is sitting in the garden of the Casa Purina when Des Prado bounds through the adjoining lumberyard crying, "Battle stations!" Des Prado is a young man of vaguely Okie origin who gives the unmistakable impression of having spent a great deal of time on Highway 101. He has also done some time in the can, along with one hitch in the navy and one in the marine corps, so he can shout "Battle stations!" with professional zest. And, indeed, something like a combat situation seems to be developing.

There is a dapper Mexican lurking in one of the bungalows under construction across the road. The Mexican is equipped with an elegant and complex camera and is covertly taking pictures of the house and its occupants.

One of the Pranksters has seized a camera which is even bigger than the Mexican's and is pretending to photograph him, although there is no film in the Prankster's camera. The Mexican lowers his and looks thoughtful. He is about thirty, casually dressed in the style of the Mexican tourists who regularly come down from Guadalajara to vacation on the Colima coast.

Kesey sits tight in the yard, a baseball cap pulled low over his eyes. There is a possibility that the man with the camera represents the press, but it is more likely that he is a policeman or an advance man for the American bodysnatchers.

Babbs and George walk across the road and hail him. He is now making awkward conversation with the Indian laborers who are building the bungalow. He will not look at the Americans or reply to them. The Indians are clearly embarrassed at the turn things have taken. Some of them have removed their hats. The camera man answers no questions in any language. After a while he gets into a white Volkswagen parked down the road and drives off. It is the same car that has been seen regularly on the road.

The siesta hour passes tensely. Everyone has assembled at the main house for desultory speculation on the stranger's intentions. A few optimists express confidence that he will turn out to be a journalist, but this is not the prevailing opinion. Kesey leans against one wall sipping Coke. Every now and then he looks out the window.

When siesta is over Kesey looks out of the window again and sees that the man with the camera has come back. He has come directly to the house and is standing before the door, looking about him with an amiable expression.

Kesey turns and walks into a room where Faye is making

Prankster costumes on a sewing machine. They exchange looks, say nothing.

Two or three Pranksters go outside to say hello. One of the Pranksters who goes out is Neal Cassady of song and legend, the companion of Kerouac and Ginsberg in the golden days of Old San Francisco. He has been a sidekick of Kesey's for years, functioning as chief monologuist and Master Driver for the Acid Test. Now, without a word (most unusual for him) he walks into the road and constructs a little brick target. He had been carrying a six-pound hammer in his belt for days, and he begins to throw his hammer at the target with a great deal of accuracy and control. The dapper Mexican watches Cassady's hammer-throwing as though he finds it charming. Three other Pranksters are standing around him and they are all taller than he is. Babbs is much taller than he is. He seems to find this charming as well.

He has learned English during the siesta.

"Well," he says, "I guess you guys were wondering what I was doing out there with the camera."

Cassady continues to throw the hammer, but now he accompanies the exhibition with a rebop monologue. When there is no one else around, Cassady practices his routines with a parrot named Philip the Hookah. Philip and Cassady discuss automobiles or books of current interest, and since Philip is rather a nonverbal parrot, Cassady does most of the talking. Occasionally, the question arises of what to do with a parrot who will talk like Neal Cassady. Kesey suggests that it would make an Ideal Christmas Present.

"Um yass, quite indeed," Cassady says, retrieving his hammer. "Quite a setup, yaas, yaas. Bang, bang, bang," he sings, "bang, bang, went the motosickle."

The dapper Mexican tells an astounding story. He is from Naval Intelligencia. He is looking for a Russian spy whose description is incredibly like Kesey's. The Russian spy is spying on the coast of Mexico. Occasionally, Russian ships appear off the bay and they flash lights to him. Russian spies are Commies, the man explains, and mean America no good. The Pranksters are Americans, no? Ah, the man likes Americans very much indeed. He hates Russians and Commies. Might the Pranksters assist in investigating this nastiness?

Ah, now the dapper Mexican sees musical instruments lying on the porch. The Pranksters are musicians, are they not? He seems to find this charming as well. He is watching Cassady's hammer from the corner of his eye.

And how long have they all been in Manzanillo?

Kesey stands in the room with Faye and the sewing machine. Faye continues to stitch costumes from the forthcoming Manzanillo Acid Test while Kesey looks through the blinds.

Faye Kesey is a woman of great beauty, the sort of girl frequently described as radiant, possessed of a quiet vivacity and a dryad's grace. It is said that the meanest cops refrain from giving Kesey's handcuffs that nasty extra come-along twist once they've seen Faye. Fourteen years ago, she and Ken were steadies at Springfield High, and they have come a long way together since. Her name was Faye Haxby, she was a dreamer, and she was of the legendary and heroic race of women who, appearing delicate and fragile as ice cream swans, were yet prepared to accompany some red-eyed guzzling oaf over frozen passes and salt flats, mending axles, driving oxen, bearing children and nursing them through cholera. Faye has never driven oxen, although she can be a handy mechanic, but she has come over some strange passes in some funny mountains and, with Kesey, she has been out in all the weathers.

Faye leans forward over her machine for a look at the man with the camera, smoothing out the colored cloth on the table before her.

Kesey watches the Mexican intently, trying to gauge his size, weight, intelligence. He does not know what will happen or what he will do. There is a little song he likes to sing, a cowboy-style ballad called "Tarnished Galahad." It has that title because a judge in San Francisco so referred to him when he disappeared and Mountain Girl remained in the coils of the law.

Down to five pesos from five thousand dollars
Down to the dregs from the lip-smacking foam
Down to a dopefiend from a prizewinning scholar
Down to the bush from a civilized home.

What people once called a promising talent
What used to be known as an upstanding lad
Now hounded and hunted by the law of two countries
And judged to be only a Tarnished Galahad.

Tarnished Galahad — did your sword get rusted?
Tarnished Galahad — there's no better name!
Keep running and hiding 'til the next time you're busted
And locked away to suffer your guilt, and shame.

He accepts the turns of the outlaw game, but he does not want to go to jail. He is not the type.

Just beyond the doorway, the agent with the camera is still talking Foreign Intrigue. When his conversation with the Pranksters lags, he revivifies it by asking questions.

Now it is Babbs's turn to be uncommunicative.

How about him, the agent wonders. Does he play a musical instrument?

Babbs nods his head affirmatively.

The agent looks him in the eye. In order to do this, he must bend his head backwards and stare almost straight upward. So, the agent says, Babbs prefers not to talk. He prefers simply to watch? He wants to just listen?

Babbs nods and scratches his nose.

Cassady is still performing the hammer throw. Babbs belches. The Mexican agent smiles the grim smile of Montezuma. But he does not go away.

Inside the house Faye sews and Kesey watches. It is now a year and a half since the night when several varieties of law enforcement officers, human and canine, dashed into his house in La Honda to arrest him and thirteen of his friends on charges of marijuana possession. The cool Mexican operative outside is only the latest in a long procession of agents, DAs, sheriffs, snoops, troopers, finks, and detectives who have peopled his fortunes since 10:30 p.m. on the night of April the twenty-third, 1965.

Kesey recalls finding little piles of cigarette butts and Saran Wrap on the hillside across from his property several times during the weeks preceding the raid. He had, he says, taken all possible precautions against being accused of marijuana possession. Nevertheless, on that night the officers struck. Kesey says that he, Mountain Girl, and Lee Quarnstrom, a former newsman, were painting the toilet bowl in the bathroom when Federal Agent William Wong sailed through the door, clapped a Federal Agent lock around his neck, and commenced to beat on him. (The bathroom at Kesey's was—and thanks to the simpatico sensibility of the house's present tenants, remains— a remarkable pop composition. Much painting and pasting was done on it at all hours.) The police maintain that Kesey was trying to flush his marijuana down the toilet.

A fracas ensued, police guns were drawn, an alleged attempt was made by one of the Pranksters to grab a deputy's service revolver. The occupants of the house were collared, busted, and taken away. Faye Kesey and the Kesey children were off visiting relatives in Oregon at the time of the arrest.

Ken Kesey has always maintained that the bust was queer. "We'd been warned by three people to expect a bust that Saturday night," he says. "Not a bad trip if you're expecting it. You can set up to film and record the cops' frustration. You can even have your lawyer forewarned. But some way, they boxed us and showed up a day early. They blew our cool for a while, I have to admit. I'm in the bathroom with Mountain Girl and Lee. Page is standing in the bathroom shaving. Other people were out sewing, working with tapes, wiring, and like that. "Suddenly I got a guy beating on me from behind and chaos all around. Babbs snatches him off me onto Page, who falls on his back in the tub. Then follows the whole search, question, banter, and looking ceremony. Other events happened that I tell no more because they have been so often sneered at as likely stories from one side — or nodded at as 'what else can you expect from those bastards' from the other. Like the business of painting the toilet, a beautiful double-edged paradox. One side: Okay, but why would you just happen to be painting the can — the most likely place for a man to be disposing of contraband just when the cops busted in? Other side: Okay, but if they were watching and waiting for the best chance to make a good case, wouldn't they wait for the most incriminating scene to bust in on? And this I believe is the true price of justice — the amount of time wasted justifying."

The net took Mountain Girl, Des Prado, and Neal along with Kesey and various other Pranksters. The "contraband" assembled by the arresting officers ranged from "one disposable syringe" to "one Western Airlines bag" and included one pint jar and two and a half lids of grass in addition to "marijuana debris."

One of the principals in the first Kesey arrest was Agent William Wong of the Federal Bureau of Narcotics, the officer whose flying tackle opened the Battle of the Bathroom. Agent Wong, who is no longer with the bureau, was then working as Federal liaison officer with the San Mateo County Sheriff's Department Narcotics Division. Wong seems to have become convinced that Kesey was, in addition to being a novelist, a dealer in both marijuana and heroin on an international scale — in any case, he seems to have conveyed this conviction to officers of the county. Just how the Federal presence was introduced into the case is a question that no one involved feels quite able to answer. Some local detectives remember a story that Wong had been working on a heroin case in the area and had come to believe that Kesey was connected with it. Kesey's lawyers aver that Wong told one of the girls he was grooming as an informer that he believed it was Kesey's practice to lure girls into his house, get them "hooked," and then sell them into prostitution.

According to a San Mateo officer, Wong, as Federal liaison man, would frequently drop by the bureau to "bullshit." The Great Raid seems to have developed from one of these "bullshit" sessions, more or less as a law enforcement caper. And there are persons officially connected with the legal apparatus of San Mateo County who feel that Kesey's prominence as a novelist and "nonconformist" was not wholly unconnected with the zeal with which his arrest was sought and obtained.

According to the affidavit submitted by the police to obtain a search warrant, Agent Wong was working "undercover" in the North Beach area of San Francisco. In what must be imagined as a low dive frequented by twilight figures without hope, he chanced to overhear the following remarkable conversation:

FIRST MALE: Hey, man, did you hear?
OTHER TWO PERSONS: What?
SAID FIRST MALE: At Kesey's. La Honda, man—a swingin' pad!
OTHER TWO PERSONS: Yeah! Yeah!

The said persons continued to address each other enthusiastically in this manner; the connoisseur will recognize their frenetic mode of speech as the argot of the so-called hipster. Agent

Wong, who doubtless does a great deal of listening, seems to possess a gifted amateur's ear for dialogue, for here again the imagination takes wing. One pictures the agent, inconspicuous as hell; perhaps his hat brim is pulled low across his countenance, perhaps he counterfeits the stupor of narcosis. In the next booth sit the said persons—and, man, you *know* how they look. They wear berets and sandals, the girl has stringy hair, and like all three of them are carrying a set of bongo drums.

In any case, as the incident is rendered in an affidavit, the first male conveys to others, in the colorful speech to which he is given, intelligence that Agent Wong interprets to mean that Kesey is going to have a party at which dope is served.

Kesey, whose point of view is admittedly subjective and who is perhaps overly given to regard comic strips as vehicles of contemporary reality, professes to believe that this conversation never took place. He holds that Agent Wong lifted the whole number from a recent installment of *Kerry Drake*.

After relating the agent's North Beach adventure, the police affidavit goes on to record the alleged statement of a coed who reportedly admitted to officers that she has been "furnished" with marijuana by Kesey, and the account of a surveillance mission during which the police encountered several persons who appeared to be under the influence of a "narcotic, dangerous drug or other stimulant." The document also records the police's belief that Kesey was a drug dealer, on the evidence that "said Ken Kesey has written two books, one dealing with the effects of marijuana and one with the effects of LSD, namely *Sometimes a Great Notion* and *One Flew Over the Cuckoo's Nest*."

The point seemed to be that Kesey was so confirmed a dope

pusher that he felt able to devote his spare time to enriching the literature of narcotics, perhaps with an eye toward drumming up a brisker business.

Signatory to the affidavit and a participant in the raid and arrest was Deputy Sheriff Donald Coslett, a pleasant, crew-cut young man whose office is decorated with assorted buttons of the kind favored by youthful narcotics offenders, examples of psychedelic art, and a *Ken Kesey for Governor* sign. Deputy Coslett is what might be termed a "head buff," and it is fitting that he should be such, for he is assigned to the Narcotics Division of the San Mateo County Sheriff's Department. At the time of Kesey's arrest he had served some ten months on and off as a narcotics officer and attended a Federal training course for narcotics officers. As a result of his training and experience, the deputy had a simple method for detecting probable violations of the narcotics laws.

"Whenever you get a person who has a bohemian-type house," he declared, "weird paintings on the wall, nothing made out of coat hangers hanging from an oak tree, and people around banging the bongos all night—nine out of ten somebody's blowing grass."

It has been a year and a half since Kesey bolted, and now they are back. The Mexican with the camera means he has been found, or is about to be found.

Kesey peers through the window, thinking of Lenny Bruce. ("Bruce was *courted* to death," Kesey says. "He got tripped out on the law as though that would help him.") Kesey will not let them court him to death. He will do something they do not expect, something superheroic.

Babbs and the Mexican walk off down the road together. Kesey waits a few moments, borrows someone's hat, and goes outside cautiously. One of the Indian workmen in the bungalow across the road makes the sign of the slit throat and smiles sadly. Kesey waves.

He walks down the road, his shoulders thrown back, his pace determined. With the postman's whistle around his neck he looks like a soccer referee about to make an unpopular decision.

A friend walking with him remarks that this latest of cops is pretty cool. Kesey agrees. The cop is very cool, he has talent. The thing would be to fuck him up.

"Remember the *Casablanca* routine?" the friend asks. "Humphrey Bogart? Claude Rains?"

"What was that?" Kesey wants to know.

Kesey's friend does the *Casablanca* routine. Claude Rains is a Vichy policeman. Humphrey Bogart is Rick, the owner of Rick's. He's in trouble with the Vichy police for his suspected Allied sympathies. "Why did you come to Casablanca?" asks Claude Rains. "For the waters," says Bogart. Rains is urbane but puzzled: "But there are no waters here. We are in the desert." Bogart tells him, "I was misinformed."

"Yeah," Kesey says.

He looks around, surveying the quiet beach. When they come, he thinks, they will materialize out of the sand, they will scamper down from the palm trees, they will emerge from lidded baskets holding tommy guns. Perhaps they will have dogs again.

When Kesey was arrested for the second time, it was on a rooftop in North Beach. On that occasion, fortune dealt Kesey a slice of whacked-out reality exceeding the most freaky delirium he had ever dispensed at the Acid Test. He was so impressed with it that he decided to compose the event into a scenario.

It was the night before the Trips Festival Acid Test. Kesey and Mountain Girl were free on appeal bond and plotting the doings. They got together on the roof. Someone didn't like the sound of falling gravel and called the cops.

The cops went up and found a cellophane bag of grass near their reclining mattress. Kesey attempted to fling the bag off the roof. One of the policemen attempted to prevent him and a wrestling match ensued. Kesey, having been an All-American wrestler at good old Oregon U, looked like a winner. The other cop thought everything was happening too close to the edge of the roof and drew his gun. The match ended with the police in possession of their evidence, and of Kesey and Mountain Girl.

It was at this point that Kesey decided he had detected a trend. A short time later, his Acid Test bus was discovered abandoned near the hamlet of Orick, in far northern California. Inside the bus was an eighteen-page letter that began, "Last words. A Vote for Barry is a Vote for Fun. Wind, wind send me meee not this place though, onward . . ."

The letter proceeded to convey Kesey's respects to the principals in his life and career, and went on, "Ocean, ocean, ocean, I'll beat you in the end. I'll go through with my heels your hungry ribs . . ."

As Kesey sped south toward the border, he might have heard what Tom Sawyer heard on his disappearance, for the press lost no time in firing cannons over his wake. Everyone seemed to believe him a suicide except those who had heard otherwise, and this category included practically everyone concerned. All agreed it was a Prankster's Prank.

"Hey," Kesey calls to the people of the house, "where'd they go, Babbs and the Mexican?"

"Up the road," someone says. "They went off to the Hawaiian joint for a beer."

Things have taken a Prankster-like turn. The agent has not arrested anyone, but instead he has gone with Babbs to an elegant Polynesian-style roadhouse. Kesey looks around and sees the margin of reality widening.

"All right," he says. "Let's go do that *Casablanca* thing." The Mauna Kea is quite the right place. It has thatch and palm trees, it has little tables with coconut candle holders. It has a bamboo bar behind which there is a tank of gorgeous tropical fish and a fat bartender who wears a loud sport shirt. Continental music purrs from the leafy loudspeakers. There is even a beaded curtain to glide through.

The Mexican agent has bought two beers; he and Babbs are sitting at the bar, sharing a small plate of spiced shrimp. Kesey waits before the beaded curtain and measures the scene.

He will be Humphrey Bogart. The Mexican agent is no Claude Rains, but he will do for the smooth foreign cop. Kesey eases through the beadwork, slicing it with the edge of his hand.

Babbs and the Mexican agent are now on speaking terms; the agent is buying beer and telling stories, presumably Mexican naval yarns. He looks up with interest as Kesey joins them on a stool.

"Hi," says the agent, "how are you?"

"Well, just fine," Kesey says.

Babbs introduces him as Solomon Grande. The Mexican's name is Ralph.

"Grande?" he inquires. "Grande? What is that? French?

"American."

"Fine, fine," says Ralph. He is quick to buy another beer. He seems in a mood to drink beer himself.

"A guy in Sinaloa," Ralph declares, apparently resuming an anecdote, "one time swears he's going to kill me. He believes he's more man than me and that he could do it. One time I'm in the office and the chief says to me, You know what? Old what's-his-name in Sinaloa wants you to come see him. He wants you to be the godfather of his child.

"I say, Good—I'll go.

"The chief says, Man, you're crazy. He wants to kill you.

"I say, He can try.

"I went. I'm godfather to his child. Now he's my compadre. He was going to kill me. He's my compadre now."

"Huh," Babbs says. "Was he in trouble with the navy?"

"Naw. He was a big dealer in marijuana. We sent him up."

Kesey frowns. "Marijuana, huh?"

"Yeah. You know about that? Marijuana?"

"Yes, I have heard of it," says Kesey. "But I don't believe it's as much of a problem in the States as it is down here."

"Is that right?" the agent asks. He is very cool indeed. "But I thought it was."

Babbs and Kesey shake their heads furiously.

"No, no," they assure him, "it's hardly any problem at all." More beer and more shrimp arrive. Someone else pays for it and the Mexican agent is much put out. He is sensitive about his salary.

"So you investigate dope-taking too?" Kesey asks.

"Sure." He goes into his pocket and produces a badge emblazoned with the rampant eagle and struggling snake. He is a Federale, and his badge number is One. He is Agent Number One.

"Numero Uno," Kesey says. He looks at the badge. Babbs whistles softly through his teeth.

"Do you have a license to kill?" Babbs asks.

Agent Number One cocks his head in the Mexican gesture of fatality.

"Sure," he says. "Sometimes people try to escape." Someone buys another round of beer. Agent Number One seems to grow very angry.

"Don't do that again," he tells them. When that round is over, he buys the next.

He tells them that at the office they call him El Loco. They call him that because he takes on the cases that no one else wants, the cases you really have to be tough to handle. It was he, he informs them, who followed Lee Harvey Oswald through Mexico City. In Puerto Vallarta, he met Elizabeth Taylor in the course of a secret investigation.

"There was an American who was one of the movie company stooges," Number One recalls. "He tells me that it's impossible for me to see her."

He leans forward, almost snarling into Kesey's face. "I told him, You don't tell me it's impossible!" Babbs and Kesey nod in spontaneous approval.

"By the way," the agent asks, "have you ever been in Puerto Vallarta?"

"No," Kesey says. "And I've always regretted it."

"You'd like it," Agent Number One says. "It's beautiful." There is a short pause as everyone sips their beer and takes a reality break.

"By the way," Babbs begins, and commences to tell outrageous stories involving Russians and people who appeared to be Russians whom he has encountered in and around Manzanillo. There have been many. Sometimes it has seemed that there were more Russians than Mexicans about.

Agent Number One receives the intelligence soberly. He keeps saying "Wow!" and seems always about to write something in his book. Kesey joins in telling of his encounters with Russians.

"Wow!" Number One says. He tells them that this information will set one hundred and fifty Federal agents in motion.

"Wow!" Babbs says. "A hundred and fifty!"

"Sure," the agent says.

Des Prado comes into the bar and the Federale buys a final round of beer for everyone.

Kesey and Babbs present the agent with one of their Acid Test cards. Number One looks at it incredulously.

"Acid?" he inquires. "Acido?"

"Sure," Babbs says. "We say that if you can stand our music, then you've passed the Acid Test."

"Wow!" the agent says.

They walk outside and stand in the sun beside Number One's white VW. There will be an Acid Test at their house on Saturday, the Pranksters tell him. He is invited. If the hundred and fifty other agents have nothing special to do that evening, they are invited as well.

Agent Number One looks at them strangely and says he will try to make it. Also, he has one favor to ask. Might he take their picture? For his collection. He already has Elizabeth Taylor's.

Kesey shrugs, confounded. Why not? Babbs, Kesey, and Des Prado throw their arms about each other's shoulders and strike superheroic poses. The agent, all business, photographs them.

He gets in his car and Babbs climbs in beside him. They are going for a drive so that Babbs can show him all the places where the Russians have been seen.

Kesey and Des Prado walk back down the road to the house and sit down outside.

After a while Babbs appears, grinning.

"What a great cat!" Babbs says. "How about that guy?"

"Definitely a man with something going for him," Kesey says. "Definitely."

—In *One Lord, One Faith, One Cornbread*, 1973
(a version also appeared in *Free You*, 1968)

THE BOYS' OCTET

I t's always extremely difficult to try to look back on some-one's life, to choose the aspect of it that seems most to lend itself to celebration. I have a copy of *Sometimes a Great Notion*, which I have always felt was Ken Kesey's greatest novel. It shows a picture of that intense, thoughtful Kesey who's gazing into space, who seems to be stalking something, who seems to have spotted something. The Kesey who is always associated with quotes around his picture that said things like, "There is a great ear out there, and it's always open."

And I remember him saying that to me once, that there was a great ear out there, and it's always open. To tell you the truth, this is not the kind of thing that I enjoy people telling me. I'm uneasy with that kind of cosmic ambition, even in ordinary conversation. But I know the level on which Kesey believed that, and the ways in which he chose to pursue it, ways in which he tried to come to terms with those forces in the world that were beyond us, were very special and, in a way, unique to him. I don't think anybody ever struggled so hard, so overtly, so *physically*, with the forces beyond us, since Jacob at Peniel.

The dedication in *Sometimes a Great Notion* is "To my mother and father, who told me songs were for the birds, then taught me all the tunes I know, and a good deal of the words." And his dedication in *One Flew Over the Cuckoo's Nest* is to our mutual friend Vic Lovell, a psychologist in California, and that dedication reads, "Vic, who taught me that dragons did not exist, then led me to their lairs." There is a kind of contradiction, the idea of a young man—a boy who was turning into a young man—who was ready to see through all these pretensions that the world made for creation and the act of creation, until he could experience it himself—until he *did* experience it himself. In other words, until he made it his own. Until he made the process his own. I think belief was a very important thing to him, but I don't think he believed in anything that he couldn't somehow make his own—not dominate, but simply make his own.

I first met him in 1962. He'd published two novels, in what seemed to be an amazingly short time, two years, and then set out on that original bus trip. It was 1964, and we were going to the World's Fair. Those of us who went along had that as their purpose. Probably it was the absolute zenith of American power and wealth. At the same time, it was an era of tremendous discontent, which he represented. He felt and represented that discontent. In the very nature of the prosperity, of the tremendous feeling of power, there was a kind of discontent. I don't think he could quite put his finger on it. I think he wanted to go to New York, to the World's Fair, to protest the nature of these blessings that we were all enjoying.

I think he tried somehow to short-circuit the necessities of art. He believed that he could somehow invent a spiritual technology, an applied spiritual technology, somewhere between Silva mind control and the transistor, that would spare all the humiliating labor that went into the creation of art. He somehow thought that a lot of basic metaphysical mistakes had been made about the world, and that they could be righted. And when he came into the world of drugs, he really saw in them a means, a formula. *Doctor Jekyll and Mr. Hyde*, one of the greatest books ever written in English, is both a Calvinist moral story and a science-fiction story. It would apply very well to Kesey, because those were elements that made up his life.

But when you went out with him, he always had this sense of doing something as *setting forth* — you didn't just go somewhere, you *set forth*. And it was as though we were out to resolve whatever had been overlooked between where we were and where we ought to be. I never knew anyone in my life, then or since, who was a dreamer on that scale, who really believed in Possibility, the great American bugbear Possibility, to the degree that Kesey did. I never knew anyone who had his ability to communicate that sense of Possibility.

He was not, I think, enough of an individualist by nature to want to be a novelist. Starting out, he had preferred acting, because I think he disliked the loneliness and isolation of the writer's life. He was determined, somehow, to make it all happen faster, for everybody.

At the start of that bus trip, just as the trip gets under way, the nature of America begins to change. The Kennedy assassination takes place, and then the others. All of the feelings of security and certainty that Kesey was rebelling against are taken from us, and we're visited with confusion, which Ken refused to accept. Ken saw somehow — or believed — that America, in the late first half of this century, had reached a point where it was meant to be at, and that its arts, its thinking, all of these things, could be carried, almost by main force, if enough people believed in it, into another dimension.

He was a true dreamer, but unlike a lot of dreamers who had dreams of his scale and dimension, he was also a person of innate goodness. This is tremendously important to remember, because Kesey can be quoted out of context in ways that make him seem more purely interested in power than he was. He had a good heart. He desired good things for people, for all sorts of people.

I remember we were both reading here at the Y one night in 1992. We were introducing each other, and he recalled a night in the Albert Hall in London. He was telling a humorous anecdote about me, which isn't always easy, and he said, "It was Christmas Eve, and the Beatles were there, and everyone was having fun, and Stone started singing 'Deutschland über Alles.'" I almost died, you will understand. I was not happy. Finally I got to straighten it out. I started singing "The Internationale," not "Deutschland über Alles"! I'm happy to finally clear that one up.

But he was a great artist whose best work is going to last as some of the exemplary work of the twentieth century. I think anybody who met him and had to do with him has got to say, "Thanks. Thanks for that encounter."

Ken once had a little joke, a little jingle, on himself. He said, "Of offering more than what I can deliver, I have a bad habit, it is true. But I have to offer more than what I can deliver, to be able to deliver what I do." Maybe that's true of everybody.

There was another nonsense song that we used to sing. We

decided—there were about eleven or twelve of us, boys and girls—we decided we were a boys' octet. So we had a little anthem that we sang, our mixed-gender, eleven- or twelve-member company, the Boys' Octet. We used to sing,

I never had such a good time yet
as when I was a member of the Boys' Octet.

And on these cryptic and meaningless words, a tribute to Kesey, I'll close.

—Tribute to Ken Kesey, 92nd Street Y, New York, 2002

KEEPING THE FUTURE AT BAY

The late, great journalist A. J. Liebling, who imagined the city of New Orleans with the intensity of a true lover, once described it as a combination of Paterson, New Jersey, and Port-au-Prince. Liebling was conjuring up the city before 1960, in most of which Stanley Kowalski would still have been comfortable without a shirt. The high life and the low life were curiously turned and very restricted. It was a poor, peculiar, happy place, where the fateful gaiety of Carnival really did last all year long—an antic spirit that savored very much of mortality and the imperfectness of things. Only local black people and a handful of hipsters knew to call it the Big Easy.

With the oil boom, New Orleans acquired a belt of Chiclet suburbs where alligators fled the new white middle class that fled the inner city, divided, ironically, by integration. Million-dollar condominiums were nailed together everywhere in the Vieux Carré. Until 1960 a French Quarter address still carried with it more than a suggestion of bohemian impropriety, and the Monteleone was the only big hotel actually in the Quarter. A few years later there were half a dozen, all of them oozing old-timeyness and simulated essence of magnolia, with menu prose that implied they had been standing at least since Kate Chopin's day. One of them, the Bourbon Orleans, occupied the shell of the convent of the Sisters of the Holy Family. The sisters were small brown Creole ladies of an ineffable delicacy, and I have often wondered whither they were removed. The convent, as I remember, had fewer stories than the hotel has, although the hotel is no higher. Above Canal Street, the city acquired several brutal square skyscrapers of the sort that seem to require a rooftop sign reading BULLSHIT WALKS — they manage to be tall and squat at the same time.

The New Orleans of my recollection ascended no higher than the white cupola atop the Hibernia Bank Building. I remember chimes that sounded "Abide with Me" over the rattle of the St. Charles streetcar and the newsie's cry and the police whistles. I'll never be sure how much of what I remember is imagined, so readily does this city lend itself to dreams. Memory is subverted, tainted by fantasies that thrive in the languid shadows. People who grew up here tell me it is the same for them, that the way in which they recall lining up for frozen Sno Balls or going to parochial school takes on a certain spin.

At the same time, reality has always been relentless in New Orleans. My daughter was born in Huey Long's Charity Hospital under legal segregation, which meant that everything was done twice, separately, often cheerfully and in theoretical equality, but under circumstances that are horrible to contemplate today. There was nothing insubstantial about the poverty, violence, and general squalor that poor people, white or black, endured in the land of dreams. Yet in the worst of times an absurd magic might intrude itself. In the waiting room outside the maternity ward, I fell into conversation with a Cajun farmer who assured me that Saint Joseph took special care of firstborn children. It was good to hear a friendly word in that hard-boiled but unsanitary place.

Politics have a way of coming to you in Louisiana, circa 1960, even of coming at you, no matter how you tried to hide. For one thing, the desegregation battles were being fought in the streets and in the small towns of the Deep South. About the time I showed up, other young people from the North were appearing all over the South to help in the struggle for black civil rights. I was not among them; instead I was ingloriously supporting my new career as a beatnik, selling encyclopedias door-to-door in towns such as Bogalusa and Picayune. By some perverse synchronicity I always seemed to appear with my cheap suit and dissembling sales pitch at the very moment when the townsfolk had sworn unspeakable violence against the next fast-talking scut of a Yankee agitator with the nerve to show his nose. Northern accents were instantly detected and explanations urgently required. In several places I was rescued by the police; in others, I was not. I got to see the inside of a couple of Mississippi and northwest Louisiana jails. To this day, when people from the movement tell war stories and talk of Southern prisons, I'm tempted to casually put in my observations on the St. Tammany Parish lockup compared with the jail in Pearl River County. But at the time I was a subscriber to art for art's sake, wanting to be left alone.

The last thing Louisiana needed in 1960 was a few more beatniks, but there we were. It was existential. We got by with odd jobs and passing the goblet after poetry readings. There was a bar on Burgundy Street that featured bunches of bananas as part of its decor; on evenings when the paying customers found our performance insufficiently stirring, they would toss bananas at us to indicate their displeasure. A poet I know would take the bananas home and eat them with rice and Worcestershire sauce. In those days, the *vie de bohème* was undertaken without state assistance. The only thing forthcoming from the municipal welfare authorities, should we have been rash enough to approach them in our penury, would have been a couple of expletives and the advice to get out of town. We went from day to day, eating when we worked, fasting otherwise. Our poverty was not a game; there were no rich relatives back home to bail us out. On the other hand, we always felt just on the edge of vision, an available cop-out, shameful but perhaps eventually necessary. One could always go home, get a steady job, maybe save enough to go to college. Our style, if not our lack of means, *was* voluntary.

But around us in those years another kind of poverty ruled, one that afforded its subjects no redeeming posture. The timeless poverty of the Deep South had not been relieved at that time, if indeed it has since. For all that things had improved since the Depression of the thirties, poverty lay like a dark enchantment over that part of the country, laving the edges of the city and flourishing well inside it. Its victims were more often black than white (although plenty were white). This poverty was deathly mean and formidable; it embittered people and made them dangerous; it stunted hope and destroyed even the imagination. Because I was young and male, the aspect of the poor South that most arrested my attention then was its anger and violence. I was looking for experience, wanting to learn. I got it and I learned. Eventually I saw that poverty and the culture it promotes have a political dimension. Politics, it turned out, was not something I could ignore.

Of course it would have been hard to ignore politics in New Orleans in any case, if in a definition of politics one chooses to include the caperings and adventures of Louisiana politicians. When I first came to the city, Huey Long's younger brother Earl was at the end of his long career, and his eccentricities were prized and recounted angrily or affectionately all over town. When I came to write my first novel, which like all first novelists I made the receptacle of every single thing I knew, I found Louisiana and its politics inevitable. I thought *A Hall of Mirrors* was quite fair to America in important ways, although probably unfair to New Orleans in unimportant ones. I tried never to let on how in love I was with the big soupy city, but it came through anyway. The idea of the Republicans convening in the Superdome aroused in my breast a fierce possessiveness to which I was not in the least entitled.

The town the Republicans came to was a poor place again. Ten years ago, when I had last passed through, New Orleans was on a roll. The squat skyscrapers were shinier and the Quarter was extremely spiffy; some residents worried that progress might sweep the old city beyond recall. Preservation has always been a little difficult in New Orleans, where politicians have traditionally been available for a good time. The old breed of shady white politician had been replaced by a new breed of shady black politician, but money was still green. Subsequently, however, oil took its downturn and the city went back to living off the out-of-towners while waiting for the wheel to come around. In the Vieux Carré, the old walls looked patched and peeled now, and balconies were sagging. The *Times-Picayune* ran a story on the "demolition by neglect" of some of the older buildings. The owners of these buildings, the story said, "either didn't want to spend the money or hoped to let an old building decay so badly that the city would finally allow the owner to tear it down and put the property to more profitable use, such as turning it into a hotel or a parking lot."

My personal standard of measure is the building my wife and I lived in on St. Philip; ten years ago it had been newly renovated, but this August it looked worse than it did when we moved in. Some New Orleans residents I talked to say that the hard times have at least served to maintain the Quarter's character—which depends somewhat on its characters, many of whom may be priced out when the boom comes back. But in the quiet streets away from the hustle and din of Bourbon, the steamy air hung timeless and fragrant and it might have been long ago. You could hear children playing on some of the patios, and caged canaries sang in the balcony windows. All over town the ironwork was dressed in patriotic bunting as the city got itself up for the Republican Convention, the old soul sister never more herself than when getting ready for a party. Even good-time girls have their authenticity.

The Louisiana Superdome, the actual site of the four-day convention, is a wonder of the modern age. If the purpose of the vaulted Gothic cathedrals was to remind humanity that God was above, the Superdome serves to remind us that what yawns eternally overhead today is space. Together with the Hyatt Regency and an adjoining shopping mall, to which it is attached by a concrete caul, the Superdome forms an air-conditioned island of spic-and-span order right in the middle of funk's own hometown. Within this bastion you can watch the NFL Saints, go to bed, or sip an aperitif at a sidewalk café the temperature of a meat locker. During the convention, the entire complex was as busy as a hive, with delegates, guests, and journalists lining up for food and drink. In the shopping mall, the outer reaches of the Hyatt, and all around the Superdome itself, hucksters were selling Ollie North videotapes, Ronald Reagan masks, political tchotchkes of every kind. It would not be too much to say that a carnival atmosphere prevailed. Strolling this enormous carnival, I saw ghosts. I took the 1960 census here.

Yes, right here, house-to-house in the summer heat, I carried my census book, knocking on doors when there were doors to knock on, yoo-hooing into shanties, poking my nose into people's kitchens. The people endured my questions: Place of birth? Estimated yearly income? Mother's full name? Father's? Condition of residence? We didn't ask that one; the answer was always "dilapidated," and we checked the appropriate square.

Where the counter dispensing libertarian Republican literature stood was once a row of shacks before which half-naked children played among rusting automobile skeletons. On the site of the campaign-button boutique was a storefront church, the Sanctified Temple of the Lord God, in whose window was the painted text "Sufficient unto the day is the evil thereof." (When I first saw that text in the church window, I didn't understand what it meant, though I've since learned.) Under the dome itself, where the band played "Happy Days Are Here Again," was a kind of hotel, unlike the Hyatt Regency, in which solitary people lived in rooms divided at the top by chicken wire, and with candles for light. Where the podium was erected

—of course I exaggerate here, but not by much, a block or two —was the house in which I apprehended one of the very few political truths I know. Let me describe the scene.

It is July 1960 and I am alone, deep in the heart of the black slum where many years later the Superdome will rise. I am not, as I certainly would be today, afraid. Not at all, in fact. I've been coming back here for weeks and everybody knows my white face by now. Some people are rather short with me, but many others sit me down with a cool drink and tell me the story of their lives. Never have I known heat like this. Never have I seen such poverty.

I am Tail-end Charlie for the census; I get the hard cases —the brothels, skid row, the B-girl dorms, the transvestites who scared the last census taker away. It's an aspiring young novelist's dream. I'm also assigned to the poorest black areas back-of-town, to get people the regulars have missed. The fact is, I'm having a rather good time of it. I have taken to the South in a big way. I feel very romantically about it. I've also fallen hard for blackness, in the mindless, old-time, hipper-than-thou beatnik way. In the weeks I've been in this back-of-town, I've been listening to black speech and watching black moves, and I dig it. It's ringing my young literary bells. It's got something, all right; the rhythms and the raps are sounding in my dreams; I think I'm ready to signify.

Late one afternoon, up against the Illinois Central yards, I check out a ramshackle wooden house suspected of being a household. No one, over the summer, has responded to the bureau's attempts at communication. So I knock ... and this time there's an answer, a female voice asks me in. Inside, half a dozen people are gathered around a bed. Beside it, a single candle burns at the feet of a plaster Virgin. Cloth blinds have been drawn over the windows to keep back the killing sun, and the candle provides the only light in the room. I advance on the bed. The people in the room have turned to watch me. Looking over their shoulders, I see that lying there, with clean white sheets drawn up almost to her chin, is a very old woman. Her skin is a café au lait color and engraved with fine wrinkles. Her toothless face is like an old turtle's. She breathes slowly and with difficulty. She's clearly dying.

I am delighted to learn that the folks in the room are attendant relatives from two different households, an overwhelming tactical coup, census-wise. In my brisk impatience to record the statistical details of everyone's life, it takes me a moment to register the fact that these people are strangely unforthcoming. Looking up from my forms, I confront their eyes. Their eyes are calmly questioning, almost humorous. I stand and stare and return to my jottings, and then suddenly it hits me: someone is dying here. These people have come to attend a death. Perhaps this is not the best of times for census taking? After this death-defying leap of understanding, the rest follows unbidden.

That had this been a white middle-class household, I would have never been allowed past the door.

That had this been a white middle-class household, I would never have dreamed of entering a sickroom, approaching a deathbed, asking cold, irrelevant questions of people who had come to mourn and pray.

That what has happened here is entirely determined by the politics of race and class—how blinding it can be, how dehumanizing, how denying of basic human dignity.

So I left, and walking along Dryades Street in the paralyzing glare, the rest of the wave hit me. The question of why I, a white person from out of town, should have been taking the census here. That there were no black census takers.

So the voice of God was in that wave. A poor thing, a less than dazzling exercise of the social sensibilities, but mine nevertheless. In the many years since then, I have tried to keep that frail candle of insight flickering. Through the absurdity and bloody-mindedness of Race Relations in America, a subject so double-dipped in hype, phoniness, hustling, hypocrisy, lies, stupidity, malice, blind ambition, ignorance, groveling, sniveling, and foolishness that it defies coherence, I've tried to keep it burning. Life doesn't often pause to allow us a moment of common sense. Watching the Republicans convene among the ghosts, I tried to hold it to my heart.

The hotel in which I stayed was beside a freeway and of a singular crumminess. Unluckily for the management, the New York delegation was housed there, and in no time at all, a media blitz of ridicule descended on the unfortunate place. A block the other side of Canal stood the Iberville housing project, another place I remember from long ago. In my memory, the Iberville project had both black and white tenants, the officially segregated housing blocks alternating racially, so that passerby could see poor Southern kids, black and white, playing together. Now the project was officially integrated — and all black. Unemployment there ran up to 70 percent. Late one night, in a welter of blue lights visible from the hotel bar, the police picked up the body of an unidentified black male in his twenties. He had been shot through the head, apparently another victim of the crack wars. It occurred to me that I might have counted him back in 1960; he might have been one of the babies. There were so many.

At the Calliope Street houses, a project that stands in what's left of the slum the Superdome replaced, residents had their usual route to Canal Street blocked by chain-link fences installed around the Dome for security purposes. Forced to walk the long way round, they were able to see the limousines scooting past, creating a significant juxtaposition no self-respecting reporter could resist. To Calliope Street went the working press, eliciting forlorn quotes. These are from the *Times-Picayune:*

> "Ask the politicians if they can cut out the shooting out here," said Mayola Brumfield, 40, cradling her granddaughter on a porch step.
> "Tell them I need a job—bad," said Brenda Sumling, 26.

To all of which the unwritten coda was: Good luck.

A few hundred yards and a world away from Calliope Street, the president was now speaking. I missed a bit of his speech; I had decided to walk from the hotel to the Superdome and cover some of the old ground. This foolish exercise in nostalgia soon found me wandering through Fritz Lang's worst movie, a godforsaken wilderness of cement over which whirled a vortex of ascending and descending freeway ramps. Ghostly figures darted at the edge of the open spaces. I hurried, sweating mightily in the heat, feeling whiter than Moby-Dick and equally pursued. Imagine my relief, then, when I gained admission to the great stadium and heard the dear, familiar voice.

It is not entirely facetious to speak of the president's voice as dear and familiar. Ronald Reagan is one of the most interesting phenomena this country affords, and no examination of contemporary American reality should be undertaken without reference to him. In the Superdome on August 15, he was giving the assembled delegates and their guests enormous pleasure, making them laugh, bringing them to their feet with fierce patriotic cries, and occasionally reducing them to tears.

"Twilight? Not in America. Here, it's a sunrise every day — fresh new opportunities, dreams to build."

One had the feeling he might have gone on and on and on. What could be dearer or more familiar, a happy mating of *Ursprache* and Muzak, the refined essence of every sunlit daydream crooned in a reassuring, cheery baritone.

Where have we heard it before?

But where have we *not* heard it?

It's the primal voice of the electronic age, the medium *and* the message, the voice that never sleeps, that cajoles, inspires, and commands wherever cathodes glow. We can no more resist it than oncoming night. For just about as long as Ronald Reagan has been alive, his voice has whispered in our dreams, a manifestation of American reality. Flick a switch and there it is, unresponding but constant, everywhere, every hour. It seems to emanate from some invisible consensus, the voice we have all agreed to hear. It is not the voice of a man; its name is legion. It is inside us. Our consciousness ebbs and flows to its undulation, obedient as tides to the moon. Hearing it, we mistake it for our own.

Dutch Reagan, the man on the radio, is speaking in the voice of American popular culture. No one does it better. One of American popular culture's principal artifacts is a sentimentalized view of America, touched by the dreams of the immigrants, rubes, and carnies who created it. Its media are semaphores, not much good for conveying subtleties. In the language of American popular culture, words cast no shadows. The land to which it speaks is a land without irony, a land without contradictions, a land in fact that doesn't exist and never did. All the same, it's the real thing, the McCoy. That's a paradox, the only paradox you have to know in Ronald Reagan's business.

He was a poor kid, his old man drank. God knows what he's really like. But now he's American popular culture's greatest creation since the Wizard of Oz, another glib midwesterner. Only Reagan's charm is authentic. Otherwise, as a voice or an image on a screen, he's always been the agent of someone else's agenda. Part of America's willingness to forgive him for the disasters of his administration may relate to the sense he gives of having been dragged in arsy-varsy, a secondary figure in his own career, along for the ride. His most effective public gesture is that humorous shrug of incomprehension, a mannerism that appears strangely genuine. To see him do it is to laugh with him, to share his amused befuddlement at the mess the world's in. It's also reassuring. If things are this bad and he's not worried, why should we be?

Inside the Superdome on that Monday night, he was breaking their hearts for a while. And why not? He had perfected his routine before a lot of them were born. Then a balloon popped. For a fraction of a second his rhythm broke; he seemed to lose forward motion. He misspoke a word or two. People looked from the monitors to the podium, but the man himself was too far away, a tiny figure.

It's difficult not to speculate on his inner life. Everybody has one. What resides at the core? What does he mean, "It's morning again in America"? Why should it be morning?

Suddenly he regains his timing, and I have the answer to that. I have only to look at him on the monitor and I know. It's because morning is time for brunch. Brunch is what he's making me think of. Maybe everyone in the audience all across America is listening and thinking of something equally scrumptious. I see it shining plain: it's 11 a.m. and we're in Pacific Palisades and the sun is sparkling on Santa Monica Bay. There will be croissants and honeydew. It's brunch, the California Eucharist, the sustaining reality at the president's core. It makes me feel like cheering, but when the monitors fade, he's gone.

Off the convention floor there were a few swell parties. One was thrown at the Fairmont Hotel by the National Rifle Association, a luncheon with free booze. From the very beginning of the convention, a certain coldness had been in evidence between the working press and the convening Republicans. At the NRA party, this mutual lack of appreciation occasionally threatened to bear fruit. The electronic media had stashed their equipment in the center of the hired ballroom, and the resultant mountain of hardware served as a rallying point for the reporters. From within the laager, a newsman might proceed in reasonable safety to the bar and then, fortified, venture forth in search of a survivalist troglodyte who might be baited into grunting threats and imprecations against decent folk.

In fact there were no camouflage suits to be seen at the NRA's party, the celebrants being, on the whole, better dressed than the press. But though the scene was mainly good-natured, there were volcanic domes of anger over which the crust sat lightly. Among the angriest were the several divines the NRA seemed to have assembled. There was a priest of the old school with a face that would have looked a lot more appetizing on a plate with parsley and horseradish than it did on the front of his head. There was an intense young man in a yarmulke who seemed ready to cast the first stone. I asked the priest if he was a member of the association, a question that reduced him to inchoate rage. He eyed my press pass as if it were a turd or a squirting boutonniere. He was not a member. Before long he was at the podium telling jokes, and I got the feeling that he and I went back a long way together and it was time to go.

The religious dimension was not overlooked in New Orleans. On Tuesday morning, Jerry Falwell spoke to a student symposium on the Tulane campus on the subject of the Moral Majority. Falwell was dapper, brisk, and genial. He allowed that the folly of the Bakkers and Jimmy Swaggart had "hurt the cause of Christ." He said he found the fall of the Bakkers unremarkable; he had been detecting a materialist element in their theology for a long time. In response to a question, he hinted, as he has several times lately, that he was about to undertake a program of civil disobedience. He compared *Roe v. Wade* with the Dred Scott decision. He sounded less like the leader of any "majority" than like the organizer of a major pressure group setting out to make trouble for the misguided.

Generally the convention was short on conflict. One of its minor dramas was the public fall of Falwell's fellow preacher Pat Robertson. Robertson's camp had harbored the only organized disgruntlement left alive by convention time. Over the course of the year his delegates in states such as Michigan and Georgia managed to threaten the seamless fabric of Republican good fellowship. But in the end, Robertson simply failed to gather the money or the votes to back up his candidacy. The opening of the convention found him in the position of a man who had thrown a roundhouse right at the bouncer and connected with the incorporeal air. A muted anticlericalism prevailed among the party pros. On Tuesday night, Robertson took his wages in the form of an opportunity to address the convention. He was less than electrifying. As his speech progressed, it was possible to stand at the exits and watch the crowds streaming out into the night, bound for Antoine's and Mahogany Hall. His press conference the next morning at the Intercontinental Hotel had a somber, penitential tone.

Barely a dozen reporters were present. These were equally divided between the Old Sweats, who had followed Robertson through the primaries, and the Marginals, who included this writer and an amiably nerdish young man in a baseball hat inscribed with the words ATHEIST AND PROUD. The young man described himself as "Chicago bureau chief" for the American Atheist Press. A beefy front-page type from USA Today asked him if there are also Rome and Jerusalem bureau chiefs. While waiting for Pat, several journalists interviewed the bureau chief, who recounted for them the variety of insults, threats, and put-downs visited upon him over the previous two days by godly Republicans. Presently Robertson arrived, smiling his smile and looking philosophical. He and the atheist were old pals; indeed, Robertson looked grateful for the company. Most of the reporters wanted to know about Robertson's plans for the future; they were assured that he would carry on. It was hard to believe, though. As Robertson left the room, the Chicago bureau chief of the American Atheist Press was pursuing his press secretary, Barbara Gattullo.

"Barbara, can Pat be on my radio show?"

Iowa was long gone. It was deepest Palookaville.

On the very same morning that Pat Robertson was facing the music, a state judge on the other side of the Mississippi was writing a footnote on another American religious career. Debra Arlene Murphree, the temptress before whose allure the redoubtable Jimmy Swaggart's Christian resolve did a fast fade, was dispatched to the Jefferson Parish Jail for six months, having copped to a misdemeanor for prostitution. This timely retribution at the height of the convention may have preserved the career of some anonymous Republican state committeeman, who, atremble with self-destructive lust, might have flung himself on her scented settee down there on the Airline Highway.

As the convention opened, the Republicans had little to offer sensation seekers except a degree of suspense over George Bush's choice of a running mate. Bush himself had said that he would not announce a choice until Thursday, whereupon, it was thought, the selection might be dramatized at the anointing ceremony that evening. But as early as Sunday, rumors began to fly, and their flap and flutter was distracting. It was also believed that the notables on Bush's shortlist were not happy about having to spend the week standing around in their bathing suits. Robert Dole, who seemed to move through the convention in a storm of smiling, saturnine rage, made his displeasure public. Finally the rumors began to hint that Bush had not made up his own mind, a notion that invited mental images of the vice president in one of his screwball-comedy states, dithering fatuously and plucking daisy petals. So on Tuesday, when the mighty paddle-wheeler *Natchez* brought Bush down from Belle Chasse Naval Station to Spanish Plaza, he introduced Dan Quayle to the welcoming crowd and the word spread around town. Not all delegates, to say the least, were pleased with Bush's decision. Some of Jack Kemp's supporters, who were young, energetic, and numerous, cried real tears.

But the blow fell hardest on the remnants of what used to be called the Eastern Republican Establishment, now reduced to a grim band of *conversos* practicing their ancient faith in secret. For at least the last four years, they had been sporting kelly-green slacks and white loafers, trying to pass as right-to-lifing Holy Rollers, while stealthily sipping scotch and dreaming that Nelson Rockefeller was alive in the heart of a mountain somewhere. Throughout the convention they had been buttonholing media acquaintances with assurances about George Bush's personal excellence. At any moment, they held, Bush would come into his own and reveal himself as the sensible and sophisticated Yalie he truly is. What they got was Quayle.

On Wednesday, while Pat Robertson was sparring with

the Chicago bureau chief of the American Atheist Press, the conventional press was slapping Quayle around the grand ballroom of the Marriott. He was then hustled over to the Sheraton for a friendly session with the California Republican Caucus. Outside, party flacks were pointing out Quayle's valor in choosing to help defend Indianapolis from the San Francisco Mime Troupe. Inside, all was groovy. Jack Kemp, a native Californian, signed on enthusiastically, prompting a few more tears from the young surfers. Senator Pete Wilson spoke. Quayle declared his ferocious impatience to campaign against Dukakis and Bentsen.

The press joke about the selection of Quayle was that "George Bush wanted a George Bush," but that wasn't it. Quayle had none of Bush's Washington experience. According to Germond and Witcover's piece in the *National Journal Convention Daily*, Quayle's name did not appear on a shortlist of pickable senators compiled by Senator Mitch McConnell of Kentucky. Many people at the convention attributed the choice of Quayle to Roger Ailes, George Bush's media consultant, who happens also to be a consultant for Quayle. A dream deal in the Hollywood mode, a media fix so pure it could almost be called nonpolitical.

The following day, Thursday, the Republican Mainstream Committee met at the downtown Howard Johnson's. The mainstream Republicans were many, but the room in which they met was very small indeed. The chairman of the meeting was Congressman Jim Leach, from the First District of Iowa. The press attendance was meager, featuring those birds of ill omen, *Harper's Magazine* and the American Atheist Press. Many present at the mainstream meeting were young, and they seemed idealistic in an old-fashioned, innocent way. Discussion tended to be rather abstract; there was talk of a struggle for the soul of the party, and of the necessity for a Republican Party with some social responsibility. There were general expressions of support for the ticket and attempts to find common Republican ground. The only tangible expression of common ground expressed was an opposition to taxes. The libertarian tendency seemed to predominate.

One of the Republicans at the meeting was Harriet Stinson, of the California Republicans for Choice. The CRC had prepared a flyer it intended to distribute arguing a pro-choice position on the abortion issue. The flyers bore a few signatures that had once meant something in the party—Barry Goldwater, Charles H. Percy, S. I. Hayakawa, and Rebecca Q. Morgan of the California State Senate. Harriet Stinson had FedExed her flyers to a convention hotel, where the entire consignment disappeared. Asked if she believed that the consignment had been hijacked by an anti-abortion faction, she replied that, indeed, she suspected that was the case.

Celeste King of the California Black Republican Council pointed out that when Vice President Bush landed at Spanish Plaza the only black on the platform was a high school kid playing the trumpet. King called the situation unacceptable.

So the mainstream Republicans got nothing from George Bush's post-Reaganite Republican Party. Black Republicans got practically nothing but the brief presence of Coretta Scott King in Bush's gallery, where she and the candidate acknowledged the applause of the convention. The Wall Street *conversos* got to hear the languid upscale tone of Governor Tom Kean's keynote address. Regarding the platform and the vice presidency, the right had everything its own way, and with the candidate's enthusiastic blessing. The moderates could lump it.

"The damn thing is," remarked one mainstreamer, an alternate at the convention, "those people never could stand George Bush." She meant the religious right and ultraconservatives. "He was always our man." By "our" she meant what the Robertson people like to call the country-club set. She was watching "her man" being borne forward on the shields of the barbarians. Later in the week, mainstreamers were speculating that everything might be different when Bush won election.

The delegates, alternates, and guests present in the Superdome performed a function somewhere between that of a studio audience and a laugh track. The audience could hardly behold the physical presence of its heroes; as mentioned, each speaker was a tiny figure unrecognizable across the Superdome's great spaces. Huge Orwellian monitors displayed talking heads at various points around the arena so that, in the stands and on the floor, people faced in different directions, watching different screens. As a result, there was little sense of unity, no true crowd to become a single animal with a single voice in the grand old style. There were milling, isolated groups. The sound system that carried the speeches was particularly poor. In some parts of the Dome the speaker's remarks were absolutely inaudible. For this reason, the prepared tapes that introduced the president on Monday night and George Bush on Thursday provoked a more emotional reaction than their remarks. Television speaks to isolation, and the 1988 Republican National Convention was television and little else. Being in the

Superdome was a bit like being on a movie set or behind the scenes at a television studio.

Late one night, CNN showed some footage of the 1952 Republican Convention, at which General Douglas MacArthur was the keynote speaker. Plummy and orotund, the general's style was not well suited to a "cool medium." The cameras saved him from absurdity only by keeping their distance. The world that this footage evoked seemed hard to imagine. It appeared to be a grayer, riskier, and somehow more serious place, more than a little frightening. The Republicans in New Orleans thirty-six years later were trying hard not to affright a soul. As noted earlier, it was morning—all week, around the clock. The background colors on the monitors could adjust themselves as if by magic to tones complementary to the flesh and apparel of the speaker. The effect sought was similar to that of a beer commercial.

Amid this kind of flummery, it can be extremely difficult to maintain consistent standards. How to tell the wax from the Shinola? How to react when references to love of country, honor, courage, and fidelity are shoveled into the hopper and ground into televised gruel to the throbbing of strings? Nihilism gapes beneath the pilgrim. The mind becomes taxed with the necessity of correctly perceiving the apparently obvious. Is American politics all a deception, designed to clothe a system of patronage? If it is, is that all right? And if American politics is all a deception, does not modern history show other systems to be equally so? Are we not apes with flags and speeches? Surely it will be necessary to go away somewhere and think about all this. Seen from within the core of its creation, such a media event reduces everything to the significance of Michelob Light.

No nation whose people are unable to recognize their own social superiors can be said to have lost its innocence. So the convention, like the country, continued to puzzle over George Bush's attempts to be a regular guy. Most of the week, the press eyeballed him like so many shrinks at a lunacy hearing, watching for popped synapses, spasms, and false moves. It must have taken considerable nerve to endure. There was a lot of slightly hysterical finger-pointing when he referred to his grandchildren as "the little brown ones"; fortunately, it soon stopped. Eventually, to the relief and disappointment of many, he more or less made it through. By the time he stepped away from the podium on Thursday night he appeared to have weathered the passage from goofy diffidence to button-eyed vulgarity.

The speech he made was of the sort generally described as effective. Bush delivered it convincingly, and it was extremely optimistic, from a certain point of view. It described America as a rising nation and predicted a second American Century. That is certainly a sort of patriotism, although not necessarily the sort we require at this period in our history. At one point, in summing up our country's achievements, he said we had "lit the world with our culture." I thought "lit" sounded a trifle electric. Later in his text, the vice president was made to describe himself as a "quiet man," and this seemed an inspired phrase. "Quiet" is not entirely the word for the way George Bush appears, but it is a sympathetic way of describing it.

"You are history," said George Bush to "the drug dealers,"

those swart banditos of American political song and legend. "Read my lips," he declared to any who might doubt his resolve to hold the line on taxes. This colorful lingo was a property of the new Bush, the one with the common touch, capable of exchanging the idiom of the country day school for that of the regional junior high.

So who is this George Bush? You have to believe he's a man who does good by stealth. No one in American public life is surrounded by so many favorable rumors and benign innuendos. Almost everyone who knows him personally says he's wonderful. Yet publicly he appears . . . "quiet."

The real point is that in order to become the Republican candidate for the presidency, the vice president has embraced some very intolerable and retrograde elements with whom he has not heretofore been associated. Perhaps, as he says of his stand on abortion, he has "changed his mind" on various issues.

Bush may well ride his successful convention appearances all the way to the White House. Then, perhaps, the inner excellence he's said to have will emerge in the fullness of time, expressed in policy. Perhaps not. And if George Bush doesn't care what he's really like, why should anyone else?

In August of 1988, Bush took charge of a Reagan-enchanted party, rigid with complacency. Against the backdrop of contemporary New Orleans, the party's convention looked even more unreal than its media specialists sought to make it. There are many other American landscapes upon which it would have appeared ephemeral and fantastic, not because of the lights and the music but because of what Bush might be induced to call "the vision thing." Again and again at this convention, speaker after Republican speaker affirmed that his party would carry this country into the future, as though it were a trick only they could manage. In fact, they were promising to keep the future at bay. The future does not require the Republicans; it will come.

As the convention drew to a close, Bush left the podium and they released the balloons. It was a moment we'd all been waiting for, and it was quite amusing to watch the balloons and confetti drift down past the cold ironical smiles of the foreign press corps. Not all of them looked ready for another American Century. Guests, the press, the delegates, and alternates began filing toward the exits. Outside, the air was heavy with impending rain, smelling of history. People went in groups, searching for their buses or peering anxiously up Loyola Avenue for a taxi. The future we'd heard so much about was gathering in the darkness. The evening was ending as so many contemporary evenings do, in the search for a safe way home.

—*Harper's Magazine*, 1988

EAST-WEST RELATION:
SUMMIT ON FIRST AVENUE

Early last summer, I spent a few days in one of the capitals of the "socialist" bloc, an ancient and mellow place under the rule of cynical and arrogant bureaucrats. The principal form of the class struggle in that place at the moment is the authorities' resistance to the influence of Gorbachev and *glasnost*. The fear to which the intellectual and artistic communities are subject there is of a sort I hope we may never experience here. It is difficult to visit places like this central European capital without reflecting on how undeserved America's promiscuous freedom sometimes seems. Then it's necessary to remember that people's fundamental rights mainly *are* undeserved, and that's as it should be.

A reading at the city's medieval university accidentally put me in touch with some student dissidents, to whose underground newspaper I gave an interview. The interview was conducted in a pleasant city park beside the ubiquitous river, with much scouting around and looking over the shoulder. The publication in question was produced for my brief inspection, then hurriedly stashed in someone's bag. It consisted of the customary typewritten sheets, covertly reproduced by someone with access to a copier. I very much doubt that there was anything in it that threatened the governance of the Communist Party in that country. In a superbly reflexive fashion, it offended by virtue of its existence, regardless of what it contained. So we were all criminals that afternoon.

The government of that country has long been known for its morbid sensitivity to any vein of independent thought. An acquaintance of mine from there, a world-famous author now in the West, likes to tell a story from his early days. He and some other youthful spirits had a program on the state radio that afforded them a vehicle for general riffs, routines, and madcap hilarity. For the program, they invented a revered personage named Zimmerman. Zimmerman, a native son, was the inventor of everything; his discoveries included the goose-quill pen, the cannonball, the diving bell, aloe shaving cream, and raspberry syrup. On their program he became a running gag. After not too long a time, an utterance issued forth from the mouth of the state: Knock it off about Zimmerman. It's not funny. Nothing is funny. Moreover, anything funny is proscribed.

That was the way it was then and how it is today.

After my reading, I had the kind of milling, hurried, postlectoral conversations one has in those circumstances, and in the course of it a young woman whom I took for a student informed me that she would presently be in New York. And, as one will in certain circumstances, I found myself saying, Oh-really-well-do-give-me-a-call. I felt undeservedly privileged among those quiet, avid students. I wanted to do something about it, something for them. And that was why I said it.

When I arrived home two weeks later, a message from the young woman awaited me, and, as may be imagined, I had no idea who she was. I remembered many people very vividly from my visit to the riverside socialist capital; for whatever reason, she was not among them. But I remembered the reading and the students and my feelings of obligation. During a week when I had no time whatsoever for excursions, it seemed to me that I had better make some.

When I called the apartment where she was staying, to agree upon a meeting, I thought she sounded surprisingly impatient and overbearing. I put it down to cultural differences. We agreed to meet for a few hours in New York on a day when I had an errand in the city. We arranged to meet at the Museum of Modern Art. From there we would spend two hours or so flitting around New York, until such time as my errand came due.

I found her outside the museum cafeteria. She recognized me. She was attractive and sympathetic in appearance, seemingly both serious and youthfully enthusiastic. I'll call her Eva. Eva and I had MOMA's equivalent of *Kaffee und Kuchen*, and I also ordered a soda water, which in my general and unfocused haste I drank from the can. That was our first difficulty. With a subtlety hardly to be limned, Eva conveyed her disapproval of the practice of from-the-can soda drinking. Her disapproval was a particularly concentrated substance, an airy sub-rosa essence like a petard, slight but highly significant. To command such a resource, it seemed to me, a young person would have to spend an inordinate amount of time disapproving, having learned the science from skilled disapprovers.

Just as these insights were occurring to me, Eva told me a

little of her life. She was not quite the student waif adrift in the free-thinking, unfeeling West that I had imagined. She had stories from Canada, from Japan, from Sweden. She had been everywhere. And as we discussed art and literature and other topics appropriate to the heady ambience of MOMA's snack bar, I came to realize that I was entertaining not one of the students of whose lot I had been so solicitous but a child of the regime, a state princess, whose interest lay, inevitably, in the very conditions I had been deploring over there. Of course I had neither the brutality nor the courage to heap my politics on the head of a kid nearly young enough to be my daughter. I did what most people would have done: I kept smiling and grew discreet in my discourse. I did regret not having accompanied her through the museum's exhibits. It might have been interesting, I thought, to hear her comments on the state of Western art. Convinced socialist realists are lately thin on the ground.

Refreshed, Eva and I hit the streets of the Big Apple. Since we had decided to tour buildings of architectural interest, I found myself conducting her toward Trump Tower. On the way, we passed one of Fifth Avenue's premier celebrity panhandlers, a man whose props included a long, hand-painted chronicle of his woes and who I swear had been working the corner of Fifty-Sixth and Fifth since I was in high school. As we drew closer to the old boy, I sensed Eva's interest quickening.

"There are so many poor," she said happily, and took his picture.

I allowed there were, but insisted the chap on the pavement wasn't one of them. I bade her imagine the volume of cash that would pass through his frail hands if only one in a hundred passersby gave him a quarter. I suggested that he probably led the Internal Revenue Service a merry chase. But it was impossible to dampen her spirits.

Not far from Tiffany's we encountered another indigent, this one truly in want, and the juxtaposition cheered Eva further. From building to building we went, with Eva shutterbugging their contours. By that time, I knew she was in search of more subjective and colorful material.

As we waited at Fifty-Seventh and Lexington, Eva watched the alienated hordes jaywalking in the teeth of the yellow and red lights. It all reminded her of a remark her father had made about people's attitudes toward traffic signals in North America: "The yellow means 'Run, run, the Reds are coming.'" I thought the anecdote had a slightly complicated aftertaste.

On First Avenue in the upper Fifties we turned downtown, bound for the United Nations. By now, I felt, Eva was alert to every touch of the squalor and misfortune with which New York is so richly endowed. There's nothing like walking in Manhattan with a Communist to bring out an endless procession of the untended lame, the halt, the homeless, and the unconfined insane. Before long, First Avenue was transforming itself into an outsized outdoor production of *Marat/Sade*, so many were the lunatics, junkies, and *clochards*. Eva began to take pictures. But when we came to the site of the Chinese and Chinese-American demonstration against the government in Beijing, a kind of night descended on her eyes. We breezed past the posters and the Goddess of Liberty and the demonstrators, and Eva saw none of it. She was as good at not seeing un-Communist demonstrations as you and I are at not seeing the poor.

We stopped for a cold drink at what must be the last of the old-time First Avenue candy stores and sipped our sodas in front of the magazine rack. Eva asked about the magazines. Which ones, she wanted to know, are devoted to art and literature? Art was easy enough, but literature a little dicey. *Penthouse*, so prominently displayed, is definitely not a literary magazine, and *Playboy* is not; and *Vanity Fair* is not about literature. Eva ran her eyes over the rack, unsurprised by the sleaze and concupiscence, and I was momentarily at a loss. *The New Yorker*, *Harper's Magazine*, the *Atlantic*—they're not quite literary magazines either. So I was reduced to telling her that while literary magazines were in plentiful supply, there just didn't happen to be any available in this particular store—which is what they tell you about meat in Bucharest.

At that point Eva had something to ask me. What did I think, she wanted to know, about communism? No one had ever asked me that before. It's a question you hardly ever hear. I replied that since we had spent virtually the entire twentieth century living out the gruesome side effects of nineteenth-century prescriptions, it was time we came up with some of our own. While Eva knit her brow to digest this intellectual dumpling, I looked across the store and saw Edwin Newman, the television commentator, on his way to the door. Clearly he had overheard my snappy bon mot. Inexplicably, he seemed unamused; if anything, gloomier than usual.

We hit the street again and walked a block, and that was where she saw the man. He was sitting on the sidewalk with his back up against the wall opposite the UN, the wall inscribed with Isaiah 2:4, the one about beating swords into plowshares. He was stoned and out of it, ragged, impoverished, an utter mockery in that landscape of right-mindedness and good intentions. He was a natural photo opportunity for Eva.

All the time, I swear, I had a feeling. There was something about him that gave me pause, and I like to think that I was just about to suggest that Eva turn her socially conscious lens elsewhere when he spotted her from the short end of the camera. He let us have it.

I think he may have used the acoustics of the glass building across the street. Maybe he'd done it before. New York is too hip—how can you tell the spontaneity from the routines? Suffice it to say that there on the sidewalk he raised the most dreadful, soul-withering shout that ever echoed in an urban nightmare. When I say shout, I mean *shout*, because the Baptist Church lost a great preacher when that man took his first swallow of bad whiskey. Over the river and off the wall, resounding in the midtown towers, the man on the sidewalk wailed. His song was of death and fornication—you didn't want to hear it. At the top of his considerable voice, he gave us some traditional advice. He advised me that any attachment I might have formed to the lady's person should not blind me to the physical perils attendant upon her conduct. He reminded us that death is sudden in the city, that protection is often unavailable, and that heedless behavior sometimes destroys its author. A man can be dressed up, he pointed out to us, and in the company of a handsome young woman one minute, but cooling his dice in a rubber bag the next. He invited us to consider the sound of a shell entering the skull. He reminded us that the morgue was not far away, and beyond it the cemetery and bereavement for our next of kin, in whose grief he would rejoice.

I've worked with the best, I've listened to the rest, and he was good. At the height of his rap he was stopping pedestrians in their tracks three blocks away, his phrasing so sophisticated that he could operate at the top of his voice with perfect control. I should point out that not once in the course of this dreadful encounter did the man's sorry ass disconnect from the pavement. But Eva didn't notice that. She was seeing him astride the building across the way, three hundred feet high, baring his teeth and snatching at airplanes. Her camera hung limp, her eyes were wide, and her knees were close together. I escorted her across the avenue and into the visitors' center of the United Nations, where we both endeavored to refrigerate our psyches in the Eskimo art.

When we came out she said, "My father says most of them could find work."

By then it was past time for Eva to go back to her digs and pack, and past time for me to be about my errand. I wondered aloud if she would like a taxi. As I should have realized, it was a point of proletarian honor with her to ride the subway. I didn't at the time see any use or any need to argue her out of it, but it did occur to me that I ought to go down with her to see that she got on the right train. So at Grand Central, the two of us descended into the IRT.

The subway was in its state of high-summer ripeness that afternoon. It isn't much to see at the best of times, but seeing it through Eva's eyes was daunting. There was so much I wanted to explain. What I mainly wanted to explain, though, was how I, a lifelong subway rider, managed to get us lost in the familiar maze under Grand Central. I wanted to tell her that it was all because they changed the route of the IRT uptown express. I wanted to, but the infernal roar prevented me. Sweating, dispirited, our vacant faces and tentative steps attracting malign attention, we soldiered through the IRT until I found Eva's train and bade her farewell. Making for the surface, I didn't want to even think about how New York looked to her that day. But her vision of things had somehow stayed with me.

In the middle of Grand Central Terminal, beneath the vast vaulted roof that still displays its patched, peeled zodiac, some advertising types were doing a shoot. A model posed under the lights, looking extraordinarily cool and disdainful. Around the lighted rectangle, a crowd of men stood watching—commuters, muggers, addicts, policemen, all of them displaying slackjawed, lascivious smiles. It was like a scene from some dark age, not in the past but yet to come.

In the adjoining waiting room near the Forty-Second Street doors, a mob of the ragged and deranged sat waiting for no earthly train, though a few looked as if they might be hearing some lonesome whistles blow. Presently, I thought, Eva would be on her way home to sleep in the bosom of state security, safe within a fortress of police spies and informers, propaganda and lies. Though that system might oppress millions of her countrymen, it would work perfectly well for Eva. No doubt it would seem doubly vindicating in her eyes after her distressing New York adventure.

Eva knew where she could run that afternoon; I wasn't so sure about myself. I found myself walking in long circles among the streaked marble and corroded brass. In the tunnels under the terminal, any number of human beings were said to bed down. Just as on any other day, there were bad sights to endure, hard ironies to ignore. The terminal had outlived its vital age just as surely as Marxism had outlived its own romantic, Wagnerian improbabilities. Its heroic space had ceased to function as a monument to speed, commerce, and sleek convenience, home to the aptly named Twentieth Century Limited. What it celebrated now was the egotism, violence, and uncertainty of the city, with which I had long ago made my peace. Nothing is free, and that relentless law of life surfaces again and again to our eternal disquiet. Eva had her walled city; I had mine.

—Harper's Magazine, 1989

A HIGHER HORROR
OF THE WHITENESS

One day in New York last summer, I had a vision near St. Paul's Chapel of Trinity Church. I had walked a lot of the length of Manhattan, and it seemed to me that a large part of my time had been spent stepping around men who stood in the gutter snapping imaginary whips. Strangers had approached me trying to sell Elavil, an antidepressant. As I stood on Broadway I reflected that although I had grown to middle age seeing strange sights, I had never thought to see people selling Elavil on the street. Street Elavil, I would have exclaimed, that must be a joke!

I looked across the street from St. Paul's and the daylight seemed strange. I had gotten used to thinking of the Wall Street area as a part of New York where people looked healthy and wholesome. But from where I stood, half the men waiting for the light to change looked like Bartleby the Scrivener. Everybody seemed to be listening in dread to his own heartbeat. They're all loaded, I thought. That was my vision. Everybody was loaded on cocaine.

In the morning, when I drove into Manhattan, the traffic had seemed particularly demonic. I'd had a peculiar exchange with a bridge toll taker who seemed to have one half of a joke I was expected to have the other half of. I didn't. Walking on Fourteenth Street I passed a man in an imitation leopard-skin hat who was crying as though his heart would break. At Fourth Avenue I was offered the Elavil. Elavil relieves the depression attendant on the deprivation of re-refined cocaine —crack—which is what the men cracking the imaginary whips were selling. Moreover, I'd been reading the papers. I began to think that I was seeing stoned cops, stoned grocery shoppers, and stoned boomers. So it went, and by the time I got to lower Broadway I was concerned. I felt as though I were about to confront the primary process of hundreds of thousands of unsound minds. What I was seeing in my vision of New York as superstoned Super City was cocaine in its role of success drug.

Not many years ago, people who didn't use cocaine didn't have to know much about it. Now, however, it's intruding on the national perception rather vigorously. The National Institute on Drug Abuse reported almost six million current users in 1985, defining a current user as one who took cocaine at least once in the course of the month preceding the survey. The same source in the same year reckoned that more than twenty-two million people had tried cocaine at least once during their lives.

So much is being heard about cocaine, principally through television, that even people who live away from the urban centers are beginning to experience it as a factor in their lives. Something of the same thing happened during the sixties, when Americans in quiet parts of the country began to feel they were being subjected to civil insurrection day in and day out.

One aspect that even people who don't want to know anything about cocaine have been compelled to recognize is that people get unpleasantly weird under its influence. The term "dope fiend" was coined for cocaine users. You can actually seem unpleasantly weird to yourself on coke, which is one of its greatest drawbacks.

In several ways the ubiquity of cocaine and its derivative crack has helped the American city to carry on its iconographic function as Vision of Hell. Over the past few years some of the street choreography of Manhattan has changed slightly. There seems to be less marijuana on the air. At the freight doors of garment factories and around construction sites people cluster smoking something odorless. At night in the ghettos and at the borders of ghettos, near the tunnels and at downtown intersections, an enormous ugly argument seems to be in progress. Small, contentious groups of people drift across the avenues, sometimes squaring off at each other, moving from one corner to the next, the conformations breaking up and re-forming. The purchase of illegal drugs was always a sordid process, but users and dealers (pretty much interchangeable creatures) used to attempt adherence to an idealized vision of the traffic in which smoothie dealt with smoothie in a confraternity of the hip. Crack sales tend to start with a death threat and deteriorate rapidly. The words "die" and "motherfucker" are among the most often heard. Petty race riots between white suburban buyers and minority urban sellers break out several times an hour. Every half block stand people in various states of fury, mindless exhilaration, and utter despair—all of it dreadfully authentic, yet all of it essentially artificial.

On the day of my visionary walk through the city I felt beset by a drug I hadn't even been in the same room with for a year. New York always seems to tremble on the brink of entropy —that's why we love her, even though she doesn't love us back. But that afternoon it felt as if white crystal had seeped through the plates and fouled the very frame of reference. There was an invisible whiteness deep down in things, not just the glistening mounds in their little tricorn pyramid papers tucked into compacts and under pocket handkerchiefs but, I thought, a metaphysical whiteness. It seemed a little out of place at first. I was not in California. I was among cathedrals of commerce in the midst of a city hard at work. I wondered why the sense of the drug should strike most vividly on Wall Street. It might be the shade of Bartleby, I thought, and the proximity of the harbor. The whiteness was Melvillean, like the whiteness of the Whale.

In the celebrated chapter on whiteness in *Moby-Dick*, Melville frequently mentions the Andes—not Bolivia, as it happens, but Lima, "the strangest, saddest city thou canst see . . . and there is a higher horror in the whiteness of her woe." Higher horror seemed right. I had found a Lima of the mind.

"But not yet," Melville writes, "have we solved the incantation of this whiteness, and learned why it appeals with such power to the soul . . . and yet should be as it is, the intensifying agent in things the most appalling to mankind . . . a dumb blankness, full of meaning, in a wide landscape of snows—a colorless, all-color of atheism from which we shrink."

I was in the city to do business with some people who tend

toward enthusiasms, toward ardor and mild obsession. Behind every enthusiasm, every outburst of ardor, every mildly obsessive response, I kept scouting the leprous white hand of narcosis. It's a mess when you think everybody's high. I liked it a lot better when the weirdest thing around was me.

We old-time pot smokers used to think we were cute, with our instant redefinitions and homespun minimalism. Our attention had been caught by a sensibility a lot of us associated with black people. We weren't as cute as we thought, but for a while we were able to indulge the notion that a small community of minds was being nurtured through marijuana. In a very limited way, in terms of art and music, we were right. In the early days we divided into two camps. Some of us were elitists who thought we had the right to get high because we were artists and musicians and consciousness was our profession, and the rest of the world, the "squares," could go to hell. Others of us hoped the insights we got from using drugs like pot could somehow change the world for the better. To people in the latter camp, it was vaguely heartening when a walker in the city could smell marijuana everywhere. The present coke-deluded cityscape is another story.

Cocaine was never much to look at. All drugs have their coarse practicalities, so in the use of narcotics and their paraphernalia, dexterity and savoir-faire are prized. Coke, however, is difficult to handle gracefully. For one thing, once-refined cocaine works only in solution with blood, mucus, or saliva, a handicap to éclat that speaks for itself.

I remember watching an elegant and beautiful woman who was trying cocaine for the first time. The lady, serving herself liberally, had a minor indelicate accident. For a long time she simply sat there contentedly with her nose running, licking her lips. This woman was a person of such imposing presence that watching her get high was like watching an angel turn into an ape; she hung there at a balancing point somewhere midway along the anthropoid spectrum.

The first person I ever saw use cocaine was a poet I haven't seen for twenty-five years. It was on the Lower East Side, one night during the fifties, in an age that's as dead now as Agamemnon. Coltrane's "My Favorite Things" was on the record player. The poet was tall and thin and pale and self-destructive, and we all thought that was a great way to be. After he'd done up, his nose started to bleed. The bathtub was in the kitchen, and he sat down on the kitchen floor and leaned his head back against it. You had to be there.

Let me tell you, I honor that man. I honor him for his lonely independence and his hard outcast's road. I think he was one of the people who, in the fifties, helped to make this country a lot freer. Maybe that's the trouble. Ultimately, nothing is free, in the sense that you have to pay up somewhere along the line.

My friend the poet thought cocaine lived someplace around midnight that he was trying to find. He would not have expected it to become a commonplace drug. He would not have expected over 17 percent of American high school students to have tried it, even thirty years later, any more than he would have expected that one quarter of America's high school students would use marijuana. He was the wild one. In hindsight, we should have known how many of the kids to come would want to be the wild ones too.

A few weeks after my difficult day in the city, I was sitting in my car in a New England coastal village, leafing through my mail, when for some reason I became aware of the car parked beside mine. In the front seat were two teenage girls whose tanned summer faces seemed aglow with that combination of apparent innocence and apparent wantonness adolescence inflicts. I glanced across the space between our cars and saw that they were doing cocaine. Their car windows were rolled up against the bay breeze. The drug itself was out of sight, on the car seat between them. By turns they descended to sniff. Then both of them sat upright, bolt upright might be the way to put it, staring straight ahead of them. They licked their fingers. The girl in the driver's seat ran her tongue over a pocket mirror. The girl beside her looked over at me, utterly untroubled by my presence; there was a six-inch length of peppermint-striped soda straw in her mouth. There are people I know who cannot remove a cigarette from its pack with someone standing behind them, who between opening the seal and lighting up perform the most elaborate pantomimes of guilty depravity. Neither of these children betrayed the slightest cautious reflex, although we couldn't have been more than a few hundred yards from the village police station. The girl with the straw between her teeth and I looked at each other for an instant and I saw something in her eyes, but I don't know what it was. It wasn't guilty pleasure or defiance or flirtatiousness. Its intellectual aspect was crazy and its emotional valence was cold.

A moment later, the driver threw the car into reverse and straight into the path of an oncoming postal truck, which fortunately braked in time. Then they were off down the road, headed wherever they thought their state of mind might make things better. One wondered where.

Watching their car disappear, I could still see the moment of their highs. Surfacing, they had looked frosted, their faces streaked with a cotton-candied, snotty sugary excitement, a pair of little girls having their afternoon at the fair, their carnival goodies, and all the rides in a few seconds flat. Five minutes from the parking lot, the fairy lights would be burned out. Their parents would find them testy, sarcastic, and tantrum-prone. Unless, of course, they had more.

The destructiveness of cocaine today is a cause for concern. What form is our concern to take?

American politicians offer a not untypical American political response. The Democrats say they want to hang the dealers. The Republicans say they want to hang them and throw their bones to the dogs. Several individuals suggest that the military be used in these endeavors. Maybe all the partisan competition for dramatic solutions will produce results. Surely some of our politically inspired plans must work some of the time.

I was recently talking with a friend of mine who's a lawyer. Like many lawyers she once used a lot of cocaine, although she doesn't anymore. She and I were discussing the satisfactions of cocaine abuse and the lack thereof, and she recounted the story of a stock-trading associate of hers who was sometimes guided in his decisions by stimulants. One day, all of his clients received telephone calls informing them that the world was coming to an end and that he was supervising their portfolios with that in mind. The world would end by water, said the financier, but the right people would turn into birds and escape. He and some of his clients were already growing feathers and wattles.

"Some gonna fly and some gonna die," the broker intoned darkly to his startled customers.

We agreed that while this might be the kind of message you'd be glad to get from your Yaqui soothsayer, it hardly qualified as sound investment strategy. (Although, God knows, the market can be that way.)

We agreed that what cocaine mainly gave you was the jitters.

"But sometimes," she said, "you feel this illusion of lucidity. Of excellence."

I think it's more that you feel like you're *about* to feel an illusion of lucidity and excellence. But lucidity and excellence are pretty hot stuff, even in a potential state, even as illusion. Those are very contemporary goals and quite different from the electric twilight that people were pursuing in the sixties.

"I thought of cocaine as a success drug," one addict is reported saying in a recent newspaper story. Can you blame him? It certainly looks like a success drug, all white and shiny like an artificial Christmas morning. It glows and it shines just as success must. And success is back! The faint sound you hear at the edges of perception is the snap, crackle, and pop of winners winning and losers losing.

You can tell the losers by their downcast eyes bespeaking unseemly scruple and self-doubt. You can tell the winners by their winning ways and natty strut; look at them stepping out there, all confidence and hard-edged realism. It's a new age of vim and vigor, piss and vinegar, and cocaine. If we work hard enough and live long enough, we'll all be as young as the president.

Meanwhile, behold restored as lord of creation, pinnacle of evolution and progress, alpha and omega of the rationalized universe, Mr. Success, together with his new partner and pal, Ms. Success. These two have what it takes; they've got heart, they've got drive, they've got aggression. It's a no-fault world of military options and no draft. Hey, they got it all.

Sometimes, though, it gets scary. Some days it's hard to know whether you're winning or not. You're on the go, but so's the next guy. You're moving fast, but so is she. Sometimes you're afraid you'd think awful thoughts if you had time to think. That's why you're almost glad there isn't time. How can you be sure you're on the right track? You might be on the wrong one. Everybody can't be a winner or there wouldn't be a game. "Some gonna fly and some gonna die."

Predestinarian religion generated a lot of useful energy in this republic. It cast a long December shadow, a certain slant of light on winter afternoons. Things were grim, with everybody wondering whether he was chosen, whether he was good enough, really, truly good enough and not just faking. Finally, it stopped being useful. We got rid of it.

It's funny how the old due bills come up for presentation. We had Faith and not Works. Now we've got all kinds of works and no faith. And people still wonder if they've got what it takes.

When you're wondering if you've got what it takes, wondering whether you're on the right track and whether you're going to fly, do you sometimes want a little pick-me-up? Something upbeat and cool with nice lines, something that shines like success and snaps you to, so you can step out there feeling aggressive, like a million-dollar Mr. or Ms.? And after that, would you like to be your very own poet and see fear—yes, I said fear—in a handful of dust? Have we got something for you! Something white.

On the New York morning of which I've spoken, I beheld its whiteness. How white it really is, and what it does, was further described about 130 years ago by America's God-bestowed prophet, who delineated the great American success story with the story of two great American losers, Bartleby and Ahab. From *Moby-Dick*:

> And when we consider that . . . theory of the natural philosophers, that all other earthly hues—every stately or lovely emblazoning—the sweet tinges of sunset skies and woods; yea, and the gilded velvets of butterflies, and the butterfly cheeks of young girls; all these are but subtle deceits, not actually inherent in substances, but only laid on from without . . . and when we proceed further, and consider that the mystical cosmetic which produces every one of her hues, the great principle of light, for ever remains white or colorless in itself, and if operating without medium upon matter, would touch all objects, even tulips and roses, with its own blank tinge —pondering all this, the palsied universe lies before us a leper; and like willful travelers in Lapland, who refuse to wear colored and coloring glasses upon their eyes, so the wretched infidel gazes himself blind at the monumental white shroud that wraps all the prospect around him.

All over America at this moment, pleasurable surges of self-esteem are fading. People are discovering that the principal thing one does with cocaine is run out of it.

If cocaine is the great "success drug," is there a contradiction in that it brings such ruin not only to the bankers and the lawyers but to so many of the youngest, poorest Americans? I think not. The poor and the children have always received American obsessions as shadows and parody. They too can be relied on to "go for it."

"Just say no!" we tell them and each other when we talk about crack and cocaine. It is necessary that we say this because liberation starts from there.

But we live in a society based overwhelmingly on appetite and self-regard. We train our young to be consumers and to think most highly of their own pleasure. In this we face a contradiction that no act of Congress can resolve.

In our debates on the subject of dealing with drug abuse, one of the recurring phrases has been "the moral equivalent of war." Not many of those who use it, I suspect, know its origin.

In 1910, the philosopher William James wrote an essay discussing the absence of values, the "moral weightlessness," that seemed to characterize modern times. James was a pacifist. Yet he conceded that the demands of battle were capable of bringing forth virtues like courage, loyalty, community, and mutual concern that seemed in increasingly short supply as the new century unfolded. As a pacifist and a moralist, James found himself in a dilemma. How, he wondered, can we nourish those virtues without having to pay the dreadful price that war demands? We must foster courage, loyalty, and the rest, but we must not have war. Very well, he reasoned, we must find the *moral equivalent of war.*

Against these drugs can we ever, rhetoric aside, bring any kind of real heroism to bear? When they've said no to crack, can we someday give them something to say yes to?

—*Harper's Magazine,* 1986

THE MORNING AFTER

B y the third day of the Republican Convention in San Diego last August, the superficial air of decorum and tolerance had smothered any prospect of adventure, and although the rough beast of reaction might have been off thriving in the dark somewhere, everything in view was moderation. A virtually Japanese aura of hollow courtesy was made manifest for televisionland, and what with the bright colors and corporate beneficence, we might all have been up the road at Disneyland. A tootling goodwill prevailed, intercut with a kind of juvenile, improving right-mindedness, a chipmunk-like, helium-tasting rapture. Dissent seemed to have been vaporized and consensus oppressed like the light of a flawless California afternoon.

Failing to find even the semblance of political argument—"conflict," as they say in the movie business—I remembered how much I had enjoyed the performance of the religious right at the 1988 Republican Convention in New Orleans. Swinish, ham-faced priests with morning whiskey breath and National Rifle Association buttons had staggered from behind every free lunch buffet. Minyans of wild-eyed desert rabbis of the thornin-the-eye school, lapel slogans reading EVERY JEW A .22, had interrupted invocations of the avenging angel Metatron to include me and my press pass in their Kabbalistic interdictions. Brigades of smiley, ill-dissembling Ku Klux Klergy, snake handlers, weevil sniffers, and pretend lunatics in Armani suits had recalled their conversations with God before my treacherous, respectful attention. Where were they now?

The very possibility of conflict had been exiled to San Diego's geographical margins. Pat Buchanan had been consigned with his followers to a site thirty miles up Route 15, in Escondido, at a place called the California Center for the Arts. Had the venue been designed as a further insult? Was an attempt being made to associate Pat and his movement with an institution virtually every syllable of whose name suggested abominations? Everyone at the convention knew that artists were faggots who kept crucifixes in little vials of piss.

But with nothing but concord in and around the San Diego Convention Center, I decided to set out for Escondido. It was a sad trip. When I had first come that way, in the early 1960s, the Pauma Valley was a stretch of avocado groves and wild-flowering semidesert hillsides from which it was possible to see, through the clear air, to distant snow peaks, to the Laguna Summit and the Santa Ysabel Mountains. The skies over Mount Palomar aren't clear anymore, and along the road to Escondido, which is now called the Escondido Freeway, there are no snow peaks visible through the smog, no avocados, and no flowering hillsides — except those with blossoms spelling out the corporate logos that prospered mightily during that bright Morning in America of which President Reagan was so fond.

Since then it's been morning in America a lot. In fact, it's been morning in America damn near a thousand times, and while some mornings were perfectly acceptable, most of them were like the ones being celebrated at this particular Republican Convention, the ones in which the Ronald Reagan fan club fixed the tax laws and set up the savings-and-loan swindles and blessed the real estate developments on the road to Escondido with names like "Applause" and "Rancho Superior" and "Imperial Canyon Mews."

Outside the sleek campus of the California Center for the Arts, the California Highway Patrol, looking more than ever like some multisex unit of the Uruguayan Presidential Grenadiers, was effortlessly containing a horde of aging malcontents doing their best to work up the kind of rage toward Pat Buchanan I choke down a couple of times each day before breakfast. There were tie-dyed graybeards and their favorite nieces and nephews costumed in period garb, and keen-eyed elders with Aztec eagle cloaks and VIVA LA HUELGA buttons left over from the days of the grape strike and the sixties protests against short-handled hoes. There were chants like "Power to the people." The CHP treated the protesters with rare interplanetary courtesy, employing virtual speech and microamplifiers, as though trying to avoid a misunderstanding with Martians.

Inside, it was not much better. The house was less than three-quarters full; there was hardly anyone present younger than myself. They were the opposite numbers of the people outside. If out in the sculpture garden the style was Spanish Civil War commemorative, the people in the hall were dressed for golf. People cheered Buchanan, but many heckled and booed Ollie North, who was there to introduce the headliner.

I asked one man why. He refused to tell me. He said it was for him to know and me to find out.

Other reporters discovered political sophisticates in Escondido, and the media quoted some who were quietly satisfied that their clerico-fascist agenda had been more or less smoothly inserted into the Republican platform the week before. And so it had, there to incubate on rich Republican blood until the angels of apocalypse called it forth, which the Buchananites hoped would be in November, or at the latest four years from now, and which the money-interest, class-conscious Republican pros hoped would be never. In the meantime, it was to everyone's advantage that the thing lie there forgotten.

At Escondido they responded to cues; it was plain they loved Pat and his wife and his sister and his cousins and his aunts; also that they hated Dole more than they hated most Democrats, and hated Kemp more than they hated Hillary Clinton. Buchanan was not in his fire-breathing mode. He announced a truce with the Dole-ites, an act that was not particularly well received by his supporters. The following day he would endorse Bob Dole.

Still desperate for controversy, or maybe just in search of a cause, I took myself the next evening to Lemon Grove, ten miles inland from downtown San Diego, where Operation Rescue, the radical and militant anti-abortion group, had been more or less confined for the duration of the convention. Lemon Grove is the sort of town it sounds like. The ocean is far away, and the sun hasn't twinkled on many live lemons there since well before the end of Reagan's first term in the White House. The bus-stop benches carry undertakers' ads and the buses never come, the lawns are as neat as pool tables, and the homes are of the sort usually described as modest. There are empty sidewalks and drive-by shootings, alienated Latinos, some blacks, Asian strivers, and whites who've dropped out of the white flight for lack of means. Their flight is internal now, toward the mythical past; they think John Wayne lived in Montana, and they think they'd like to live there too. They watch a lot of television commercials for damage-suit lawyers with conveniently located offices who might make them rich enough on their grievances to buy a little spread on the Salmon River, which they'd then defend to the death with rifles. They wonder about Jesus, whether he'll really come again, and what that could mean for them.

It was there, deep in the dry, sour heart of Lemon Grove, that I entered the Skyline Wesleyan Church for one of Operation Rescue's pep rallies. There must have been mountains somewhere to constitute a skyline, but you couldn't see them for the smog of Skyline Drive.

The people at the rally were the people of Lemon Grove and environs, maybe two-thirds Anglo and a third Chicano. There were a few fairly obvious police spies who scratched their crotches during the singing of "Abide with Me" and "The Old Rugged Cross," and a scattering of the mad who talked permanently and persistently in vanished tongues. Two sorts stood out: young couples, strangely joyless, who looked poor but honest; and lone women, many of whom seemed to be nursing a wound. They had left their wounds behind for the occasion, reclining on a litter in their modest homes like the wound of King Amfortas in *Parsifal*, but their lips were tight with pain. The two factions apparently shared a solidarity with the unborn, an identification of the sort animal rights fanatics feel for creatures. One could also sense, as one can with some animal protectors, a scorn for the nonanimal, for the empowered human. Their option was for the lifeless over the undeserving life.

There was also a cadre of transient true believers. A young blonde in the pew in front of me wore a pair of tight faded jeans on the back pockets of which were sewn the words "God Is Love" and a heart. The pocket message came in two sections, one on each buttock, like Urim and Thummim on the breastplate of the high priest, now reproduced on the great seal of Yale. "God Is," and then, on the other side of the center seam, "LOVE" and the heart. And sewn, mind you.

Call her Perpetua. She didn't remember precisely how she knew life began at conception, although she knew lots of people who did. She thought there was something in Psalms and something in Isaiah.

"Anyway," she said, "the Lord wouldn't give life to those little children if he didn't love them. He wants to see them alive, running and playing."

And robbing 7-Elevens, I refrained from adding, and shooting one another for laughs, and doing time.

None of the Convention Center Republicans went to Lemon Grove. Not Ralph Reed, not Pat Buchanan, not even Gary Bauer, the pro-life movement's commander in chief— not after his reasonable appearance on Jim Lehrer's news show. He was containing his inner demons in exchange for television time, and in Lemon Grove there were no cameras.

The only big-ticket pro-lifer to turn up was the strangely distinguished Alan Keyes, a black man who keeps attempting to force his unwanted presence on the GOP, going so far as to run for their presidential nomination and to win 7 percent of the vote in this year's Iowa caucuses. He possessed great presence and dignity, and was a better and more persuasive orator than Dole and Kemp put together. Needless to say, he wasn't allowed to speak at the convention. But there he was out in Lemon Grove, talking to its people, banished like them. To the GOP regulars they were nothing more than an embarrassment, lumpen, losers.

The 1988 convention in New Orleans took place in the Superdome, a space so vast it turned its occupants to antimatter. In Houston in 1992, the convention was held in the similarly enormous Astrodome. The San Diego Convention Center, by contrast, resembles a junior college modeled on the Sydney Opera House. No one can accuse it of excess.

Many of the conventioneers were housed in the part of town known as the Gaslamp District, San Diego's old tenderloin, a once run-down neighborhood of seamen's bars and brothels, many of which have been restored to their original elegance. The lamps that lit it seventy years ago have been recreated, and while some seediness persists, today it is the kind that results from too many overproduced restaurants.

In the middle of the district is Horton Square, a nicely maintained, palm-fringed park. Toward midweek, Charlton Heston took it over to inaugurate his new political action committee, an organization designed, presumably, to make the American Dream work for him too. The uninvited gathered in the darkness outside, trying to get a look at Heston, while various fat cats and moneyed rabble staggered about under the palm trees.

I think it was on my way back to my hotel from this wing-ding that I finally encountered a little of the conflict I had been pursuing. A thuggy flatfoot challenged me for reasons now obscure and began imitating my stammer. Maybe he was drunk. He was the kind of cop who made you feel as though you ought to be slipping him a twenty for no particular reason, just to keep the world turning and everyone in his place. At first I thought he might have a stammer too. Then I realized we were doing a Lenny Bruce routine and he was doing me, doing me for the amusement of his slack-jawed colleagues. Later it was explained to me that San Diego cops were tough and mean and no more honest than they should be.

For the rest of the evening, every time I looked out my hotel room window I saw him standing there. He was a distressing presence down among the cavorting Republicans. But what a jolly arrangement! He owned the street, and they owned him.

At about this point, I came to understand why everyone was so happy at the Republican Convention of 1996. Like the double-sawbuck's worth of law enforcement in the street, everyone who mattered had been fixed.

A week before the big television show that no one much watched, the party faithful had held the real convention, the one that decided the platform, the most reactionary in modern Republican history. But once the business was done, once the right-to-lifers and neo-segregationists had been bought off with the platform, there would be no embarrassments along the lines of the 1992 convention. No dervishes would dance to spoil the deal.

It didn't matter what was said during the second week, the visible one, carried live to snoozing audiences over CNN and

C-SPAN and Pat Robertson's Family Channel. The conventioneers paraded on television didn't care much about anyone else's right to life. These children of Morning in America, these prosperous baby boomers who had made their pile doing things like destroying California, had found their hidey-holes. Even crime couldn't get at them now. They hadn't a clue what it said in Psalms or Isaiah, or whether it was AD or BC. They lived in houses that faced the ocean or the river or the lake and gave their backs to the developments along the canyon, down the valley, up the slope they'd denuded forever. They were prepared to leave ideology to the hard right, as long as it had the sense not to raise the specter of jihad and cultural revolution. And after all those mornings in America, mornings of flash and hustle and shortsightedness, mornings of betting the come (as they say in Las Vegas) and blighting the land behind them, mornings of deregulation and fast cash, they knew a deal when they had one.

So the platform fixed the right-wingers; the deals within deals and the tax cuts within tax cuts fixed the Children of Morning; and the consciences of the party, the likes of Christine Todd Whitman, were fixed by being allowed to appear each and every day on the floor and by the assurance that ladylike behavior will make her political fortune one leap year down the road.

So who wasn't fixed? Lemon Grove. Lemon Grove, and maybe Bob Dole.

A few years ago, the actor Paul Newman conceived an odd notion. He was about to perform in *Mr. and Mrs. Bridge*, an adaptation of two novels by Evan Connell Jr. Newman would play a Kansas lawyer who recites Shakespeare aloud to his daughter. Driven by his notion of verisimilitude, Newman wrote to Robert Dole and asked him if he would tape a little Shakespeare for the actor to work with. Without question, Dole knew that Paul Newman's politics were very far from his own, and Newman had to wonder if he would receive a serious response or any at all. But what he got was a tape, and on it was the voice of Bob Dole, the mock-taciturn, embarrassed throat-clearing so often rendered as "arghh."

"Arghh . . . Don't know whether this is any worthwhile here, probably sounds pretty damn ridiculous, probably no good at all . . . But anyhow . . ."

And in the voice of a man reading a farm-subsidy bill into the *Congressional Record*, Dole begins to recite: "But, soft! what light through yonder window breaks? It is the east, and Juliet is the sun. Arise, fair sun, and kill the envious moon, who is already sick and pale with grief, that thou, her maid, art far more fair than she."

A riot. Not since Victor Mature got to recite Hamlet's soliloquy in *My Darling Clementine*, one might think, has the Bard been so subject to crude buffoonery.

"Be not her maid, since she is envious," Dole continues. "Her vestal liv'ry is but sick and green and none but fools do wear it; cast it off. It is my lady, O, it is my love!"

And then it isn't funny anymore; it's every bound copy of Shakespeare hauled west in the 1840s in a wagon from New York State or New Hampshire or Ohio or Pennsylvania to bleeding Kansas, every copy tucked away next to the Bible in those sod huts on the edge of the plains, every shiny schoolchild with hay behind the ears standing to recite for the schoolmarm the stuff of our language, the inner life of our new land.

A tough-talking, word-loving man of grim affairs taking a moment to read and remember. A touchy, good-hearted, wounded man.

The way he sounds reading Shakespeare, and how he comes across at close quarters, is why the press likes him, why people, even those who live in fear of his black anger, talk about him affectionately. He gives the sense that behind his irascible and saturnine manner he has concealed something decent and sound.

But the man reading Shakespeare remains rather difficult to put across as a candidate for president. There was a particular contrast in the films shown to the convention crowd. Ronald Reagan appeared in his film as a grand, twinkly old fellow (like the long-lost lemons of Lemon Grove), stirring every heart and flag. Dole's film was less well received. It began with silos and then, after a lot of the John Ford western sky, switched to the Ken Burns school of iconography.

The same sentimental tone defined the acceptance speech written for Dole by the novelist Mark Helprin. It was as if Dole were reading the voice-over in a fable about the storied American West. "The first thing you learn on the prairie," he read, "is the relative size of man compared to the lay of the land. And under the immense sky where I was born and raised, a man is very small, and if he thinks otherwise, he's wrong."

So Mark Helprin, from Ossining, New York, dreams of the West, and Bob Dole renders his dream as biography and reaches out for the brass ring of our collective memory and imagination. There's an old tradition of eastern money interests selling the romance of the West to suckers. Frederic Remington, another son of the Hudson Valley and a propagandist for Teddy Roosevelt, painted all that western art in Yonkers. Mark Helprin, who is, among other things, an operative of the *Wall Street Journal*, now packages Bob Dole as the son of the middle border.

"Age has its advantages," Helprin has his candidate say. "Let me be the bridge to an America that only the unknowing call myth. Let me be the bridge to a time of tranquility, faith, and confidence in action. And to those who say that it was never so, that America has not been better, I say, you're wrong, and I know because I was there. And I have seen it. And I remember."

He may remember it a little better than it was. Our America may look a little paltry in comparison with his because ours lacks a Steinbeck. The America Bob Dole remembers is the America John Steinbeck has remembered for us. Steinbeck's America was no paradise. Neither was Dole's, but it was a beautiful place in a lot of its corners, corners that became less beautiful with the advent of that "Morning" that made all these Republicans rich. And Senator Dole was there, the archbroker of deals, the intermediary. If America is different today, it's because he was instrumental in making it that way.

One thing Dole knows is that you go along with the power, with the people who control things, and that it is always wise and proper to slip a twenty to the wagonmaster on the Oregon Trail or the cop in the Gaslamp. If you don't know that, you're a fool, and Kansas never had any use for fools. Even the kids learning to recite the speeches in *Romeo and Juliet* and *Julius Caesar* knew that to do any good you've got to get in good with the folks who run the town. You have to play ball, like Harry Truman did over in Kansas City. Harry Truman who didn't always say what he believed and sometimes changed his policies, just the way Bob Dole changed his understanding of the necessity for a tax cut.

For all his thirty-five years in Washington, Dole, a true son of Kansas, has been a dealmaker, a master of compromise, and the advocate of corporate interests he has seen it as his job to serve. For that, and for the wound he incurred in his country's service, he thinks he should be president.

The gift of the Republican presidential nomination is *the* deal for Bob Dole; to get it, he agreed to run on a platform that contradicts many of his lifelong principles, a platform he admits to not having read. More than anything, he wanted to be the candidate. And now he is.

And yet, in the general air of I've Got Mine, the strange complacence with which everyone in San Diego savored his arrangement, there seemed to be an unlikely odd man out. In the bars, the hotel lobbies, one often heard the phrase "down the road." You had to think that meant after the election, when Dole, the unpalatable candidate, had been disposed of. Everyone in San Diego had his fix in, finally, but Bob Dole—the dealmaker without a constituency, the dealmaker in desperate haste for a last deal.

—*Harper's Magazine*, 1986

HAVANA THEN AND NOW

Late one sad Thursday night in October, two Americans retired to the bar of the old Hotel Inglaterra in Havana. We had spent the evening in a suburban apartment, watching a speech of Fidel Castro's on television. At the Inglaterra, among the tiles and potted palms, an orchestra in Cuban costumes from a forties MGM musical, faded and shiny with too much dry cleaning, was playing "Siboney." Three young Germans were cuddling with some local lovelies in spangles and mascara. A lone, gaunt Irishman sat taking pictures of the band. The light was yellow and smoky, the streets outside unlit and sinister. A man in dark glasses sat by the entrance door.

One day there may be a market for Soviet-bloc nostalgia; movies will delight audiences by reproducing the hotel lobbies of late-twentieth-century Communist capitals. At the Inglaterra that night everything was in place — the bored tourists, the hookers, the hokey native orchestra, the watcher at the door. Also the hustlers and black-marketeers in the blacked-out adjoining streets. All that was missing were the official Gypsies and the Arab thugs chain-smoking under fringed lampshades.

In terms of the big picture, of course, a lot was missing—namely, the Communist bloc, of which the Inglaterra lobby had become a melancholy souvenir. It was a rather obvious irony. While Eastern Europe whirled between the future and Bram Stoker's Baedeker, Havana, Cuba, of all places, was imperfectly replicating Warsaw or Bucharest in the age of Brezhnev.

There were a few local touches. *Granma*, the Communist Party daily, was the only newspaper available at the hotel kiosk that evening. It had a tiny item on the Clarence Thomas affair. The item informed readers that Judge Thomas had displayed his sexual organ to Anita Hill. *Granma* had subtly improved on events to underline the contradictions of bourgeois society and, perhaps, to make the whole thing comprehensible to Cuban readers.

If the walls of the Inglaterra could bear witness, they would attest to countless journalistic misrepresentations, slight liberties with the facts, colorful invocations of reality. During the 1890s, when the American yellow press was hounding the Spanish rulers of Cuba into an unequal war, Hearst's and Pulitzer's star reporters pioneered the Ramos gin fizz at the Inglaterra while calling on heaven to witness Spain's supposed atrocities. And from the hotel the Hearst artist Frederic Remington, lacking the verbal resources of his colleagues, sent the famous complaint to his boss: Everything was quiet, Remington told Hearst, and there would be no war. More American schoolboys today probably know Hearst's celebrated reply—that if Remington furnished the pictures, he would furnish the war—than know who said, "Don't give up the ship."

"No man's life, no man's property is safe," wrote the *New York World*'s James Creelman, a frequent Inglaterra guest at that time. "American citizens are imprisoned and slain without cause . . . Blood on the roadsides, blood in the fields, blood on the doorsteps, blood, blood, blood!" In the face of these conditions, American reporters could be seen daily on the hotel's terrace, composing their dispatches, having their shoes shined.

The Inglaterra was always the stuff of dreams, celebrated for its formal elegance and its misunderstandings. Insults in the lobby led to duels, wars were conceived, American misconceptions and gaucheries gave way to more exotic ones, Russian or Chinese.

From my own room at the Inglaterra later that night, I could look out on the spires of the Teatro Nacional next door. It took me back. I had been in Havana once before, more than thirty-five years earlier, in another world. The theater's preposterously heroic mass still towered over the old city. There are no white skyscrapers in Havana. That Havana rose elsewhere, in exile across the Straits of Florida. Seeing all that stone heraldry of the theater in the tropical moonlight, Castro's Victor Hugo–like cadences still sounding in my brain, I felt absurdly complicit in Cuba's fortunes.

Havana was my first liberty port, my first foreign city. It was 1955 and I was seventeen, a radio operator with an amphibious assault force in the US Navy. For most of a month we had been engaged in war games off the Puerto Rican island of Vieques. On moonless nights we would pretend to sneak ashore and kill enemies and then guide in aircraft that shot up the island at dawn. The World War II navy wanted the Pacific war, in which it had performed so well, never to end.

Sunday afternoons on Vieques we got to go swimming. The

blue-green water and the palm trees were wonderfully exotic to me, like Treasure Island. On the other hand, there were sand fleas and barbed wire, so it was pleasant and exciting when the operations were over and we were told that we would have liberty nights in Havana.

One of my mentors in those days was our chief radioman, Schultz. I asked him what Havana was like.

"In Havana," Schultz told me, "you can get an around-the-world for a dollar."

My sensual horizons were still rather limited. On long weekend passes from the base in Norfolk I would go up to New York City and date my girlfriend in Yorkville. To avoid brawls, I would not wear my uniform, and we would go to the tenement apartment she shared with her parents and neck to Frank Sinatra records. Each week she would attend confession, and the priest would tell her not to do it anymore. On my next leave, we would have to murmurously negotiate the whole thing over again. I suppose we enjoyed ourselves.

Anyway, I had trouble picturing myself suavely handing over a dollar for an around-the-world. Essentially, I had no idea what an around-the-world was, although the phrase sort of made a picture. I wasn't about to tell that to Schultz.

"As a city, though," I persisted. "What's it like?"

"Like all of them down here," Schultz said. "Crummy. Fucked up."

I remember that as we steamed past the ramparts of El Morro Castle, into Havana Bay, an elderly Cuban couple stood applauding on the opposite shore of the narrows, in the park around the Castillo de San Salvador. I reported the incident to Schultz.

"They must own a whorehouse," he said.

They hadn't looked to me like the sort of people who owned a whorehouse. Neither then nor since could I altogether reason out a political position that would lead citizens of Havana to applaud the visit of a US Navy transport. It seemed to augur well, though.

The USS *Chilton* was not an attractive vessel, and the navy did not offer it for display. We tied up at one of the docks at the south end of Habana Vieja, Old Havana, not far from the railroad station and the old city walls. Walking out of the shadows of the covered wharf and into the bright sunlight of the street, I took my first step into that problematic otherness that would so tax our country's moral speculation: the un-American world.

Touts were everywhere and the streets smelled weird. Led by the old hands, a bunch of us made our way to the Seven Brothers bar. The Seven Brothers was an old-time waterfront saloon with a big square bar, a jukebox, and a fat central European bartender whom I later liked to imagine was actually B. Traven. It had everything but women. After a great many cuba libres, it was decided we would go to the Barrio Chino, Chinatown, for more serious action.

On the way to the Barrio Chino, we stopped at the Bacardi distillery and drank free daiquiris. I looked younger than anyone else in the outfit. I probably *was* younger; in any case, I had the role of comedy virgin thrust on me.

I still recall the name of the cabdriver who took us to the brothel in the Barrio Chino; it was Rudy Bradshaw, and he was a Jamaican immigrant and spoke English with us. The place was called the Blue Moon. It had a curving wall of trans-

lucent glass bricks and a bar with a travel-poster photo of the
Havana skyline. Young women came out to be bought drinks
and taken upstairs. One of them approached me. I have many
recollections of that day, but I can recall neither the woman's
face nor her name nor the details of our encounter. I do recall there was a certain amount of laughing it up and pretending affection, and also that there was paying. The bill came to
quite a lot of money. I presume I was cheated in some way, but
everyone was nice.

Afterward we went out into the streets of the Barrio Chino.
The Barrio Chino in those days was large, and thousands of
Chinese must have lived there. (Today, all that remains are
a few worn pagoda roofs and sun-faded signs offering phan-
tom *comidas chinas y criollas*.) Many had settled in Havana after
working as plantation laborers, and some of them no doubt
hoped to slip into the United States, smuggled over by characters like Hemingway's Harry Morgan. There were many
good Chinese-Cuban restaurants and curio shops and Chinese
markets, but what the world knew best about Havana's Barrio Chino was the Teatro Shanghai. The Shanghai was a blue-
movie parlor and burlesque house that was home to the Superman Show, the hemisphere's paramount *exhibición*. Viewers of
The Godfather: Part II will have some idea of what the staging
of the Superman Show was like, since part of the act is briefly
reproduced in that film. One of the performers was always a
nearly naked blonde whose deportment was meant to suggest
wholesomeness, refinement, and alarm, as though she had just
been spirited unawares from a harp recital at the public library.
What on earth, she seemed to be asking the heartless, brutal
crowd, am I doing onstage in a Havana pork palace? Another

performer was always a large, muscular black man who astonished the crowd and sent the blonde into a trembling swoon
by revealing the dimensions of his endowment. There were
other performers as well, principally a dog and a burro. Suffice
it to say that the show at the Teatro Shanghai was a melancholy
demonstration that sexism, racism, and speciesism thrived in
prerevolutionary Havana. I hasten to add that during most of
the time this vileness unfolded, I was blessedly asleep, having
drunk myself into a state of what might be described as American innocence.

At the end of the show, we all staggered into the night and
got into taxis and hence home to the battleship-gray womb of
our mother fleet. When I woke up the next day my mood was
penitential. At the commencement of liberty I joined forces
with my best buddy, a bookish electronics technician who had
the kind of reverence for Ray Bradbury that I had for Hemingway. Abandoning our role as boozing, wenching buccaneers,
we resumed existence as high school dropout teenage savants.
Instead of carrying on in the red-light district and having our
picture taken with parrots, we were determined to behave like
proper expatriates. We would go and do some of the cool, for-
eign-type things experienced world travelers did, like drinking
black coffee very slowly from very small cups. At dusk we set
out for the Paseo del Prado, the grand boulevard that runs between the seafront and the Parque Central.

In memory, it is probably too good to be true — the crowds
ragged, elegant, ebullient, restrained; the graceful women
variously haughty or laughingly unselfconscious; the men in
guayaberas and straw hats, gesturing with cigars, greeting one
another and parting with quick handshakes and *abrazos*. The

coffee in small cups was fine, the air was sensuous and fragrant. The park was full of almond trees and poincianas. There was music everywhere; conga bands filled the street with metal syncopation and the flatted wail of African flutes. There were fortune-telling parakeets. A delicious breeze rustled through the foliage from the seafront. At the time I also noted the beggars, blind with untended cataracts or crippled by polio, squatting in doorways. (Unless something unforgettably bad happens, better memories always prevail.)

For me, in 1955, this Havana served as an introduction to the older, unreformed world. In fact, things were changing ruthlessly in the mid-fifties. A line of towering new hotels stood in the Vedado section of the city, a couple of miles west along the seafront from the end of the Paseo del Prado. An extension of the Florida Gold Coast, the Vedado casinos went a long way toward financing the mob's expansion on the mainland. In 1955 they represented someone's bright dream of the future. Reflected in the silver surf, they twinkled at night like the *Playboy* Philosophy itself. George Raft actually ran the casino at the Capri. Howard Hughes would have been at home atop any one of them.

For the most part, sailors stayed out of Vedado, where their troublesome, penniless presence was unwelcome. At the time, I was struck less by the frivolity of Havana than by its unashamed seriousness. It was then that I first saw the façade of the Hotel Inglaterra. Its formal elegance and polite luxury embodied something I had never quite experienced outside of books. Beside the Inglaterra stood the overdone but monumental Teatro Nacional, a structure besotted with its own aspirations toward high culture, fearlessly risking absurdity, all trumpets, angels, and muses. It was a setting whose pleasure required a dark side —drama, heroism, sacrifice. All this Spanish tragedy, leavened with Creole sensuality, made Havana irresistible. Whether or not I got it right, I have used the film of its memory ever since in turning real cities into imaginary ones.

Literature had always pursued this Havana, and literary perceptions of the many-layered city at that time centered on the work of two English-speaking foreigners, Ernest Hemingway and Graham Greene. Somewhat puerile sophisticates, already insulated by their superstardom, they were the great exploiters of Cuba's conduciveness to melodrama and its aspect of "playground." Romantics, erstwhile Catholics, and pro-Communists, both found in Cuba an ambience to reflect the minor-key stoicism and sadomasochistic violence they employed in fiction.

Hemingway dominated the world's sense of Havana then, less through his work than through his much-publicized presence in the suburb of San Francisco de Paula. Neither of his Cuban settings—the early pages of *To Have and Have Not* and *The Old Man and the Sea*—actually invoke Havana. But it was not necessary to be bookish in the mid-fifties to be aware that "Don Ernesto" was in town. His bearded, bare-chested figure was part of the pop iconography of the period. Magazine pictures sometimes showed him with his wife, entertaining US servicemen at his house, the Finca Vigía. There—in our imaginations—he dwelled, chief of all worldly American expats, hanging out with bullfighters, jai alai players, and ex–Spanish Loyalist guerrillas, awash in drink and worldly women, fishing by day, partying by night, writing the whole time.

Compañero Graham Greene was a higher-class act. In the ✓
summer 1991 issue of *Cuba Update*, a quarterly published by
the Center for Cuban Studies in New York City, the travel
writer Tom Miller describes his contemporary quest for
Greene's city of the 1950s, celebrated so memorably in *Our
Man in Havana*. "His life," Miller writes of Greene, "held an
intoxicating mix of literature, espionage, revolution and sex;
all of these he found in the final years of the Batista regime."
This is a fine advertisement for a life, if not for a regime, and
it sounds almost as perfect as Hemingway's. One of Greene's
favorite haunts, according to Miller, was the aforesaid Teatro
Shanghai; there he "enjoyed what he called the *louche* atmosphere." If the Shanghai, with its live animal act, was Graham
Greene's idea of ambiguity, it's hard to imagine what he might
have considered down and dirty. It's even harder to imagine
how he could have endured the sweaty proximity of all us loud
Americans, ruining the *louche* with our snores and braying. It
must have been enough to drive a sensitive traveler to Russian
roulette.

In *Our Man in Havana*, Greene describes a dive called the
Wonder Bar, a saloon where all manner of depravity is catered
to. Apparently the place was purely fictional, despite the fact
that a number of Cubans in Havana today claim to remember it. Such is the power of legend, especially the cinematic-
cum-existentialistic legend of Hemingway-Greene, two macho coxcombs who had so much trouble staying at the right
end of their own firearms. Both were elaborately proclaimed
Hispanophiles, famous for their Latin friendships. Hemingway favored toreros and waiters. Greene, in his later years as
nemesis of the American Century, became a junketeer and rosy

ornament to the *cuadrilla* of Omar Torrijos, in whose translated conversation he professed to detect profundities.

NO "Both of them spoke exactly two hundred words of Spanish," the Cuban émigré novelist Guillermo Cabrera Infante told me once, speaking of Hemingway and Greene. Cabrera Infante had been a Cuban diplomat during the early years of the Castro regime; today he is an opponent of Fidelismo. "But Greene and Hemingway could never have conversed," he went on to say. "Each knew two hundred different words."

The Cuban novelist Antonio Benítez-Rojo, who during the seventies and eighties ran the publishing division of the state-run cultural center, Casa de las Americas, remembers Greene's hobnobbing visits with Castro in Havana; he recalls, too, how Greene and other distinguished foreign guests were referred to ungenerously as *come mierdas.*

Returning to Havana late in 1991, I'd felt by the end of my first day in the city like a petty harbinger, a terminal gringo whose marginal appearance augured the ungood. As I stood on the Malecón at dusk, looking toward the lights of Vedado, it was incredible that so much time was lost to me, or at least had gone by. Somewhere out on the Gulf of Mexico, Hurricane Fabian was scattering the flying fish, and a vast tower of white cloud, trailing dark wisps like telltales, had appeared to attend to the sunset. Breaking waves lashed the seawall, drenching loiterers, splashing the windshields of passing cars. The Vedado lights were fewer and dimmer than the ones I remembered—sacrificed, like so much else, to shortages. It seemed I would miss out on the good times again.

A rush hour of sorts was under way. In the evening's strange storm light, the promiscuous whirl of odd contraptions rattling past the proud street's crumbling arcades had the aspect of a dream. There were Plymouths with looney tunes curves and fanged, finned De Sotos, not to mention Soviet-made Ladas and the largest number of motorcycle sidecar combos assembled since the Blitzkrieg. The defiant posters in front of the old American embassy were exercises in socialist realism, but magical realism seemed more appropriate to the frame. Everything in the early evening's landscape appeared fantastic. The painted slogans above the crumbling buildings were like artifacts from the past. Havana was an exercise in willpower, a dream state being grimly and desperately prolonged.

Earlier that day I had seen Hemingway's house for the first time. Surrounded by ceiba, fig, and flamboyant trees, it was a ghastly sight, moldering indecently in full view like an open grave. In the living room, ancient bottles of rye from long-defunct distilleries had gone cloudy white. Newspapers and old magazines were piled in hideous yellowing stacks: *Look*, *Collier's*, and, at the top of the stack, *Soviet Life*, as if it had been Papa's special reading treat. Then there were the animal heads, absurd and obscene, looking less like trophies of the field than something a mafioso would send his least favorite Hollywood producer. That had been the first vertiginous moment, seeing the room imperfectly embalmed in the past yet seeing it with the eyes of the present: realizing that the front ends of twelve antelope pasted to a single wall no longer look the way they did in the fifties, when such a sight suggested virile jollity and Old Grand-Dad.

The most cheerful thing about the house was the neat line of cats' graves outside, each with its cute name; it was reassuring to witness decent interment. The scariest was the presence of pale Cuban maidens who sat presiding in each and every room, as even-featured, silent, and unsmiling as cemetery angels. I would like to think I imagined them, although I know full well why they were there. Their supervisor was a middle-aged lady who had been one of the Hemingway household's young servants. Brisk and officious, the sort of ladies' maid turned martinet who appears in the wake of revolution, she was thoroughly in charge, supervising the tentative visitors, issuing observations and commands. She spoke of her late employer with a certain suppressed humor and without affection.

It seemed both ironic and fitting that this regiment of women represent Hemingway's persona in custody of the revolution. He who played at causes has one imposed upon his memory. The severity of the maidens also suggested the ambiguous relationship between Castro's Cuba and the Hemingway myth. He was, *enfin*, just another rich American who came to fish and drink. It is unlikely he would have thought well of present-day Cuba. Plainly, the Cubans, without quite letting on, understand this.

I spent a week, often accompanied by an American supporter of Fidel who lives part of every year in Cuba, listening to the residents of Havana. In the Vedado apartment an old Spanish Loyalist refugee expressed determined devotion to Castro and the regime. A writer's wife reverently showed us a photograph she owned of Che Guevara, taken while he was ill in the mountains, looking Christlike and sacrificial. Another woman, the wife of an official, showed me a picture she had taken of Fidel at rest, displaying it with moving, motherly affection. Many of those I spoke with were artists and professionals whose attachment to the government ranged from enthusiasm to sympathy to resigned acceptance. In a comfortable farmhouse outside the city I talked with members of a family whose large landholdings had been taken over by the state and who had seen numerous relatives flee to the United States. It was clear they felt that the revolution had given them more than it had taken away. The same seemed true of another family I was introduced to, in the old slum of the Barrio Chino. Many of the enthusiasts were people of principle who resembled not at all the cynical apparatchiks I used to encounter on visits to Eastern Europe.

Still, the mood of the city seemed forlorn and surly. In the downtown streets youths hassled tourists for dollars. Prostitutes were out in numbers near the Vedado hotels, and there were endless lines in front of the ubiquitous "pizzerias" in which scorched cheese concoctions were dispensed, uninteresting but filling meals to augment the rationed goods available in state groceries. In one of those consumer crises that bedevil socialist economies there was an absence of soap in the city, eroding morale among the fastidious Habaneros, forcing people to wash their clothes, their dishes, and themselves with Chinese toothpaste. A surprising number of young people, encountered casually on the street, denounced the government in bitter and obscene terms. Many of these youths were poor and of color—the very people who, in theory, benefited most from the revolution. A story was making the rounds. A little boy stands on the Paseo del Prado watching the tourists comfortably sightseeing. Whatever he wants, he finds, is on sale only for dollars, to foreigners. Asked what he wants to be when he grows up, the boy replies, "A foreigner."

One aspect of the situation in Havana was brought home about the middle of the week, after I had dinner with two other Americans in town, a man and woman around my age, at Hemingway's old haunt in Habana Vieja, the Floridita. Lobster was on the menu at $35 a claw. There were daiquiris. Musicians played "Guantanamera." Outside, we started walking the streets of Habana Vieja, as romantic a collection of Spanish colonial buildings as the hemisphere affords, but in the present circumstances crumbling and run-down. About two blocks from the Floridita, on the picturesque Calle Obispo, we were jumped and knocked to the pavement by four or five youths who grabbed the woman's bag and disappeared down the cobblestone streets.

It was a fairly noisy business, with shouts and curses and laughter from the kids who had the bag. Police state or not, no cops were forthcoming. If the Calle Obispo had a branch of the feared Committee for the Defense of the Revolution, the committee was either in recess or had decided to exclude *yanqui* visitors from its protection. The few cautious citizens who appeared were curious but fearful. They conveyed a sense of not really requiring our presence and expecting the same. Back at the Floridita, a bartender poured free drinks. Someone called the police, who eventually arrived.

As I walked into the old Spanish fortress that serves as headquarters for the city police in Habana Vieja, it occurred to me that no tour of the twentieth century could be complete without a visit to a Communist police station. This one was the traditional precinct green. Behind the desk was a sergeant who looked for all the world like a New York Irish cop, complete with jug ears and an attitude. He was smoking a cigarette under

a sign that said NO FUMAR. A few locals were standing against
the walls, looking as though they foresaw some unhappy outcome.

One of us pointed out to the sarge that his smoking was a
violation. He grinned at this piquant demonstration of North
American political correctness and explained that the sign was
for people in front of the desk, not for him. There was a second sign behind him that read PROHIBIDO ENFADARSE, "It is
forbidden to get mad."

Presumably this was also directed to the public.

As Che Guevara, Frantz Fanon, and Lenin himself would
have agreed, there's nothing like a little violence to define the
propositions—the mugging was trivial, a sign of discontent
dismissible in terms of human nature. But there were others
in Havana during my visit whose discontent and opposition
to the status quo were as principled as anything I heard from
Fidel's supporters.

José Lorenzo Fuentes is a novelist and journalist who fought
with Che Guevara in the Escambray Mountains at the time of
the revolution. In May 1991 Lorenzo Fuentes, together with
nine other Cuban writers, signed a declaration in the form of
a petition to the government. It reads, "We, Cuban intellectuals, profoundly worried about the dangerous situation in which
the country [finds] itself, have decided to try to promote a reasonable and moderate attitude in all sectors of our society in
order to avoid amongst all of us the approaching economic,
social, political and cultural catastrophe."

The declaration goes on to ask for "a national debate without exclusions" on Cuba's future, democratic procedures, a

liberalized economic system, and freedom for "prisoners of conscience." As a result of his signing, Lorenzo Fuentes was subjected to harassment by rapid-response brigades, organized mobs of official agitators. He counts himself lucky so far, since other signers have been arrested or harassed in more extreme ways. Lorenzo Fuentes's opinions have gotten him in trouble before: in 1968 he was arrested as the result of his friendship with a Mexican diplomat accused of being a CIA agent. He served three years in prison and was unable to publish for many years.

"A young girl came to my door," Lorenzo Fuentes explained when I spoke with him one afternoon in Vedado. He is a slight, formal man who appears older than his years. That particular day he seemed resigned and weary. His wife looked on with a nervous smile. "I read the petition," Lorenzo Fuentes went on to say, "and it seemed reasonable. I thought it was the right thing to sign. I accept the role that the writer has always had in the country." His wife permitted herself the observation that the mix of literature and politics in Cuba might be difficult for outsiders to understand.

The "young girl" at Lorenzo Fuentes's door could well have been the poet María Elena Cruz Varela. Formerly an avid Marxist-Leninist, Cruz Varela is the spark of a dissident group known as Alternative Criterion. Only a week before my arrival in Havana, her Alternative Criterion and a number of other human rights groups, which are joined together in a co-alition known as the Cuban Democratic Convergence, met at the house of Elizardo Sánchez, another veteran of the revolution. The Convergence called upon the Fourth Congress of the Communist Party "to initiate constitutional reforms and to take other steps to protect human rights and establish democratic institutions in Cuba."

Within a week of the meeting, the Convergence and the signers of the May petition had the government's reply. Speaking to the Fourth Congress in Santiago, Castro gave them what amounted to a summary answer. "Reactionaries have no role in Cuba," he said in a speech carried live on Cuban television. "They have nothing to do here." Castro went on to offer the Congress swashbuckling intransigence; blood, sweat, and tears; shortages and labor: a continuance of the revolution in defiance not only of the United States but of the times.

"*Tendremos otro Baraguá*," he told the crowd in Santiago. "We will have another Baraguá." The reference was to the stand of the revolutionary general Antonio Maceo during Cuba's war of independence with Spain. Surrounded, offered terms of surrender, Maceo defied his enemies. Fidel was announcing his intention to do the same.

Not long after, he sent a less rhetorical message to the human rights activists of the Convergence. Fourteen of them were arrested in the early-morning hours of October 9 and 10. Three of them were tried on October 16, charged with "illegal association," "clandestine printing," and "incitement to commit crime." Each was given a prison term. The signers of the May petition were accused of "treason" in *Granma*. Cruz Varela was denounced for "betraying her country" and being "in league with the CIA." On November 27 Cruz Varela and three others associated with Alternative Criterion were sentenced to prison terms of between one and two years on charges of holding illegal meetings, printing clandestine documents, and defaming state institutions.

Here is one of Cruz Varela's underground poems, as translated in the *Miami Herald*. May it be among the last to represent that uniquely twentieth-century form, samizdat.

> *Because I know nothing. Because if I ever knew,*
> *torn among the thistles I have forgotten.*
> *Here the thorns hurt. Here the brambles hurt.*
> *Here I leave my smell. The smell of the*
> *   persecuted . . .*
> *Because I know nothing*
> *Because I can hardly touch my knee*
> *   and I don't know anything else. And I am*
> *this crumbling city. And I am*
> *this country of shipwrecked fools.*
> *   Left adrift*
> *   aboard their ship.*

Downstairs, the band played "Siboney," the old stones of the city were bathed in moonlight, the scented air was full of tragedy, heroism, intransigence, sacrifice. The terminal gringos at the Inglaterra were getting it all wrong. "Literature, espionage, revolution and sex." "Blood, blood, blood!"

Ninety miles away, visible on clear nights from the Tupolevs beginning their descent toward José Martí Airport, twinkled the lights of the Florida Keys. It was all different over there: they had plenty of soap; the talk was of real estate, drugs, and T-shirt shops, and you could say what you liked. God in his mercy only knew how many Cubans were out paddling in the darkness between El Morro and Twelve-Mile Reef, thirsty, salt-poisoned, shark-stalked, in search of the less heroic life.

The aspect of militant Spanish revenger represents only one side of Cuba's personality. In spite of *Baraguá!* and *Socialismo o muerte*, Cuba's is not an apocalyptic culture. There is another slogan of sorts, a bit of folk poetry the slaves recited to keep themselves going. *Lo que hay que hacer es no morirse*—What you gotta do is, you gotta not die. Socialism or death? Why not socialism or somewhat less socialism? Why not socialism or regulated private enterprise? *Death?*

But among the ghosts of the Inglaterra, it is not hard to sympathize with Cuba's refusal of her assigned role in the American Century. A hundred years ago, in the fullness of our gilded age, we came weeping at our own propaganda, the particularly American variation on crocodile tears, reflecting the pity of the eagle for the forsaken lamb. (During the Vietnam era, I heard somebody remark that you could always tell the objects of American benevolence by the hunted look in their eyes.) Fair-haired Protestant heroes, descendants of Drake, we dashed the whip from the cruel Spaniard's hand, banished the sneering inquisitor. We announced the imminence of order, commerce, and light. But, of course, Cuba as a chaotic and materially backward country was useful to us in a variety of ways.

Descendants of Drake, it turned out, and equally of Blackbeard and Henry Morgan. What happened next is well known, and even if we were not at the root of Cuba's problems, our proximity and involvement never represented a solution to them. At best we offered Cubans an opportunity to emulate our own pragmatism, optimism, and common sense. At the same time, we offered our worst, a prolonged insult, a dehumanizing, sometimes racist condescension. Such attitudes are hard to forgive. People take them personally.*

We ought not to be surprised that, led by embittered middle-class Spanish Cubans such as Castro, Cuba took the opportunity to decline our halfhearted offer of middle-class progress. In doing so, Cuba was being true to the aesthetic and aristocratic foundations of its culture, embracing faith and heroism, declining mediocrity. Thus the enthusiasm of *compañero* Greene, who hated all vulgarity but his own, a self-indulgent mandarin who, in truth, hated democracy as well and rejoiced in Castro's regime as in the Church of Rome.

Neither Cubans nor Americans much love irony, but the ironies of the Hotel Inglaterra abound. It is unlikely that Castro, in spite of what he has since said, set out to make Cuba a formal member of the Soviet bloc. He was, as he claimed, a follower of José Martí and thus an opponent of American domination. A great dreamer, he saw himself as a hemispheric figure, a successor to Bolívar. He came to power in the post-Bandung world of Sukarno, Nkrumah, Nasser, Tito. No doubt he entertained the notion that in some Siberian vault a college of wise Marxist gnomes had it all figured out, economically speaking. He himself was a soldier, a knight of faith. He may have been the only Marxist head of state on earth who actually believed in

---

*Any reader wishing to sample some American attitudes toward Cuba from the early years of the century is advised to consult a travel guide of the period. On the subject of commercial relations, Thomas P. McCann's history of United Fruit, *An American Company* (1976), also makes lively, mortifying reading.

the doctrine. For that he probably deserves to be left holding the bag.

History loves ambiguity as well as irony. Castro's regime has caused great suffering for countless Cubans. At the same time it has destroyed much of the old political pathology in which Cuba was bound. For centuries the Caribbean crescent labored under a curse concealed beneath its loveliness. Like much of America, its conception had a dark aspect, the shadow of genocide and slavery. What it offered to the world was not nourishment but the things of appetite. The Spaniards who came for spices tortured the Indians for gold. When the gold was gone, there came tobacco, sugar, coffee, cocaine, emeralds, and marijuana, the very names of which suggest violence and greed, Latin tyranny, and Yankee filibustering. Graham Greene might have called them *louche*.

Under Castro, ordinary Cubans grew healthier; many learned to read and write. However passively, Castro involved the mass of people in the political process. This may not justify his regime, but it is true all the same. Perhaps it is philistine to hope for happy endings in Cuba, a place so steeped in short-term gaiety and long-term tragedy. It is possible, however, to hope for new beginnings. The final drama of Fidel Castro's Cuba may be that he has prepared a future for his country in which he and his ideologues serve no purpose, have no place.

At the same time, while Fidel and the Communists were trying to reshape Cuba, a second Havana was rising in Miami. The Cuban Americans there are often presented as an intransigent monolith committed to violence, a mirror image of the present Cuban government. Reality has proved more complex. Last spring, Liz Balmaseda in the *Miami Herald* described increased cultural contacts between the two centers: "Quietly, history is being made beneath our noses. The cream of Havana's cultural crop is flocking to Miami. Most go back but some defect. More importantly they are talking, sparking the sort of contact some Cuban-Americans have always feared. Neither Miami nor Havana will ever be the same."

In the same piece Balmaseda describes the reaction of a visiting Cuban artist to the general *cubanía* he encountered in Miami — the Spanish billboards, the huge Cuban-owed shopping centers and banks: "[But] all I kept thinking as I rode through the city was, why couldn't we do this in Cuba?"

On irony's head, more irony. The speaker was Tomás Esson, a black Cuban of peasant origin. It may have been only the Castro revolution that enabled a man like Esson to study and become an artist. Enfranchised, he was able to see American shops and banks as something belonging to his world, as achievements in which he shared. Thus Esson remains in Miami, where he has the freedom, denied him in Cuba, to paint as he wishes.

At the end of my stay, I got tired of the bar at the Inglaterra, so I walked down the Prado to the Wonder Bar for a final daiquiri. As Graham Greene reported in *Our Man in Havana*, all the appetites of the Antilles are catered to there. You can get anything, nothing is changed. Errol Flynn is the bartender. Remember him? He claims Hemingway still comes in. And George Raft too, he says. The music's great, and Havana's just the way I remember.

It's a very romantic place, the Wonder Bar, though *louche* as can be. It's where Cubans and North Americans meet. Everybody gets what they like, but nobody gets what they deserve. The Cubans are always talking about the United States, and the Americans talk about Cuba. Everyone's an expert and gets everything right. People's eyes are bright with dreams. Everybody's beautiful.

Some people say the Wonder Bar doesn't exist, but don't believe it. They say the same thing about God and the Dialectic, without which any kind of coherent history would be impossible. You have to have things like those, especially in the Spanish-speaking world where it verges on the United States.

They're going to open a place like the Wonder Bar in Miami one day soon, with the music and the dreams. There has to be one. I wonder if it will ever be the same.

—Harper's Magazine, 1992

JERUSALEM HAS NO PAST

Tip O'Neill liked to say that all politics is local. In Jerusalem, politics is local but also moral and cosmic. Of course, politicians everywhere employ an ethical diction, however ungrammatical. And the reality of power in every city has its source in a measure of combat. But nowhere is this as true as in Jerusalem. Millions of us, raised in the three major faiths, grew up believing that even apparently trivial encounters in Jerusalem's narrow streets and within the shadows of its walls determine the human condition. Its sparrows were no mere sparrows. A broken promise in the Holy City, a night of lovemaking, an act of mercy, might be studied for centuries to come as a guide to the will of the universe. The story of a nocturnal arrest and a felon's execution there might change eternally the notion of human responsibility.

The exile of the Jews from Jerusalem became the central metaphor of the Hebrew faith. At the center of the metaphor was the city. Its stones were to be built anew in a perfected world. Or it was to be the place of ingathering and redemption.

Now, after fifty years of the Jewish state, what does the future hold for this city? Anyone walking the streets of Jerusalem today, covering the relatively short route from the American Colony Hotel, through the Damascus Gate and along the Via Dolorosa to the Jaffa Gate, across the valley of condominiums at David's Village and to the adjoining Hilton through Yemin Moshe, can see how intrinsically mixed are the spiritual and temporal traditions of power in the city.

The pious Hellenistic tombs from Hasmonean and Roman days and General Gordon's Garden Tomb both reflect the influence of world empires. The exquisite Church of St. Anne was built by warlike crusaders, converted into a mosque by Saladin, then restored to its status as a church. The chambers of the Church of the Holy Sepulcher owe their construction to the Christian Roman emperors; the Dome of the Rock once supported a cross as the mother church of the Knights Templar. It remains unapproachable to Orthodox Jews, who fear to enter the site of the original Solomonic Temple's Holy of Holies. The Western Wall, part of the Herodian Temple destroyed by the Romans, later confined to the narrow Jordanian street, now stands open before the great plaza built after 1967 where the Mughrabi Gate had stood.

All of these spiritual sites followed the fortunes of earthly empires, which is to say, the fortunes of war. The glories of faith, even the most sublime, were emblems of secular triumph. The eternal question has always been settled, directly or indirectly, by force. Whose Jerusalem?

Most of the early Zionists advocated a collaborative state with the Arab inhabitants, who, it was expected, would quickly recognize the benefits accruing to them from the arrival of a dynamic, idealistic, and educated new population. One who had no such expectations was Vladimir Jabotinsky. Coming of age in the years before the First World War, he partook deeply of two elements that were stirring Europe at that time.

One was nationalism, which in its normal Eastern European form was aggressive, militant, and nurtured on a well of grievances — the insults and injuries endured by small nations at the hands of neighbors or of the great empires whose congresses had imposed the status quo. As a Jew from Russia, Jabotinsky bore grievances, personal and collective, that were not meager.

The other element was in the air, so to speak, present in art, in music like Stravinsky's *Rite of Spring*, in literature, and in the work of German philosophers. It was a certain vitalism, a fusion of Eros and Thanatos, the idea of purification through struggle, of violence as life's ultimate reality and source of wisdom.

Today, walking in Jerusalem, a visitor familiar with the city can see the changes under way. The intifada is over, for the time being, and the Old City's street stalls are no longer subject to sudden strikes. Unarmed religious Jews walk to the yeshivas they've opened in the Muslim quarter of the Old City, and there seem to be more tourists, in their identical pastel baseball jackets. The street stalls outside the Damascus Gate have been cleared away. A move toward sanitation and order? A better field of operations for the police?

Centuries ago, when King David took Jerusalem, he did so by a skillful manipulation of the water supply, inspired construction, and main force. To some extent, Teddy Kollek, the city's mayor from 1965 to 1993, followed a similar policy. But there was a difference between Kollek's philosophy, that of an old socialist who knew a war when he was in one but who believed in the possibility of peace, and that of the present Likud government. Kollek may be criticized for many things, but he loved Arab Jerusalem as a wonder of the world; it was a treasure of his city and he never wanted to destroy it.

The same could not be said for the Likud Party, which took office as a result of Benjamin Netanyahu's 1996 victory. It should be noted that under Israel's new electoral system, the victory was not a parliamentary one for Likud but a personal win for Netanyahu, who ran on the slogan "Peace with security." There are many Israelis who interpret this result as reflecting the desire of a majority of the country's people for peace. The security aspect loomed large in the wake of the multiple bus bombings that took so many lives in Jerusalem and Tel Aviv after the Oslo Accords. Recently, on April Fools' Day, students at Hebrew University carried white balloons that read "Peace with security," a gesture reflecting less than reverence for Netanyahu and what he claims is his program.

The changes in the city are there to see, some subtle, some obvious. Ehud Olmert, the Likud mayor, has been enlarging the political boundaries of Jerusalem proper in a gerrymandering technique aimed at establishing a clear Jewish majority in the city. In some cases, this has meant driving out Arabs from their neighborhoods in order to build government housing for recent immigrants.

Since the Oslo Accords and in violation of them, life has been made more and more difficult for Palestinians. A Palestinian living in one of the autonomous territories needs a permit to enter Jerusalem or, for that matter, any part of Israel. This policy is an echo of the South African pass laws, and carries about as much of a guarantee of real security. Jerusalem can be closed for days at a time even to permit holders with jobs in town. Resident Palestinians who marry nonresidents lose their residential rights. Little by little the center of Palestinian Jerusalem is being choked off. Palestinians en route through Jerusalem—from Ramallah to Bethlehem, for example—can be arbitrarily refused passage.

What, then, does the future hold? Likud, secure in something very like racial superiority, seems to feel convinced that the Palestinian population, subject to pass laws, denied permission for house repairs, harassed in scores of petty ways, will somehow decide to fade away, or at least to accept conditions that would have been unacceptable to African Americans in Mississippi in the early 1950s. The religious settlers of Kiryat Arba turn to the Bible and profess to detect there texts commanding them to harry the Arabs out of the land. The hard-right Moledet Party, meanwhile, has made Arab expulsion an official party position.

Would the Arabs, given the opportunity, drive Israel into the sea? Geronimo or Crazy Horse undoubtedly would have welcomed the opportunity to burn Washington. In other words, the Palestinians can be credited with a certain comprehension of their situation. However, the overall Arab position is sometimes hard to discern.

The Palestinians of Jerusalem and the West Bank may absorb any number of insults and indignities, but no one who knows the Arab people expects them to leave their homes until they are, as proposed by Moledet, evicted by force. Nor will their increasing hopelessness and despair make them somehow more tractable. The Israeli policy of meeting Arab violence with more violence is understandable given Jewish history, but it is not necessarily the wisest solution.

This is something the Labor Party in Israel, for all its faults, understands. The Labor bloc recognizes the continuing existence of an Arab presence in Jerusalem and the West Bank. It will never agree to any formula that implies a division of the city, but it will, many Israelis believe, in some fashion accept a responsible Arab entity in exchange for peace and security. The policies of Likud and Labor are not the same, not interchangeable, not beyond the consideration of foreign observers. Their differences, and the Arab response to these differences, is the largest determinant of Israel's future.

If the walker in the city extends his perambulation to the western hills beyond Rehavia, he will encounter the perpetual lamps and massive blocks of hewn stone at Yad Vashem, the Holocaust memorial, a setting that may obviate all the rest.

An old man hands out prayers:

"O Master of the Universe, Creator of these souls, preserve them forever in the memory of Thy people."

Emerging from this great memorial to millions of innocents, the walker sees again the sweet-scented, pine-clad hills. Then he knows that nothing, nothing whatever that he has seen — St. Anne's of the Crusaders, the Dome of the Rock, the worshipers at the Western Wall and their Holy Wall itself — none of it belongs to the past. In Jerusalem there is no past, only a present, that platform between earth and heaven where history has been enacted since the beginning of time. And a future that only an all-knowing Master of the Universe, if there be One, could know.

—New York Times Magazine, 1998

CHANGING TIDES

O n a mild afternoon I watch a pretty little single-masted sailboat beat its way around the foot of Manhattan Island. Against the background of skyscraping towers, it looks absurdly delicate as it glides along, close to the wind. Between Governors Island and the Jersey piers a half-dozen more sailboats are racing over the gray water. On this particular Sunday, they appear to have the Upper Bay to themselves. Throughout its white-capped expanse, they're nearly the only craft afloat. The harbor is a stern prospect, and on it the sailboats look not only delicate but also frivolous, like tourists on a silent battlefield. One might imagine that things had come full circle, from the doughty little sailing ships of Hudson and Verrazzano to these, their lively descendants.

The European discoverers of New York's harbor were no more given to poetry than most professional sailors, but they found it marvelous. It seemed to them, in its perfection, like something engineered. The Upper Bay's topography protected it from winter storms and kept it nearly ice-free all year. The barriers of Sandy Hook and Long Island defended its approaches from the Atlantic rollers; incoming ships passed between the eminently defensible points of the Narrows to find a broad, calm roadstead five miles long, a virtual lake on which cargo could easily be transferred to lighters. There were good moorings everywhere. One of the continent's major rivers connected the harbor to the interior.

Early visitors remarked on the harbor's physical beauty. The land around it had large amounts of fresh water and abundant game. The tidal bottom was carpeted with oysters. One captain described "wild duck in immense numbers." An English clergyman named Andrew Burnaby wrote of "delightful prospects of rivers, islands, fields, hills and woods . . . and innumerable porpoises playing on the surface of the water." The cliffs along the right bank of the Hudson were much rhapsodized. The river and its course were compared to the Rhine.

New York was intended from its foundation to be a money-making operation, and the harbor was its sole reason for existence. It would stand or fall on its facility for moving goods by water for profit. The harbor began its commercial career as an outpost of the Dutch West India Company at which trinkets and simple tools made in Holland were exchanged for furs. Eventually the Dutch decided that there was insufficient profit in the trade, and the company allowed farmers to settle in the areas surrounding the harbor. When the British took over in 1664, the town began to ship flour and timber to the West Indian colonies. The slave economies of these islands produced goods that serviced the appetite, like sugar and tobacco; the plantation owners preferred to import the wherewithal of food and shelter rather than to divert land and energy from the single crops that were their mainstay.

Because of its harbor, the future held great things for New York. That future might be said to have begun on May 11, 1785, when the *Empress of China*, a ship of 360 tons, sailed through the Narrows, bound for Canton. Her cargo consisted of ginseng, the medicinal herb valued by Chinese apothecaries that then grew wild all over North America. Ginseng could be sold in China for well over a dollar a pound. Within fifteen months, the *Empress* passed through the Narrows again, inbound, with a hold full of silk, muslins, and blue-and-white porcelain.

Year after year, the volume of New York's shipping trade increased, and the maritime complex along its waterfront enlarged. By the middle of the 1840s, the shoreline of lower Manhattan displayed the forest of masts familiar to us today from old prints and the first photographs. This was the port known to Whitman and Melville; its enormously vital and brutal early industrial landscape is reflected in their work.

If New York Harbor has a single popular association it is with the immigrants who arrived here in vast numbers before the jet age made ocean-crossing a nuisance instead of an epic. The waterfront became the great spillway of immigration, and its neighborhoods always reflected the great migration in progress. An immigrant might find employment offloading the ship that brought him over. The harbor trades were as ethnically promiscuous as the whaler *Pequod*. By the 1950s, in some areas of Brooklyn and New Jersey, a New York maritime pedigree was coming into being, a mixture of Irish, Scottish, Scandinavian, and Italian.

In the 1880s, my maternal grandfather, a ship's engineer from Scotland, settled here and eventually became master of a steam tug. His boat was berthed on the Brooklyn side, near what became Bush Terminal. He was a well-read man, known for his unsentimental wit, and there are many family stories about him and some of them may be true. One concerns his encounter with Steve Brodie, the Bowery ruffian who claimed to have jumped off the Brooklyn Bridge. Hearing Brodie's tale in a riverfront saloon, he affected to understand that Brodie had jumped over the bridge rather than off it, which any fool could do. He also seems to have harbored a number of critical observations regarding the person of the Roman pontiff with which, in rare late leisure hours, he would affront his Catholic wife and children. For the most part, he was a tolerant man and endured their piety like a philosopher.

My mother used to recall going out on his tug at dawn on Sunday and looking up at the Brooklyn Bridge. Her father had seen it built during his first days in New York, and for both of them I think the bridge was the great totem of the city. Or of their city, which of course was Brooklyn. I imagine them now, a ten-year-old girl and her fifty-year-old father aboard a tug in Buttermilk Channel. Then them steaming under the bridge, the thing suspended over their heads, such a concord of the airy and the monumental. Who really can imagine what the bridge looked like to these two during the spring of 1904? Their interior landscape must have been so different from ours.

Today, equipped with Hart Crane's poem, I can hardly look at the Brooklyn Bridge without thinking of "choiring strings." But not long ago, passing under the bridge in a rowing boat in the middle of the East River, I felt a rush of the revulsion with which it used to fill me as a child. The monstrous bulk of the supports, the dizzying intervals of the span, inspired in me a fascinated loathing. I can remember the subway ride across the bridge, how the train would break into the open air and ascend over the tenement rooftops. Flocks of kept pigeons whirled against the sky. Then we'd be in the heart of a steel-webbed abyss with checkered summer sunlight. Unimaginably far below, the river ran the color of cold steel. To me, the bridge always suggested the world of my mother's childhood, a world of hoops, lace curtains, and diphtheria. With every other artifact of my grandparents' lost world, I detested it. As a very small child I used to close my eyes riding across it. When I was a teenager, during the fifties, I could never understand why they didn't tear it down along with everything else.

The boat I happened to be rowing the day I went under the Brooklyn Bridge was a coracle, an ancient Irish boat made of leather and wood. These craft are manned by teams of rowers wielding unbladed oars, and they move smoothly, at great speed, over the roughest water. The rower in a coracle has a view of things nearly at water level, and it wasn't only the Brooklyn Bridge that assumed a monstrous shape for me that day. From down in the river, the city a few yards away seems utterly inaccessible. The traffic zipping by on the FDR Drive appears to exist in a different world. I was seeing things again as they had appeared to me when I was small.

In its vital days, New York Harbor existed on an imperial scale. Its landmarks are outsized, like the Statue of Liberty and the immense self-satisfaction of Ellis Island; even the homely Staten Island Ferry coming up against its huge two-story gangways is an impressive sight. Over on the Jersey side, the Colgate soap factory's titanic clock used to be the largest single-faced clock on earth. Farther along the same shore, in

Hoboken, the Maxwell House Coffee sign was once the world's largest self-illuminated rooftop sign.

Of all the times I've been in New York Harbor, only once have I felt I was where I belonged. That was in 1958 when I was in the navy. I was a crewman on an attack transport called the USS *Arneb*, and we had come up from Norfolk, Virginia, and anchored in the middle of the Hudson. Our liberty boat ran to the Seventy-Ninth Street Boat Basin in Riverside Park.

Nineteen fifty-eight was the International Geophysical Year, and the *Arneb* was on its way to Davisville, Rhode Island, to take Seabees and their equipment aboard. We were then to convey the Seabees to the American Antarctic Naval Base at McMurdo Sound. The voyage ended up taking most of a year; we went down through the Panama Canal and came back around the Cape of Good Hope. All the way around I kept two photographs posted to my locker door: one was of Brigitte Bardot as she looked in 1958, the other was of the New York skyline. They were both close to their prime then, as far as mere appearances go.

The skyline was quite as it had been when I was a small child. Seen at its best, from the harbor at night, it was everything you could possibly imagine. The illuminated towers were lighted to colors that existed nowhere else on earth, or so it seemed. They composed the city's fantasy of itself as a place of limitless promise. Shamelessly, they invited more than admiration; they invited worship. They thrust the eye heavenward and brought the night sky into their composition, creating a mighty unity of dreams and labor. They were a challenge and a command to everyone who looked upon them. Rank on rank, they defied gravity, spinning their masses of concrete and steel into patterns of light. Onward, they said, upward, excelsior! They were the American Dream.

The sudden sight of New York's skyline from the harbor will always be one of America's great vistas, in spite of the Lego-like dominos with which it's been seeded. New York was meant to be seen that way, and it seems a shame that so few travelers today are afforded the view on their first encounter with the city. In 1958, as we came steaming up the unbridged Narrows, we saw at once that the towering buildings at the foot of Manhattan were above all a celebration of the imperial harbor.

Watching the sailboats today, I'm caught up in the strange association between water and time. Those of us who've lived a lot of our lives around the harbor can see our past reflected in it, and now a future's taking shape, a future that these Sunday sailboats portend. As the working piers pass out of existence in Manhattan, on the New Jersey side of the Hudson, and in Brooklyn, places of residence and recreation press closer to its waters. As the working port confines itself more and more to corners like Port Newark or Port Elizabeth, the waters of New York get cleaner than they've been in a hundred years. Plainly, the postindustrial waterfront of the next century will have a very different look. There's a gentrification of the harbor in progress to match the process wrought in so many of the New York area's old neighborhoods. It's visible now along both banks of the Hudson, between Battery Park City and the George Washington Bridge. Water views are hard to beat. The shores of the city have become a prime location, a property for New York's formidable realtors to price and sell, a resource for environmentalists and populists to defend from the savageries of the market.

New York Harbor grew in the name of profit, and some things, after all, don't change. In the old days, the raw business of the harbor was done right down the street; today, in our new-age fastidiousness, we prefer not to witness the primary processes of our economy. At the South Street complex, we preserve for our pleasure a fine romance of Whitman and Melville's grand, dark, Satanic mill of a seaport. I think it's too bad we could not do more to save the scale of lower Manhattan's striving towers now that the heroic age they represent is past. They expressed a great dream, commerce as a moral force, American power, an empire of peace-loving producers and traders whose ennobled common sense would astonish the world. They were cathedrals. For as long as anyone lives who understands the dreams they personify, they will stand, in good times and bad, reflecting and reflected by the great harbor whose prosperity raised them.

—New York Times Magazine, 1988

UNDER THE TONGUE
OF THE OCEAN

O ne thousand and forty-three feet below the sunny, sparkling waters off Chub Cay in the Bahamas, the external world presents the darkness of the womb or the tomb. There are four of us down here, sitting in the dark, and to me at least, it's plain we don't belong. If we tried to leave the narrow limits of our deep-sea submersible, we would suffocate far short of the surface. Here, inside the vehicle, the artificially controlled pressure is the same as that at sea level, or one atmosphere. At thirty-three feet below sea level—about twice the distance a moderately intrepid teenager would dive to retrieve her ankle bracelet—atmospheric pressure doubles.

Here, the surface is an abstraction; we know it's up there in the same sense that someone sitting in the small hours of night-time New York knows that Paris is somewhere east-northeast, bathed in daylight. But in a sense, the surface of Bell Channel overhead is much farther from us than Paris is from New York. Its distance, in practical terms, is more like that to the moon, another world. Yet, paradoxically, what's up there is not another world at all. It's our own, part of that terrestrial creation entrusted to our stewardship, not a thousand miles but a thousand feet away.

The ingenious craft inside which we have intruded to this depth, a contraption suggesting the coupling of a jumbo prawn with a helicopter, is called a Johnson-Sea-Link. It belongs to the Harbor Branch Oceanographic Institution of Fort Pierce, Florida, and its descent is part of the work of the institution's biomedical marine research division. Attached to its forward section is an assembly of baskets, tentacles, remote mobile arms, and grabbers, all operated from the forward compartment. Batteries of video cameras and xenon arc lights, deployed, replicate bright sunlight and release the blaze of tropical noon into a world designed for darkness, inhabited by creatures whose element is perpetual night.

The reasons for my being here are varied but also fairly consistent. One of the happiest days of my life was one on which I broke an eardrum scuba diving off the island of Bonaire and descending, a little too precipitously, on my first coral reef. It was as close to paradise as I ever expect to find myself. On the sheer joy of it, I made for deeper water, slipped over the reef, and kept descending until my depth gauge registered over ninety feet. At that depth, the glorious colors of the sun-dappled reef began to disappear. Parrot- and angel fish were dun as mackerel. Purple fans lost their luster. I was approaching the levels of nitrogen narcosis and also a depth at which decompression time would be necessary to prevent an attack of the bends if I spent more than a few minutes. But I also felt at the border of a great mystery.

A few years later, I went diving off Grand Turk. At the row of orange cans that mark the edge of the reef off Cockburn Town, the Puerto Rico Trench begins, and from its bright, teeming upper ledge, where happy barracuda accompany the bubbling diver, the bottom falls off quite briskly to the abyss, 30,704 feet down, more than five and a half miles, the lowest point in the Atlantic Ocean pole to pole. It's impossible to paddle around at the entryway to such a vast deep and not feel its dark invitation. Now, invited by Harbor Branch to participate in a dive, I have the chance to get part of the way down.

There are two principal crew compartments to the twenty-three-foot-long Johnson-Sea-Link. Aft, in the thorax of the crustacean, is a small oval accommodating two observers. Its external views are provided by two traditional portholes, one in each bulkhead, and a video monitor. The monitor is angled head-high to a viewer reclining on an elbow. This rear chamber is entered while the craft is still high and dry, secured to the deck of the mother ship, and the means of entry is a metal chinning bar of the sort B-29 crews used to enter their aircraft in World War II.

Last night, on the passage out from Fort Pierce, I was tempted to have a look at the rear, or dive, compartment where I find myself this morning. I decided not to. Now, after the lights go on and I'm in the dive compartment watching a big shark attack the video camera outside (at a depth that, before ocean research by submersibles, large sharks were not known to frequent), I'm glad I skipped the pre-descent inspection. If I hadn't, it now seems to me I might have passed the night worrying about both my upper-body strength and my capacity for dealing with close confinement. It's tight in the dive compartment, which I'm sharing with Dan Boggess, one of Harbor Branch's versatile sub techs. We'll spend a little more than three hours down here, slowly climbing the slope toward minus one thousand feet. Tomorrow I'll ride in the bubble up forward.

The bubble is what gives the JSL its helicopter-like aspect, and though in terms of actual operating space it is every bit as tight as the dive compartment, its all-enfolding, clear acrylic sphere presents a memorable panoramic vision of the submarine landscape. Perhaps the reason so much of the Johnson-Sea-Link's design suggests aviation is that Edwin Link, who developed it, was the very same man who created World War II's celebrated Link Trainer, a ground-bound simulated fighter plane in which thousands of Allied pilots were taught to fly.

The association between undersea locomotion and flight is extensive. Auguste Piccard, the man who gave the world Trieste, the deepest diver of them all, began as a balloonist, ascending sixteen miles into the stratosphere to track cosmic rays in August 1932. (His grandson, Dr. Bertrand Piccard, recently completed the first nonstop round-the-world balloon trip.) Piccard incorporated the principle of discardable weight that informs ballooning into the design of submersibles, which use weight to descend and can jettison it and "fall" up in emergencies.

Before Piccard, submersibles had to be heavier than water. Piccard created the "reverse balloon." As the inflatable aircraft was lighter than air and went up, the Piccard "bathyscaphes" were lighter than water and went, weighted, down. This revolution in principles has created a situation in the dive compartment of our JSL this morning whereby the writer, an unhandy technophobe, has been instructed in the means of navigating the vessel to the surface should all his dive mates be incapacitated together. The notion makes him feel all the farther from his customary skies.

In September 1953, Auguste Piccard took the most advanced version of the Trieste to a depth of 10,330 feet, far deeper than anyone had ever descended. A few years later, the United States Navy purchased the Trieste. In 1960, Piccard's son Jacques and a young naval lieutenant named Don Walsh took the Trieste on a dive to the very nadir of the living world. One South Pacific January day, the pair descended 35,800 feet below the Pacific, seven miles down into the Marianas Trench and the depth of seven Grand Canyons, the place where the Creator appointed the seas their limit, the end, the bottom. There they remained for twenty minutes. To this day, no manned submersible voyage has equaled that of Piccard and Walsh in Trieste. Their dive marked a beginning, every bit as much as the work of Wernher von Braun, commencing a future and suggesting its possibilities.

The idea of seven miles makes our one thousand feet and change seem fairly insignificant, but I'm impressed. A giant crane on the mother ship, the *Edwin Link*, has lifted the JSL from its moorings and set us sinking in a great welter of bubbles. Above the bubbles, the great glaring mirror of the surface quivers overhead. Then, little by little, we take leave of it, the looking glass so familiar to scuba divers as the shimmering, quivering skin of the home planet. That membrane, the passage through which takes us home to sweet air and all things dry, now stretches out like a vault to become our sky. Progressively, the mirror fades and the force of the Bahamian

sun drains away. As the world outside darkens and we keep on
steadily sinking, I feel us easing down into a world of which
I know nothing, into a place—and a kind of place—where I
have never been. Not many people have. And that, I suppose,
is the chief reason I've come.

Above all, it is dark here, so dark that its darkness is palpable, a principle, unearthly. We settle on some drowned shore,
visible, with the arc lights still out, only on the pilot's radar
screen. Out in the otherworldly darkness, it's as though you
can feel the weight of the real Atlantic Deeps. The place we
sit is below what the admiralty charts named the Tongue of
the Ocean. Overhead, the Gulf Stream races through the Bahamas, and to the south, the canyon on which we're perched
slants down toward the Puerto Rico Trench itself.

For a while, the only light comes from the red instrument
panels in the dive chamber, but then, through the port, we can
see strange darts and twinklings in the pitch black. Little whirls
go spinning, looking a bit like time-exposed photographs of
traffic in impossibly distant cities. This darkness, whatever else
it may be, is alive, and the light we're seeing is bioluminescence. The glow emanates from living creatures. Creatures
we can soon see liberally populate what had looked like void.
Some are called siphonophores, long, rope-like colonial animals twinkling on and off as they float by. There are cteno-
phores, incandescent jellyfish, and we see the tinted minute
flashings of the copepodes, insect-like, deep-sea fireflies.

A number of curious notions will turn in me on these de-
scents, and this is the first one—that descending into this oceanic dream world, I've located myself in the deep dark drop of
water that might be on a slide under some biologist's micro-

scope. I have a vision of this dark stuff I'm in as the primordial soup, the solution from which life was formed, from which it is being formed now. Tomorrow, sitting in the dark in the sphere, which with its panoramic surface functions like a reverse fishbowl, I'll get a clearer look at these twinkling creatures and imagine myself transported back billions of years, into a warm Devonian sea at the dawn of creation.

After a few minutes on the bottom, Craig Caddigan, the pilot, who's seated in the front with this expedition's biochemist, Amy Wright, turns on the lights. In the light of day, the sea floor sheds part of its mystery but also reveals more variety and complexity than the emptiness beyond time we projected into the darkness. Under the xenon light, we see the big shark attacking one of the video cameras. Big, upper-level fish repair regularly to these depths, research has revealed. In addition, whales, porpoises, and even turtles show up at the extreme range of the Johnson-Sea-Link's descent capacity, which is about three thousand feet. We're at the bottom of an enormous undersea cliff, a place where everything loose eventually lands for the attentions of scavengers who patrol it. Off to the south, the canyon deepens and widens in the general direction of the Puerto Rico Trench before disappearing into regathered darkness. On the other side of the porthole, "sea snow" falls, the incessant rain of dissolving grains from the lighted world's ongoing entropy. And the sandy, boulder-strewn seabed is grown with sponges and coral, some of which live only at these depths. A crab trap, a token of the breathing world, lies on a sandy patch.

After the dive, our log will report sightings of a long list of invertebrates, corals, and hard and soft sponges. I recognize sea gorgons, whips, and fans farther up the slope. Beyond them are masses of the much-valued black coral, the order Antipatharia, huddled in branch-like clusters called "snake stars." Black coral has been harvested almost out of existence at higher depths in places where preservation is lax, and the stuff's exquisite midnight sparkle and texture make it desirable as jewelry. Looking over the log weeks later, I can ponder what Wright has recorded, and it reads a little like Homer in the original: phaekelia, bubaris (both rare), siphonodictyon, cinachrya, pseudoceratina, agelas, and crinoids. There's something appropriate about these ancient life forms bearing names in the tongue of the people who first worked beneath the mirror of the sea, gathering sponges, lowering cones full of air to prolong their down time.

When, the next day, I'm in the sphere and we're waiting in the pre-xenon darkness to observe the bioluminescence, I'll have my fantasy of being in the Devonian sea where only luminous sea flies and jellyfish dwell. It's a fine conceit, but not one that conforms to reality. Bioluminescence and the resort to the lower depths by many species were survival strategies to escape ever more mobile and observant predators higher up. This biological glow itself requires for its usefulness that special miracle of perception, the eye. Some bioluminescent species use their light to lure prey; others release bursts of light to startle and escape predators, the way squid release their screen of ink.

When the lights go on and the panorama of the sphere opens up before me, I find myself taken with a school of tiny blue fish, ranging through the web of sea fan just outside the bubble. They're so small and Prussian blue, creatures of the dark. They look very much like damselfish; perhaps they are.

According to Grant Gilmore, former senior scientist of Harbor Branch, virtually every one of the institution's deep-water expeditions has resulted in the discovery of a previously unknown animal species. There is one discovery already on record that provides some idea of the promise at hand. In 1987, Shirley Pomponi, chief of Harbor Branch's biomedical marine research division, collected some samples of a deep-sea sponge called *Discodermia dissoluta* and began taxonomic examination. Pomponi's colleagues, Sarath Gunasekera and Ross Longley, eventually isolated and characterized a chemical component of the sponge they called "discodermolide." Put as simply as possible, discodermolide was observed to prevent cells from multiplying. In 1998, Harbor Branch and the Swiss pharmaceutical company Novartis Pharma AG signed a licensing agreement for the drug company to produce and market discodermolide as an anticancer agent.

The Canadian designer and builder Phil Nuytton, one of the most thoughtful and original of undersea pioneers, makes the point that, having looked at the earth from outer space, we've seen the big picture. "We've said, 'Hey, that isn't earth; that's water,' he says. "We've already fouled up the one-quarter of the earth we live on. But there are three-quarters of this planet that are virtually pristine."

Virtually pristine and virtually unknown. We know more about the surface of the moon than about what lies down in that three-quarters. In Genesis 1:6, God is described as creating the "firmament to separate the waters from the waters." It is an accurate depiction of our place in the scheme of things. While we cling to our soiled firmament, new species are being found beneath the waters every year. The generation of life itself is taking place near hot fissures miles below the Pacific, coming out of the earth, quickened without photosynthesis.

Looking back now, I try to finish the thought I was weaving around the tiny damselfish. I was, I remember, looking for its eyes. And it had them, eyes fundamentally like mine, and blood, and all the rest. It was another creature, like myself, created of the same process, bound by the same providence. What was essentially true about the firmament applied miles under the sea. What better place to turn for help, for healing —though, of course, the customary risks apply. I'm certainly glad I went down.

It is impossible to stand where we do, at this strange interstitial point in time and fortune, and not reflect on the implications. Scanning the sky, or watching the sea's horizon and peering into its depths, gives us pause. We look for origins, explanations, even resolutions, always hoping to somehow recognize something out there. Like the indigenous people of the American continents, we look for contours that, however distantly, metaphorically or otherwise, relate us to the overall structure of things. Like self-aware components of some great design, we look searchingly into vast distances like sea and sky. What we hope to locate is, finally, ourselves, our lost providence, our forgotten secrets.

—*New York Times Magazine*, 1999

DOES AMERICA STILL EXIST?

I t's boring to put one country over another," my friend said sleepily. "Everyone says, 'The Americans are all sons of bitches.' I tell them, 'So are you. So are we all.'"

She poured more schnapps over her peppermint tea and I watched her search my bland, aging face for the American son-of-a-bitch element. She was mildly drunk and so was I.

"Nor are you stupid," she declared. "And everyone says Americans are stupid."

"It's a truism," I said, "that in practical matters Americans are smart as whips. I mean, half of everything ever invented was invented in America."

"This aptitude," my friend said, "seems not to apply to you."

Earlier in the evening we had experienced a bit of car trouble, which she had largely resolved.

"No," I said. "I'm a novelist."

She poured us both more schnapps. We were running very low on tea; the tea had degenerated to the barest gesture toward salubriousness and moderation.

"Yes," she declared, "but the novelists as well—one is led

to believe—are adventurers, Indian fighters, commandos, no? They can all fix cars, no? Even the novelists."

"We are not responsible for your fantasies about us. Especially I'm not."

"Also," she said, "they say Americans are vulgar."

"That's foolish," I said testily. "It's petty snobbery and it's banal."

Even as I spoke, I saw her cornflower eyes widen in triumph. "Now," she cried, "define vulgarity! Let's see if you can do it."

"Where," I demanded, "do you get off talking about vulgarity? You're supposed to be an anarchist."

Too late-flushed with schnapps and Nordic bloodlust, she was not about to let me off. "I want to hear. This is for my education. I am all," she announced, "ears!"

"Vulgarity," I explained, assuming an educational mode, "is a word that has more to do with polemics than with the realities of human behavior."

I took a deep breath and prepared to blow her out of the water. "For example, it was a favorite epithet of Trotsky's."

"Look," she cried. "See what we have here! I am an anarchist, a woman, a working mother, and a proletarian. You—and I don't care if what you say is true, that you were raised in the gutter, grew up in the poorhouse, were beaten on the head by coppers—are a bourgeois. That is what you are now. A bourgeois with a boat and a country house." She stood up as though she were holding my severed head by the hair in her fist. "Yet I can define vulgarity and you cannot."

"I can define vulgarity perfectly well," I assured her. "I refuse to sit here and be priggish for the sake of priggishness and boring for the sake of boredom."

She pouted for a moment, yawned, and sat down. We were both going under.

"Tell me this," she mumbled. "Tell me this, old pal. When you dream the American Dream we hear so much about—the good old American Dream that's going to wipe all us poor squareheads off the map—what's it like?"

What's it like? I thought, although my insight was fading with the northern lights. What an interesting question. Naturally, I had no intention of trying to answer, certainly not there or then. Lying awake, I drifted into a curious reverie. Once, long ago, I was the radio operator on what we called a Peter boat, one of the little vessels that supervised amphibious operations. As we pitched along among the LCVs, I watched our gunner drift into sleep, lulled by the heat, the rocking, the weight of his armor and weapons. Our alert coxswain was quick to catch him out.

"Where the hell you at, Sloper?" he snarled, kicking Sloper's ankle off the gunnel with an oil-stained size twelve. Sloper, who had done time for this kind of thing, squinted at our petty officer with his Ouachita Snake Cult blue flannel eyes. It was just a maneuver. The mock enemy were US Marines on the south coast of Crete.

"Just dreamin' the American Dream, Boats."

He got off with a captain's mast.

Even twenty-odd years ago it was an old, bad joke. The American Dream—pious cant, huckster's prattle, refuge of scoundrels too numerous to mention. In the darkness of that boreal Hegelian country, in a room smelling of dope and Gauloises and cheap government liquor, my friend's question pursued me to wakefulness. Were we not, we Americans, the secular equivalent of those the illiterate Mohammed called the People of the Book, in that our way of life was founded on a scripture, a text? To our Founders, readers of the Bible—or at least of the Edinburgh philosophers—we were not meant to be just another country. We were about something, or at least were meant to be. If we put that behind us, we will become a mere geographical expression, worshipers of the Golden Calf. Martin Luther King called us on it, almost two hundred years after the text was set down. He had a Dream. An American Dream.

Across the room my friend lay, not contentious now but asleep. What remained of our Dream might indeed cause the extermination of this woman and her children; she was right enough about that. And this hoary transatlantic dialogue that the two of us were born to—a windy exchange predating Emerson and Carlyle, suffered on over the soup through the era of Mr. and Mrs. Henry Adams, perfected by Mr. James, who was capable of conducting a transatlantic misapprehension all by himself—was still in progress, now amid cannabis fumes and white booze, no longer so polite or elegant in the lengthening shadow of Absolute War.

How piquant it was, I thought, that our conversation should concern itself with "vulgarity," a conversation between two hard-living, lowborn scriveners. Then it occurred to me that though I would yield to no one in idiot patriotism, though I had sworn an oath never to curry favor abroad by disassociating myself from the United States, if I were compelled to name that aspect of herself my country had most effectively and successfully exported, I should have to say her vulgarity. And were I questioned about which elements I thought made up the Z's of our current American Dream, I should have to enumerate them as follows:

1. The Wizard of Oz
2. Uncle Sam
3. God
4. The Future, or as it was formerly referred to, Tomorrow
5. Whales

First the Wizard. L. Frank Baum, renderer of Oz, was among the wisest of our fantasts — and for all his eccentricities, an astute observer of American reality at a critical time in the country's history. He was, more or less, a contemporary of Twain, Finley Peter Dunne, and the Anti-Imperialist League. A contemporary, as well, of Bryan, Vanderbilt, and Gould; McKinley, Mahan, and Mark Hanna. "Pay no attention to that man behind the curtain." The stale effluvia that has tainted American air, from Baum's day to our own, whenever the bell-toned, friendly voice of our relentlessly mediocre leadership has delivered itself of self-serving prevarication, isn't anything vile — why, no! It's sweetness and companion light, the savor of rectitude and virtue.

As for Uncle Sam, Old Stretch, the Yankee skeptic — where might we be without him? It was Sam who proved that a citizen could rise from chiseling war profiteer to national symbol, and if that's not an American dream, what is? The rise of Uncle Sam was to be a function of the yellow press, whose mission it was to concoct a trash nationalism. America's dream was to be transmuted into THE AMERICAN DREAM, along with such artifacts of petty chauvinism as THE AMERICAN WAY OF LIFE AND ONE HUNDRED PERCENT AMERICANISM.

Then, with all due respect, neither last nor least, there's God. We are, of course, tortuously scrupulous in avoiding any acts that might be construed as homage at the public's expense— they seem to drive some people stone ape. However, in some general fashion, we give the impression of regularly requesting and expecting his blessing. He's the Creator referred to in our Declaration of Independence and the Entity to whom our un- churched hero Lincoln made occasional reference. Once we thought of him as marching along beside us, trampling out the vintage where the grapes of wrath were stored. Lately, we're not so sure who's out there on the flank or whose grapes we're walking on. There's one thing about him, though, that makes him particularly important, so important that in the face of its awesomeness we risk overstepping the hallowed division of church and state. His name's on the money—and that, by jiminy, buys him a piece of the Dream!

We come now to the Future, which may be dispensed with briskly, since it doesn't seem to be working out as well as we'd hoped. Rather, it keeps ever more receding, just as F. Scott Fitzgerald described. At one time it was very big, American Dream–wise, appearing regularly in the Sunday supplements as a network of sleek monorails that snaked their way among bright, turreted, art deco towers. It was an immaculate urban landscape inhabited by tiny figures, white by persuasion. Fu- turistically garbed, they made their way along the ramps and tubular walkways, each apparently en route to discharge some vital, remunerative, but not particularly strenuous responsibility. The Future's future in the American Dream is a bit tenuous now. Some of us can remember its heyday, and may recall the melancholy spectacle of its degeneration into sorry little numbers like Mickey Mouse in the postwar world. There's a good deal of it lying around in the neighborhood of Shea Stadium, where it may be glimpsed by visitors to New York on their way to or from the major airports. Most of the rest is owned by Walt Disney Productions or the federal government, or is tied up in antitrust suits.

We come at length to whales. The slogan "Save the Whales" is often worn on a button or displayed as a bumper sticker by young blond people with big teeth who carry their kids around in backpacks. I have no quarrel with their sentiment, but it is not on their account that I feel compelled to include whales among the totems of the Dream.

Rather, it's a single whale, a freak albino from the last century, who's responsible. In the structure of the American Dream, each facet of the Dream must confront its Antagonist. For example, God, in his day, had Emily Dickinson, whose thrashing surrender under his unmeasurable weight even she mistook for love. During Emily's lifetime, there was raised up among us a prophet (as our American Dream preachers might put it) who told the story of a mighty white whale. Although the whale's color is rendered as white, he stands, in the story, for all those people whose color was Other. He stands for all that was natural, wild, unowned, unsubdued, and ultimately un-American. For many, those properties mark him as Evil. For others, they mark him as Good. That is the way it is in our Dream; it's one or it's the other. In the story of the whale, an American man —as some say, American Man—pursued the unsubduable to their mutual undoing. There are almost as many interpreters of this story as there are people who finish reading it. For myself, that night, I decided it, too, was part of the Dream.

The next morning I resolved that one day I would try to write a few words about what had come to be known, more than half scornfully, as the "American Dream," about what was conceived before native hucksterism and the exigencies of propaganda vulgarized it into hypocrisy and blather. I never quite succeeded.

For all our moralizing, whether delivered by Webster-thunderers or Reagan-pals, we have never been the people or the nation we pretended to be. The shyster, the grafter, and the plug-ugly have always held their measure of power here, and they always will. God doesn't manifest himself in history; men do. Nor is this God's country but ours, and thus the responsibility for its ordering. If we choose to awake and see ourselves in our own baseness, we might well be a more agreeable nation and the world might be a safer place. On the other hand, the opposite might be true. Should we abandon the Dream, perhaps we'd breathe easier. We'd cease to be a People of the Book. There'd be no more cant about a New Order of Ages. Yet nothing is free, not even disillusionment. And it is just possible, as a result, that we might find our place in history as the betrayers of the noblest vision of civil order and probity that this imperfect world, and the cautious optimism of Western man, will ever be capable of producing.

—*Harper's Magazine*, 1984

The Heart of
This Strange Story

W e in the Western world are what the Muslims call People of the Book," Stone writes, in "The Reason for Stories." "The prototypical book in this culture has been the Bible, regardless of whether or not we are believers. After centuries of being Christians and Jews, our context and our perceptions continue to be conditioned by the Bible's narratives. It's hard to overestimate the impact of the Bible on our civilization and on our language. The novel came into existence with the rise of a literate mass readership, and the greatest vehicle of mass literacy in the English-speaking world has been the King James Bible. It has been the great primer. The Bible is unique among religious books in the relationship it defines between God and man, and in the view it takes of human life. The narratives about people in the books of the Bible are thought to mean something. They are thought to be significant. This implies that the corporeal world in which people live is not an illusion to be overcome, or a shadowland reflecting the void, but an instrument of God's will. For centuries we have been reflecting on peculiar things—like why Esau was disinherited, and how Abraham could have been ready to sacrifice his son —and asking ourselves: What does this mean? What is at the heart of this strange story? What can I learn from it? How does it bear on my situation?"

It's noteworthy that this discussion is framed in a context of historical religion, without requiring of writer or reader any engagement with the mystery of faith. Stone's position on these matters changed and developed over the course of his life, and across the essays in this section, with a good deal of ambivalence involved.

As for the value of stories and their telling, Stone came to his conclusions early. He liked to say that his first work of fiction was an oral performance he delivered as a boy, to get himself out of the clutches of New York's Child Protective Services. The essay "In Silence" broadens the theme: "When I began to think up stories, as a child, it was because stories were my greatest childhood pleasure. I also found that in an environment where it was very difficult to gain approval, I could get some positive reinforcement from storytelling."

Indeed. A good many contemporary writers will claim that storytelling is a survival skill—psychologically speaking, at least. For Stone, this point is to be taken more literally than for most. "In Silence" continues its account of Stone's childhood sensibility: "My interior world felt like confusion, a source of fears and unrequited aspirations and disappointment. But it was also, as far as I could determine, where joy originated, and hope for and fantasies of a different, better life."

"Capture," composed for a book of photographic portraits, allows Stone to reflect generally on the craft of characterization, which was of immense importance to him: "The artist who deals in recapitulating what is human has to be a good listener and a good watcher. He must command the facility to identify and examine all the elements, large and small—all the contradictions and passions that together make up the most ordinary person. In a way, he must deny the existence of such a thing as an ordinary person. He must understand that clichés do not exist in nature, not even in human nature, but only in art. No matter how embittered he may be, he must finally be in sympathy with humankind." Stone's own fictional characterizations are just such a cocktail of bitterness and sympathy.

In this and in all other aspects of "recapitulating what is human," whatever the medium, fidelity to truth is the most important factor. The standard here is not Nietzschean intellectual honesty, but Stone's own idea of artistic honesty, for which his mantra "nothing is free" was one form of expression. Stone won't allow any artist to put a thumb on the scale—not without consequences, anyway.

In all ways but the artistic, Stone must have thought of Malcolm Lowry as an example to avoid, although the two had much in common: both were sailors and wide-ranging travelers; both wrote with difficulty and cared about almost nothing else; both had a dire weakness for alcohol, fatal in Lowry's case. In his early thirties Stone had feared for a time that he might become what Lowry effectively was: a one-book wonder. But redemption (a topic that interested Stone increasingly as he dragged his own difficulties into the second decade of the twenty-first century) is found in Lowry's one luminous masterpiece, and in the fact that while making that work, he never did put his thumb on the scale.

"The Reason for Stories: Toward a Moral Fiction" was provoked by an essay by William Gass, "Goodness Knows Nothing of Beauty," published in *Harper's Magazine* and now considered to be a companion—or better, perhaps, a counter-weight—to Stone's subsequent piece for the same magazine. Certainly, the two essays pin down opposite ends of a particular spectrum. Gass presents the case for a pure, disembodied aesthetics: art for its own sake and absolutely nothing more. For Stone, literary art must have a larger purpose: "Stories explain the nature of things," and further, "the laws of both language and art impose choices that are unavoidably moral." A system where nothing is free "requires the artist to constantly make decisions, to choose between symmetry and asymmetry, restraint and excess, balance and imbalance. Because this law is ruthlessly self-enforcing in art, the quality of the artist's work will depend on his making the right decision. The same law operates the scales the blindfolded woman in the courthouse holds. Artistic quality is related to justice. Grammar is related to logic, which is the engine of conscience. Language is always morally weighted," because, for Stone at least, it can't not be.

Stone's argument with Gass actually is about belief, though the belief in question isn't religious—it concerns the worth and value of art. The issue can be framed religiously, though, if one believes, as Stone contends, that the fundamental purpose of art is to discover and represent whatever order may be found in our universe. The religious dimension of that enterprise gets further consideration in "The Way the World Is," a transcription of an interview for Peter Occhiogrosso's collection *Once a Catholic*. Though Stone usually presented himself as a lapsed Catholic—he was certainly not a churchgoer—he here lets it drop that "I have trouble with nonreligious humanism as an ethical system. It's not that I don't understand it; it simply doesn't have any meaning that I can respond to."

Elsewhere in the conversation, Stone points out that "there is just more religion and religious questioning in my work . . . more overt Catholicism in the stuff I write about, than in most writers' work." He was at the same time extremely conscious of the great violence and harm done throughout history in the name of organized religion, and thus wary of signing back on to it, or having his characters do so. Religious questioning in Stone's fiction is not likely to resolve in acceptance of dogma, as it will do in Graham Greene's fiction (which Stone for the most part detested).

Still, Stone felt sufficient attraction to religion to produce a constant, energetic tension—an energy constantly feeding back into his work. "I never tried to live as a Catholic adult," he tells Occhiogrosso, "which means that it can be there as a kind of illicit love for me, as a forbidden pleasure, because I never tried to live it out in a responsible, day-to-day way." The seduction of faith is powerfully present in "Coda," a very late work that Stone intended as his final *ars poetica*, though even there he still maintains, "Insight was my God when I felt deserted."

"Coda" is directly addressed to Stone's readers, although, unlike many of his contemporaries, he was not in the habit of projecting an ideal reader in what too often can be a sentimental way. In this last text he seems more to be talking to himself, or maybe he was praying.

MSB

IN SILENCE

When I began to think up stories, as a child, it was because stories were my greatest childhood pleasure. I also found that in an environment where it was very difficult to gain approval, I could get some positive reinforcement from storytelling.

My interior world felt like confusion, a source of fears and unrequited aspirations and disappointment. But it was also, as far as I could determine, where joy originated, and hope for and fantasies of a different, better life.

I made a few discoveries in the earliest stages of my reading that I never quite got over. One was that a story could be knit together in such a way that it completely dominated the mind's eye and ear and became an alternative reality. Certain books and tales seemed to accomplish this more effectively than others. It was like the difference between a good trick and an indifferent one.

I also found that a story did not have to end happily to be satisfying. That even stories that made you feel like crying, or did make you cry, like Andersen's or Wilde's fairy tales, provided a certain comfort. They were almost scary to read, because you knew that they would end in your tears. Yet the satisfaction, paradoxical but undeniable, was as intense as that to be had from any funny story. After a while I realized that their secret lay in the fact that they made the world less lonely. Almost every way one felt, it seemed, could be made into a story. About then it occurred to me that stories were about recognizing the way things were. In other words, they were about truth, and truth was important.

Very early on, I thought that the ability to combine character and incident with a measure of that truth was a very fine thing to be able to do. When I was a child, there was a children's card game called Authors that featured writers like Whittier and Dickens, Longfellow and Poe. Although I can't recall any of the rules of the game, I remember thinking that these characters with their chin whiskers and feather pens must be great men indeed. (We believed in Great Men then.) There were, as I remember, no women writers in the game, which seems almost impossible now. But I never doubted the stature of these old-fashioned gents. I had a certain sense of what they had done for a living, and I had even read some of their work.

Whittier's "Snowbound" was, I think, the first and most vivid poem I can remember, my first favorite. Like most people, I remember poetry first.

> *The sun that brief December day*
> *Rose cheerless over hills of gray*
> *And, darkly circled, gave at noon*
> *A sadder light than waning moon.*

And "The Rime of the Ancient Mariner," which I read before I could comprehend its argument but the lines of which haunted me:

> *Like one who, on a lonesome road*
> *Doth walk in fear and dread,*
> *And having once turned round walks on,*
> *And turns no more his head;*
> *Because he knows, a frightful fiend*
> *Doth close behind him tread.*

That got to me.

I thought writing was a great thing to do, and I wanted to do it too. I was unhandy and unartistic. I could not draw anything but stick figures, or fashion base materials into the shape of something greater. But I loved language; I loved its tricks and rhythms and ironies. Although I had been taught there was a time to keep silence, I thought there were times when the world, in its loneliness, required something other than the vast silence in which we labored. I knew no other way of not being alone in the world than through language.

Eventually the silence came to seem to me like an absence of something that must somehow be invoked. I knew only writing, that message in a bottle, with its artificial sounds and mimicked speech and tropes, as a means of invocation. I knew only narrative as a way of making sense of causality. Silence could be an enemy, a condition to which we had been consigned and to which we must respond. Because I respected the silence, however cold and alien and hostile, I wanted to make that with which I tried to answer it worthy of its terrible majesty.

—In *Why I Write*, 1998

THE REASON FOR STORIES: TOWARD A MORAL FICTION

Last spring the writer and critic William Gass published an essay entitled "Goodness Knows Nothing of Beauty," an essay that toyed with the proposition that art and moral aspiration were mutually distant. Statements of this view very often seek to replicate in their style the kind of cool, amoral elegance they claim for good art, and Gass's piece is not in this regard exceptional. It is characterized by paradox, alliteration, and a faintly decadent naughtiness suggestive of intense sophistication. In the end, as such pieces often do, it resolves itself solipsistically; that is, it explains itself away in terms of its own moral and aesthetic definitions. But it is interesting to see this old opposition between art and morality appear again, offered by a commentator usually wise and insightful.

"To be a preacher is to bring your sense of sin to the front of the church," Gass writes, "but to be an artist is to give to every mean and ardent, petty and profound, feature of the soul a glorious godlike shape." If this means that you get no points

THE REASON FOR STORIES · 301

in art for good intentions, no one would argue. But I find here echoes of an old antinomian tendency that goes back at least to Nietzsche. It has been argued by people as different as José Ortega y Gasset and Oscar Wilde; by Joyce speaking in character as Stephen Daedalus; and by Shaw during the period when he was writing *Major Barbara* and, it now appears, attempting to invent fascism.

In this antinomian vision, morality and art are independent and even in opposition. On the right squats morality. It may be imagined as a neo-Gothic structure—immense, ornate, and sterile. Its self-satisfaction, lack of imagination, and philistine sentimentality are advertised in its every plane and line. Architecturally it resembles the Mormon Temple, the one in downtown Salt Lake City, not the Hollywood-biblical one on Santa Monica Boulevard. It contains drear echoing silences.

And over here—art. Art is nothing but beautiful. Art is like a black panther. It has the glamour of the desperado. Art is radical, the appealing cousin of crime. Never a dull moment with art. Morality, in this view, is not only its opposite, but its enemy.

This claim of estrangement between morality and art retains its currency for an excellent reason: it's fun. It's agreeable for an artist to imagine himself as a Zarathustrian rope dancer, balanced against eternity up in the ozone and thin light, while far below the eunuchs of the brown temple of morality whine platitudes at each other in the incense-ridden noonday darkness: "Look before you leap." "A stitch in time saves nine." But let us pursue this notion. Let us imagine the novel, for example, freed completely from moral considerations. What would that be like? One thing it might be like is one of the antinovels

Robbe-Grillet gave us during the 1950s and '60s. These are novels without any moral context, but they are similarly without characters and plots, beginnings and endings. Surely such an exercise in *doing without something* serves to reinforce the idea of its necessity. Is it possible to postulate the idea of a successful novel about people, or about animals for that matter, in which the living of life, as reflected therein, exists beyond the signal area of moral reference points?

What about the comic novel? Let's eliminate at the outset the obviously sentimental or political comedies that have a message (that is, a moral point) at their core. Let's take the work of two writers—William Burroughs and Evelyn Waugh —who have written very funny books and who are not usually thought of as kindly humanistic sages.

Naked Lunch is the prototypical Burroughs novel, and like all the others it's full of cruelty—not just sadism, but cruelty. The element of sci-fi political satire it contains is sometimes claimed as representing a moral dimension, but I think that's bogus. The moral element in the work of William Burroughs is in its very humor. In the grimmest imaginable places, in the grammar of drug addiction, in the violence and treachery of the addict's world, Burroughs finds laughter. The laughter itself is a primary moral response. Laughter represents a rebellion against chaos, a rejection of evil, and an affirmation of balance and soundness. One can see this principle at work in the way that laughter undercuts superserious attempts at self-consciously "wicked" sex. I was once given a description of a waterfront S&M joint that presented itself as the meanest saloon on earth. There was a dress code, and patrons were expected to present to any observer nothing less than a grim mask of depravity. There were two house rules, according to my informant. The first was No rugby shirts. The second was No laughing. We must assume that the people who run places like that know what they're doing.

Evelyn Waugh seems to have been lacking in all the qualities we philanthropists find congenial. A bully, a coward, a fascist, a despiser of minorities and the poor, a groveler before the rich and powerful, Waugh was surely one of the worst human beings ever to become a major novelist. But paradoxically, his life and work provide us with a ringing confirmation of the dependence of serious fiction on morality. By borrowing, spuriously or otherwise (it doesn't matter), the certainties of Catholicism, he was able to infuse his best work with the moral center that makes it great. The worldly lives described in the *Men at Arms* trilogy and *Brideshead Revisited* are constantly being measured against a rigorous neo-Jansenist Christianity. In these books the invisible world becomes the real one, and its meanings constitute the truth that undergirds the confusion of desires with which the characters struggle.

Gass's essay starts by having us ask ourselves whether we'd rescue an infant or a Botticelli painting if we saw both of them being washed out to sea and could salvage only one. The Botticelli's a masterpiece; the baby's only a "potential" human being. After prescribing this antinomian exercise, he commences to deflate his own balloon by running it on the thorns of common sense. He refers to the author's historical struggle against censorship, as though this somehow establishes art's essentially unmoral character, and then admits that each censoring hierarchy reacts to whatever inadequacies of its moral system are challenged by the work in question. He reminds us that good books were written by bad people—bad people (and crafters of fine moral fiction) like Waugh, I assume. Then he ends with a truism to the effect that propaganda cannot justify bad art or bad writing.

There are few statements in the essay that Gass does not obviate or contradict, but there is one that stays, unforsworn and unqualified, in my recollection. He refers to Keats's identification of beauty with truth and vice versa as "a fatuous little motto." Now, it seems to me that Gass is being unkind to a perfectly nice axiom; surely we should meditate for a moment on this most appealing sentiment. Isn't it true?

Concerning life, it is a question we cannot finally answer. I think it tends to be true. The explanation at the core of any one of nature's mysteries is often edifying. Job cuts through to the substance of it when he questions the beneficence of God. In the end he learns that God's majesty and holiness suffuse the universe. This is what the medieval mystic Julian of Norwich was referring to when she wrote "all shall be well and all shall be well and all manner of things shall be well." In terms of Western tradition it should be true that truth is beauty. Even if you take God out of it, the grimmest principles of existence have their symmetry. All the same, there can be a hundred different explanations for things and every one of them beautiful and none of them true.

But, in art, isn't it always true? Aren't truth and beauty very nearly the same? Surely every aesthetic response entails a recognition. What standard do we hold up to art, other than things themselves? And what do we require for art if not a reflection of things, of our lives, in all their variety?

We in the Western world are what the Muslims call People of the Book. The prototypical book in this culture has been the Bible, regardless of whether or not we are believers. After centuries of being Christians and Jews, our context and our perceptions continue to be conditioned by the Bible's narratives. It's hard to overestimate the impact of the Bible on our civilization and on our language. The novel came into existence with the rise of a literate mass readership, and the greatest vehicle of mass literacy in the English-speaking world has been the King James Bible. It has been the great primer. The Bible is unique among religious books in the relationship it defines between God and man, and in the view it takes of human life. The narratives about people in the books of the Bible are thought to mean something. They are thought to be significant. This implies that the corporeal world in which people live is not an illusion to be overcome, or a shadowland reflecting the void, but an instrument of God's will. For centuries we have been reflecting on peculiar things — like why Esau was disinherited, and how Abraham could have been ready to sacrifice his son — and asking ourselves: What does this mean? What is at the heart of this strange story? What can I learn from it? How does it bear on my situation?

All our philosophies of history descend from the assumptions bequeathed by our scriptures: they profess to detect the informing principles at the heart of human events. Life matters, lives matter, because earthly human history is the arena in which the universe acts out its consciousness of itself, displaying its nature as creation. Human annals become charged, they become an entity: history. History, then, is perceived as a rational process, the unfolding of a design, something with a dynamic to be uncovered.

Stories explain the nature of things. Any fictional work of serious intent argues for the significance of its story. A reader holds the characters in judgment, investing sympathy or withholding it, always alert for recognitions, hoping to see his lonely state reflected across time, space, and circumstance. How then can fiction ever be independent of morality? To be so, it would have to be composed of something other than language.

There is no brown temple where morality resides. There is no high wire above it where the artist whirls in freedom. If there is a wire, it's the wire we're all on out here, the one we live on, with only each other for company. Our having each other is both the good news and the bad.

We deceive ourselves, we contemporary people, if we imagine that beneath our feet is a great, sound structure, a vast warehouse called civilization, chockablock with boring, reliable truths and insights. Around us there is only deep space. Out here, where we all live with each other, it's mostly impromptu. Right-mindedness is cheap—but goodness? William Gass need not worry about its coming between ourselves and our pleasures.

Most journalists who worked in Vietnam during the war were oppressed by the extreme difficulty of translating what they saw into words. It was not necessarily that it was so uniquely horrible; it was only that the brutality and confusion one experienced seemed to lose something when rendered, when written. Somehow, in describing the situation so that it could be set up in columns of type, one always seemed to be cleaning it up.

As I pondered this process, a moment of illumination struck me. We are forever cleaning up our act. Not only in describing ourselves but in imagining ourselves, we project a self-image that is considerably idealized. In all our relationships, we present idealized versions of ourselves so as not to frighten others with our primary processes. And just as we individually cultivate an elevated image of ourselves, so we conspire as nations, peoples — as humankind — to create a fictional exemplar of our collective selves, ourselves as we have agreed to imagine ourselves.

But this is not the whole story. Though we are only what we are, we have the amazing ability to extend, to transcend the grimmest circumstances. Moments occur when we amaze each other with acts of hope, acts of courage that can make one proud to be human. The fact is that we absolutely require the elevated image of ourselves that we indulge. If we did not idealize ourselves, if we only accepted the reality of ourselves as we are most of the time, we would never be capable of the extensions of ourselves that are required of us.

Things are in the saddle, Emerson said, and ride mankind. "Whirl is king." Things happen ruthlessly, without mercy; the elemental force of things bears down upon us. From one moment to the next we hardly know what's going on, let alone what it all means. Civilization and its attendant morality are not structures; they're more like notions, and sometimes they can seem very distant notions. They can be blown away in a second. In the worst of times we often look for them in vain.

Sometimes the morality to which we publicly subscribe seems so alien to our actual behavior that it seems to emanate from some other sphere. One might call it a fiction, but it's a fiction that we most urgently require. It is much more difficult to act well than we are ready to admit. It can be extremely hard to act sensibly, let alone well.

Storytelling is not a luxury to humanity; it's almost as necessary as bread. We cannot imagine ourselves without it because each self is a story. The perception each of us has of his own brief, transient passage through things is also a kind of fiction, not because its matter is necessarily untrue, but because we tend to shape it to suit our own needs. We tell ourselves our own stories selectively, in order to keep our sense of self intact. As dreams are to waking life, so fiction is to reality. The brain can't function without clearing its circuits during sleep, nor can we contemplate and analyze our situation without living some of the time in the world of the imagination, sorting and refining the random promiscuity of events.

If the practice of fiction is inextricably linked with concerns of morality, what is there to say about the writer's responsibility? The writer's responsibility, it seems to me, consists in writing well and truly, to use a Hemingwayesque locution. The writer who betrays his calling is that writer who either for commercial or political reasons vulgarizes his own perception and his rendering of it. Meretricious writing tries to conventionalize what it describes in order to make itself safer and easier to take. It may do this to conform to a political agenda, which is seen as somehow overriding mere literary considerations, or under commercial pressures to appeal to what are seen as the limitations of a mass audience.

The effect of conventionalized, vulgarized writing is pernicious. Fiction is, or should be, an act against loneliness, an appeal to community, a bet on the possibility of spanning the gulf that separates one human being from another. It must understand and illustrate the varieties of the human condition in order to bring more of that condition into the light of conscious insight. It is part of the process that expands human self-knowledge. Meretricious fiction does the opposite of what fiction is supposed to do. The reassurances it offers are superficial and empty. It presents a reality that is limited by its own impoverishment, and as a result, it increases each individual's loneliness and isolation. In the absence of honest storytelling, people are abandoned to the beating of their own hearts.

It must be emphasized that the moral imperative of fiction provides no excuse for smug moralizing, religiosity, or propaganda. On the contrary, it forbids them. Nor does it require that every writer equip his work with some edifying message advertising progress, brotherhood, and light. It does not require a writer to be a good man, only a good wizard.

Above all, what I wish to argue is that the laws of both language and art impose choices that are unavoidably moral. The first law of heaven is that nothing is free. This is the law that requires the artist to constantly make decisions, to choose between symmetry and asymmetry, restraint and excess, balance and imbalance. Because this law is ruthlessly self-enforcing in art, the quality of the artist's work will depend on his making the right decision. The same law operates the scales the blindfolded woman in the courthouse holds. Artistic quality is related to justice. Grammar is related to logic, which is the engine of conscience. Language is always morally weighted. Nothing is free.

his books

Political situations have always attracted me as a subject, and not because I believe that political pathology is necessarily more "important" than private suffering. During times of political upheaval, the relationship between external "reality" and the individual's interior world is destabilized. Revolutions, wars—such upheavals liberate some people from the prison of the self, even as they invite others to play out their personal dramas on a larger scale. People caught up in things that transcend the personal forever bring their own needs and desires to bear. They make pleasant and unpleasant discoveries about each other and themselves. The elements of drama descend on ordinary people and ordinary lives.

I wrote my first book after spending a year in the Deep South, a time that happened to coincide with the first sit-ins and the beginning of the struggle against segregation and also with the reaction to it. The novel centered on the exploitation of electronic media by the extreme right, a phenomenon we have not altogether put behind us. *A Hall of Mirrors* was not a strictly "realistic" book, but as young writers will, I put every single thing I thought I knew into it. I gave my characters names with the maximum number of letters because I thought that would make them more substantial. I had taken America as my subject, and all my quarrels with America went into it.

A few years later, working in Vietnam, I found myself witnessing a mistake ten thousand miles long, a mistake on the American scale. I began to write a novel set in Saigon. As it progressed, I realized that the logic of the thing required that everybody make his or her own way back home, into the America of the early 1970s. The early to mid-'70s still seem to me, in retrospect, like a creepy, evil time. A lot of bills from the '60s were coming up for presentation. *Dog Soldiers* was my reaction to the period.

I went to Central America in 1978 to go scuba diving while at work on a new novel, and returned to the region several times thereafter. I became acquainted with a few Americans working there. At that time relatively few people in this country knew where Huehuetenango was, and Managua, Nicaragua, was the title of an old Andrews Sisters song. The Somozas had been running Nicaragua for many years, and they seemed quite secure in their power—at least to my touristic eyes. Everything was quiet there. One day I even semi-crashed a party at the presidential palace.

The palace stood in the middle of what was literally a fallen city. From a distance, downtown Managua looked like a park —it was so green. When you got a closer look you could see that the green was that of vegetation growing over the rubble where the center of the city had collapsed two days before Christmas in 1972. The palace stood unscathed in the middle of the destruction. Around it was a kind of free-fire zone of scrub jungle where no one was permitted. The palace stood just beyond the effective mortar distance from the nearest habitation.

During my trips to Central America, I made a point of listening to as many stories as I could. After a while the stories began to form a pattern that conformed to my sense of Mesoamerica's history. This band of republics between the Andes and the Grijalva seemed placed by its gods in a very fateful situation.

The region seemed to have attracted the most violent conquistadors and the most fanatical inquisitors. When they arrived, the Spaniards found holy wells of human sacrifice. Here, racial and social oppression had always been most severe. The fertile soil of the place seemed to bring forth things to provoke the appetite rather than things to nourish—baubles and rich toys, plantation crops for your sweet tooth or for your head.

These lands were eventually yoked to labor-intensive, high-profit products: bananas, of course, and coffee, chocolate, tobacco, chicle, emeralds, marijuana, cocaine. I decided to put down the book I was writing and begin a new one. My subject was again America; the United States had been involved here for so long. The new novel became my third, A *Flag for Sunrise*.

Children of Light, a novel about the movies published in 1986, is also political, in my view. The process of creating Hollywood movies is loaded with examples of how America works. People in the film industry who see *Children of Light* as an attack on moviemaking apparently fail to see how movie-struck and reverent it really is.

I do not claim to know much more about novels than the writing of them, but I cannot imagine one set in the breathing world which lacks any moral valence. In the course of wringing a few novels from our fin-de-siècle, late-imperial scene, I have never been able to escape my sense of humanity trying, with difficulty, to raise itself in order not to fall. I insist on disputing William Gass's claim that "goodness knows nothing of beauty." Nor do I believe that, in his excellent fiction and lucid criticism, he practices the ideas he expressed in his essay of that name.

Just as it's impossible to avoid standards of human action in novels about people, it's difficult to avoid politics. But if a novelist openly accepts that his work must necessarily contain moral and political dimensions, what responsibilities does he take on?

He assumes, above all, the responsibility to understand. The novel that admits to a political dimension requires a knowledge, legitimately or illegitimately acquired, intuitive or empirical, of the situation that is its subject. Political commitment is not required, although eventually most authors maneuver themselves into a stand. I think the key is to establish the connection between political forces and individual lives. The questions to address are: How do social and political forces condition individual lives? How do the personal qualities of the players condition their political direction?

The novelist has to cast the net of his sympathies fairly wide. He should be able to imagine his way into the personae of many different people, with different ways of thinking and believing. The aspiring, overtly political novelist might spend a little time every morning meditating on the interior life of General Noriega, a man who actually exists. As far as political satire goes, it should be remembered that the best satire requires a certain subversive sympathy for one's subject.

The writer must remember the first law of heaven: nothing is free. Commitment can be useful because it brings a degree of passion to bear, but it's also dangerous. To be the contented partisan of one side or another, one has to sell something. Because so much of serious politics in this century has to do with violence, this can be a morally enervating exercise. Moral en-

ervation is bad for writers. Above all, the writer must not senti-
mentalize. He must remember that sentimentality is the great
enemy of genuine sentiment.

I believe that it is impossible for any novelist to find a subject other than the transitory nature of moral perception. The
most important thing about people is the difficulty they have
in identifying and acting upon what's right. The world is full
of illusion. We carry nemesis inside us, but we are not excused.

Years ago, a whimsical friend of mine made up a little ditty
that for me sums up the backwards-and-forwards tragicomical
nature of humanity's march. It's a highly moral little ditty, and
it may contain the essence of every work of serious literature
ever written. It goes like this:

> *Of offering more than what we can deliver, we have a bad habit, it
> is true.*
> *But we have to offer more than what we can deliver, to be able to
> deliver what we do.*

> —*Harper's Magazine*, 1986

WHAT FICTION IS FOR

In the autumn of 1981, I found myself in Bucharest, in Ceauşescu's Romania. Bucharest under Ceauşescu was one of the most ghastly places on earth. Its atmosphere partook of true horror; he was Dracula, the real thing, the Prince of Transylvania, ruler of the undead. No tour of the twentieth century would have been complete without a stop in Ceauşescu's Bucharest.

Two books of mine were being translated into Romanian because I was seen as what was locally called a progressive writer. My work was seen as critical of American society, and consequently I was perceived as a potential foreign friend.

While I was there, I got to know quite well the man who was doing the translation. Talking to a translator is almost always a pleasure for writers. You're with a person who has a special interest in exactly what you intended in a book line by line, one who is trying literally to get on your wavelength. I discovered, to my relief, that he did not find my novels particularly progressive but that he liked and understood them. So Andrei and

I became friends during the time I was there. Just before I was to leave, he told me that he was undertaking the translation of another book, one he had to work on in the deepest secrecy at that time, in that place: Thomas à Kempis's *Imitation of Christ*, the first translation of the *Imitatio* into Romanian since the sixteenth century. In undertaking this Andrei risked everything, his job, his house, the magazine he edited, and his university appointment—even, possibly, in Ceauşescu's perverse world, arrest.

Because they thought I was so progressive, the Romanian state publishers made an exception in my case and paid me royalties. There wasn't much to spend them on. I decided to take Andrei and Maria for the best meal in town. As we were dining, attended by musical Gypsies, I realized that I had no way of spending the royalties that were in the local money, the Romanian lei, which I was forbidden to take out of the country and which were worthless abroad anyway. So, like Erich von Stroheim in the bad movie version of a quaint operetta, I started handing the stuff out to the Gypsy musicians until we were surrounded by swarthy men in earrings sawing away desperately in exchange for Ceauşescu's worthless paper money, and heavily rouged ladies trying to read my palm and get a gander at my watch.

And at this point, more or less, Andrei asked me if I would take his manuscript out of the country—if I would take it to Brussels, where an émigré typesetter was waiting to print it. I felt it was the right thing to do.

I wasn't risking much. I was a more or less official guest, and I suspected that no one would search me on the way out, and in any case, the worst I could expect was an argument. The Romanians were not, at that time, looking for trouble with Americans. I spent the evening prior to departure sitting in the underlit lobby of my crummy hotel watching unshaven Arab hit men chain-smoke under fringed lampshades, and dreaming up what to tell the Securitate if they in fact found the manuscript at the airport. I was waiting for a man who worked as an electrician in the hotel to bring the manuscript to me. There was only one carbon copy in existence.

While I waited, I read a book I had brought with me called *The Execution of Mayor Yin*, written by a young woman,* an overseas Chinese from Canada who had been caught in the Cultural Revolution. The first story was set in a town beside the Yellow River sometime in the late seventies. It begins when the villagers hear that a large contingent of Red Guards is on its way. Having heard some rumors about the Red Guards, they await their arrival with some anxiety.

When the Red Guards arrive, the rumors prove true. The local party officials are humiliated. Some are beaten nearly to death. The Red Guards stage an auto-da-fé at which people denounce themselves, their friends, their spouses, their parents or children. No one will sleep for days. In the course of this visitation, which gives every sign of going on forever, excited messengers arrive from Beijing.

All at once the Red Guards begin driving everyone down to

---

*Chen Ruoxi published *The Execution of Mayor Yin* in an English translation in 1978. —*Ed.*

the riverbank. There at a splintering dock, an ancient excursion steamer is at moor. The Red Guards commence to force everyone in the village, the entire population regardless of age or condition, aboard the steamer. No exceptions. Everyone.

No one knows what will happen next. The boat has no engine, since it was removed during the Second World War. The summer sun beats down. No one may go ashore for any reason. The Red Guards never sleep, staying up on hysteria and amphetamines. By the second day, people have begun to sicken and die. Neither corpses nor the dying are removed. The Red Guards entertain with patriotic songs.

Then, on the third day aboard, the villagers see a patrol boat, commandeered by other Red Guards, coming downriver. After consultations, a tow line is set and the patrol boat manages to drag the engineless steamer out into the current. Since the rudder post has been removed, the only way to steer the boat is with giant makeshift oars made from fallen trees. In the process of trying to steer the thing, a number of people are crushed to death between the tree trunks and the rail. There is no food and no water.

But at last the boat is hurtling downstream, the current rushing it along, threatening at any moment to set it spinning in dizzy revolutions from whirlpool to whirlpool.

The Red Guards have seen something downriver. They grow even more excited. Rushing up and down the filthy, crowded deck among the prone bodies, they exhort the miserable, thirst-maddened, half-dead passengers to sing. The song for the day is "The East Is Red."

So down the river the boat careens, with everyone singing, dry dying throats raised in chorus. And the passengers see another boat approaching in the opposite direction. It is trim and clean and comfortably appointed. Aboard there is only one passenger, reclining in a cushioned deck chair. Seeing the excursion steamer filled with people singing, the passenger smiles and waves. She is Han Suyin, the Eurasian novelist. The whole show has been produced for her benefit. She will movingly recall this stirring encounter.

This story is offered as fiction, but surely it has the ring of truth. The author of *The Execution of Mayor Yin* wrote her stories while she was still in China, with little hope of ever having them published. They took on a certain piquancy in the lobby of the Bucharest hotel.

I had just finished reading the story when my Securitate escort and minder, whose name was Gabriella, appeared. The electrician with Andrei's manuscript arrived at the same moment, saw her, and set the thick manila envelope down on a sofa. Gabriella had three topics of conversation: the first involved what interesting things anyone I talked to might have said, the second was whether or not I thought she could make it in the fashion business in New York, and the third was astrology. I had to wait until we exhausted these topics before I could go over to the sofa and pick up the envelope. No one searched at the airport.

Earlier this year, I gave a reading on upper Broadway in Manhattan, and Gabriella was there, asking for a reference. I declined to give her one. For a moment I thought about reporting her as a known agent of a foreign security service, but I didn't do that either.

All this made me speculate to some degree on the role of

the writer, what stories are, what purpose art in general serves. Art, it seems, is the place where we establish a consensus about how it is with us. It is the only medium we have for removing a moment from the whirl of events and placing it under scrutiny in all its dimensions. It is the place where imagination meets the greater world and each acts upon the other.

Who knows, transporting the *Imitatio* may be the most significant literary act I ever perform. I may never again get a chance to do anything like it.

Every time I traveled behind what used to be the Iron Curtain —which I did often—I took courage from the writers I met there, from the way in which they met with adversity, from their certainty of purpose, their clear knowledge of who the enemy was, and their conviction that they were fighting the good fight. It was not quite so clear on our side.

Now we're all together in a whited-out make-a-buck world. Of course I celebrate their liberation, but I know freedom will bring them a few unpleasant surprises. Now there are no more censors to beguile and despise. Instead, there will be international publishing chains, Western media, and Western popular culture, which will bury some of them deeper than the Communist monolith ever could.

The Communist state, like all the states representing political modernism—in that I include all the varieties of Marxism-Leninism, plus the Nazis and fascists—took art and literature seriously. Why? Because all such regimes had their origin in an attempt by a relatively small number of intellectuals to transform life into art. Everyone knows that Marx began life as a poet, that Mussolini was a novelist, that Hitler had an artistic temperament and aspirations—but none of that is necessarily important. What's important is that we see how little there is to any of these ideologies beyond their aesthetic appeal.

Rationally, none of them compute, least of all Marxism, which in spite of its self-declared scientism and materialism has more to do with epic poetry and eschatology than with economics or geopolitics. The fact that very brutal prosaic people made a good living out of these ideologies shouldn't blind us to their origins in that attempted fusion of life and art. As Americans we tend to laugh off art as something harmless to the point of triviality, but this is an oversight on our part. In relatively recent history, art is what replaced God for many people. People have been living, killing, and dying for art in some form throughout the twentieth century.

The greatest piece of graffiti I ever saw was on the wall of an eastern liberal arts college where I was once a writer in residence. "There are no metaphors," it said. A nice piece of intellectual horror. The ultimate reduction of that assertion means that no word or act can represent anything more than itself. A world without metaphor is a hermetic nightmare, utterly incomprehensible, without the possibility of humor or insight. Everything would happen once. No individual or event could be interpreted in the light of another.

There are metaphors, though. Language exists, although its connection to reality is an ongoing open question. Literature exists. We are able to entertain narratives about other people's lives, imaginary people's lives, and recognize elements familiar to us from our own hopes, fears, and dreams. Past lives, imaginary lives, are seen to contain messages for us, metaphorically speaking. Our understanding may draw upon them. This is the importance of fiction, that it offers meaning. People suffer and live out their lives; they would like their suffering and their lives to mean something. This is the point where fiction and nonfiction diverge in terms of what they provide. Everyone who has ever tried to convey a situation of any complexity knows how hard it is to keep facts from getting in the way of truth. The best way of preserving truth from the hickory-dickory-dock distractions of gross phenomenology is by inventing. In the world of fiction, the author is king, the dispenser of doom and grace, the world's foremost authority on anything within the confines of his fiction. But why should one person pay attention to the vain imaginings of another? What use is it?

The Western Bible assumes that human action matters, matters even on a cosmic scale. In its view of the universe, life is not an illusion, nor does the universe consist of endless cycles eternally replaying dreams. Its God, unlike many, is directly concerned with humanity. So our ancestors examined the strange stories in the Bible for their meaning, their message. They felt certain that every story was intended as a lesson and guide. For centuries we have been reflecting on peculiar things, like why Esau was disinherited and how Abraham could have been ready to sacrifice his son, and asking ourselves: What does this mean? What is at the heart of this strange story? What can I learn from it? How does it bear on my situation? Similarly, they examined Homer's stories and Plutarch's lives. The work that survives, survives only to the degree that it remains relevant, the degree to which it contains people and situations we recognize.

All our best works of literature descend from the assumptions bequeathed by our scriptures: they profess to detect the informing principles at the heart of human events. Life matters, lives matter, because earthly human history is the arena in which the universe acts out its consciousness of itself, displaying its nature as creation. Human annals become charged, they become an entity: history. And from history, from hearsay, from experience and memory, we make stories, not only to entertain ourselves but to inquire into the nature of life, to speculate about its meaning if it has one, to imagine the lives we left unled.

A few years ago, I was involved in an exchange with the author and critic William Gass, a writer whom I much admire. Gass wrote an essay in *Harper's Magazine* called "Goodness Knows Nothing of Beauty." His position was that art and morality were mutually distant, that art was somehow a glamorous cousin of crime. He seemed to present the image of two conflicting worlds, one pedestrian, prim, and boring; the other exciting and fantastical, a high wire. Art was on the wire, morality in its brown temple far below. In the course of his presentation Mr. Gass referred to Keats's principle, stated in his "Ode on a Grecian Urn," that truth is beauty and vice versa, as "a fatuous little motto." I disagreed and still do.

The short story and the novel developed in the Western world for certain historical reasons; its readers brought to their reading certain cultural assumptions. One, which goes back to the Old Testament, was that human life had an underlying significance, even a kind of purpose. Thus the events of a human life could be examined in the name of moral speculation.

Adam is supposed to have named all the creatures of the garden in order to assert his dominion over them. Language is a way of rationalizing life, subjecting the chaos around us to the control of grammar and reason. Fiction carries this process one step further by suggesting a moral relationship between people and things. Those who assert that good fiction can work its way free of moral valences are mistaken. From the most simplistic narrative with its good guys and bad guys to the most decadent and arcane poetry, wherever fiction exists, judgment is in progress. It's inescapable, built into the language, into the grammar.

Consider what Joseph Conrad has to say about the art of fiction in his preface to "The Nigger of the *Narcissus*":

> To snatch in a moment of courage, from the remorseless rush of time, a passing phase of life, is only the beginning of the task. The task approached in tenderness and faith is to hold up unquestioningly and without fear the rescued fragment before all eyes in the light of a sincere mood. It is to show its vibration, its color, its form, and through its movement, its form, and its color, reveal the substance of its truth—disclose its inspiring secret: the stress and passion within the core of each convincing moment. In a single-minded attempt of that kind, if one be deserving and fortunate, one may perchance attain to such clearness of sincerity that at last the presented

vision of regret or pity, of terror or mirth, shall awaken
in the hearts of the beholders that feeling of unavoidable
solidarity; of the solidarity in mysterious origin, in toil,
in joy, in hope, in uncertain fate, which binds men to
each other and all mankind to the visible world.

—Bohemian Club Library Notes, 1994

THE WAY THE WORLD IS

I was born in Brooklyn, on President Street, the border of
Park Slope and South Brooklyn, in 1937. My mother was
a schoolteacher in the New York public school system. My father worked for the old New Haven Railroad. My mother's
family had been on the Brooklyn waterfront, working on the
tugboats, for several generations. When I was still small, my
parents separated. I moved with my mother to Manhattan and
grew up then in Yorkville and on the Upper West Side. My
mother was schizophrenic, and when I was about five she was
hospitalized for a while. I went to St. Ann's at Lexington and
Seventy-Seventh Street, which later became Archbishop Mol-
loy High School. St. Ann's was somewhere between a boarding
school and an orphanage, run by the Marist Brothers. I was at
St. Ann's until I was nine, and then I was out again.

I lived with my mother in SROs and rooming houses mostly
on the West Side. They weren't as bad in those days as they
later became, so I can't really say that I was in there with junkies. There was more variety in the poverty of New York at that
time—layers and layers. It was very interesting to live on the

West Side when it was only seedy, before it became totally le-thal. Now it's much more dangerous and less interesting, which seems kind of unfair.

I stayed with the Marist Brothers, as if I couldn't get enough of them. I stayed right through high school—almost through high school, actually, because I never did quite finish high school. I never got a diploma from them, and yet they have this capacity to find me—and I'm not very easy to find. But they always find me, I don't know how. They send me pitches for donations, and they send me the class list, which I am not on. They never seem to put it together; they're always try-ing to awaken my nostalgia by sending me these class lists on which my name does not appear. Every once in a while I get their alumni notes, and they always get the names of my books wrong. Such prizes as I've won, they get the names of my books wrong. It's completely scrambled. I just really don't want these people finding me. I go through a week-long depression when I see something from them in the mail. I really try to put all that *far* behind me, and it's a tremendous bringdown to see their little coat of arms with its beehive and its corny Latin motto. It awakens a kind of panic, as if there's nothing I can do to get that out of my life.

The Marists were savage, but in those days I don't know where they stood in terms of relative savagery—you were al-ways hearing about some order of Irish troglodytes down the road, you know, who were actually permitted to use flails. They certainly slapped people around right and left; it was very dreary, very tiresome. But, of course, you assumed this was the way the world was supposed to be. Where else would anybody tell you to offer your humiliation to the Holy Ghost? That always stayed with me. One of my earliest anxieties was whether I was going to be lined up outside the prefect's room at night to get my hands slapped with a razor strop. There *was* a strop, and he actually did sharpen his straight razor on it, and he had these little kids of five and six lined up outside his room, to hit them on the hands.

It's very hard to escape that take on the world. And when you come right down to it, the world is like that, after all. I mean, first you think the world isn't like that, and you feel very liberated to find that it isn't. But after a while you work your way to the point where you discover that actually *is* the way the world is. So the preparation probably had some usefulness after all, some grim utility. There are good things that you get from a Catholic upbringing, although it's the hard way to get them. Then again, life is not supposed to be easy. Anything you get, you get the hard way. In some ways, Catholicism is very good training for making the best of a hard world, which is what you have to do. That is what they're telling you, on a certain level.

My mother was Scottish and Irish, so her family was religiously mixed; I think my father's was too. But she really foisted Catholicism on me. Her father was a Presbyterian, her mother was Irish Catholic. She liked the idea of Catholicism. She thought it gave kids something to adhere to—she was quite right—so she sort of elected me to be the house Catholic. As soon as I stopped going to church, when I was about fifteen or sixteen, she immediately stopped. My high school years were a complete disaster. I don't know whether it's the result of my experiences as a kid or just because of my temperament generally, but

I was never able to come to terms with formal education. My punishment was to become a professor in later life. I went on to teach writing and literature at Stanford, UC Irvine, Harvard, Princeton, Amherst, and the University of Hawaii. Irvine was the most fun, because the students were already writers, some of whom had published in small magazines and were willing to work day jobs as waiters and mechanics and cabbies to support themselves in writing fiction. I had a lot of fun with them and actually took them to the racetrack—to Hollywood Park—to cruise for dialogue. I was always a writer in residence; my only real degree was a high school equivalency diploma I got while I was in the navy.

I joined the navy when I was seventeen, in 1955. I was a radio operator, first attached to a tactical air control squadron in the Norfolk Naval Air Station in Virginia, and then I went to sea. I was in the amphibious force and was finally rated as a journalist. I was transferred to a ship called the USS *Arneb*, an attack transport that was part of the 1958 Antarctic expedition. That trip to Antarctica took most of my last year in the navy and passed the time very interestingly. Now that I'm able to think about it with some detachment, I really had quite a good time in the navy. It just never occurred to me at the time. In 1956 in the Mediterranean, we saw the air attack on Port Said by the French during the bombing of Suez. We got caught in the harbor and were sitting right in the middle of that. We were not a target, but the Egyptians in the harbor around us, and everything that could float, came as close to us as they possibly could. We had this enormous American flag, which we were flying and which we illuminated at night. The harbor was being shot up indiscriminately; there was no attempt that

I could determine to find military targets. The firing was coming from flights of Mystère jets.

I got out after three years and started at NYU, Washington Square College. My wife worked in the Figaro, back when it was really the Figaro, when Gregory Corso used to read there. Before she worked at the Figaro, she was a guidette at the RCA Building, and she had another job at the Seven Arts coffeehouse, which was between Forty-Second and Forty-Third streets on Ninth Avenue. That was a great spot, where all sorts of celebrated events took place. Kerouac was very often there, Ginsberg read there, Corso read there, and LeRoi Jones, as he was known then. It was a great scene. I think I always had literary aspirations of one kind or another, even when I was in high school. I had read *On the Road* when I was in the navy. If I'm not mistaken, I think my mother had turned me on to it. I think I'm probably the only person who ever read *On the Road* at his mother's suggestion.

Also, my mother was really kind of anticlerical. I was the solid citizen of that duo, and I took Catholicism much more seriously than she did. It was just not in her temperament to be religious. She went to church only when she went with me. I think she went only to please me, whereas I thought I was going to please her. So finally we were both going to accommodate each other, and we both quit when I did. But I took it seriously enough to imprint quite deeply a lot of aspects and attitudes that I think are religious and Catholic. Also, I left it—at least I abandoned any attempt to practice it—when it was still unreconstructed, unenlightened, post-Tridentine, 1950s Catholicism, so the Church that I left really no longer exists. But I certainly had made an association between ethical systems and religion—an association that I think a great many Catholics make—to the degree that I still tend to associate ethical coherence and religion. It's very hard for me to disassociate the two, and I think that's a very important philosophical attitude. I have trouble with nonreligious humanism as an ethical system. It's not that I don't understand it; it simply doesn't have any meaning that I can respond to. I mean the kind of secular humanism that merely tells you to do good, as opposed to its being tied to ultimates.

That kind of secular humanism tends to make you not a bad citizen if you're brought up that way, of course. Because if, on the other hand, you lose your religious anchor, then you tend to go into utter nihilism—it certainly is an option—and you tend to go on asking the kinds of broad and total questions that you got in trouble for asking in catechism class. And you don't get any better answers from a humanistic society than you did from a dogmatic religion—which I think is good, actually. Because there is a certain aspect of Catholicism that, to me, is its most appealing and attractive tradition, and that is the tradition of Catholic skepticism, which I associate with people like Montaigne and Erasmus and Pascal. I think that's a very intellectually wholesome tradition, and I can still identify with it to some degree.

Perhaps because I left Catholicism at a relatively early time, I never really tried to make it relevant, and in a way this kept up its appeal for me. I never tried to live as a Catholic adult, which means that it can be there as a kind of illicit love for me, as a forbidden pleasure, because I never tried to live it out in a responsible, day-to-day way. So there's a kind of real-life Catholicism, as opposed to my nostalgia trip of long-vanished

Catholic comics, like *Treasure Chest* and Chuck White and all that stuff—the only secret plans and worlds that we all are party to. This new Catholicism is vaguely left wing and feminist: folk Masses. All the scorn of the ex-Catholics that I know is focused on the folk Mass as an exercise in utter fatuousness. It seemed like common sense at the time, but it turns out to have been a real mistake.

In 1962 I got a Stegner Fellowship to the writing program at Stanford. So I happened to be in Palo Alto at the right time when this strange scene was going on with Ken Kesey and the rest, and one aspect of it, of course, was psychedelics—taking acid. I think this impelled me to reexamine my attitudes toward religion, because my experiences with acid were very much charged with religion. I guess it would have been strange if they weren't. I was taking acid, and I was taking it seriously. I felt that I was consciously developing a view of the world, and when I had these religious experiences as a result of taking acid, I really felt that they demanded to be reconciled with my intellectual attitudes generally. So it made me less able to develop a totally secular intellectual system of my own. I again had to make allowance for the numinous—if not the supernatural, at least the nonrational, the extrarational. I think this probably served as a process through which my adolescent religious attitudes were transformed but somehow reinforced. My adult secular life was subverted again by something very intrusive and very strong. I began to have to afford to the extrarational a certain importance in terms of how I saw things, and as a result these religious areas of experience came to be reflected in my writing. The drug experiences forced me not to dismiss those things as simply part of my childhood gear but to realize that I had to continue to think about and deal with them.

A couple of the acid trips I had that were most memorable brought me into confrontations with aspects of things like God—or the absence of or presence of. I felt, as the result of one time that I took acid in Wales sometime in the mid-sixties, that I really was experiencing God, and I don't know where that came from. It wasn't particularly Catholic, this experience; it was as close to that celebrated oceanic experience as I've ever personally been. So I realized that I was not going to build a personal system or live in a personal system that was free of those concepts, and so I don't.

There was a night in 1963 in San Francisco when a bunch of us had bought a lot of peyote and refined it, went to a pharmacy and bought a lot of plastic capsules, and put this refined peyote in the capsules—and I swallowed twelve of them. We piled into a Volkswagen bus and headed into the city. We saw John Coltrane at the Jazz Gallery and later went out onto Broadway, and that was where I totally lost it. The rest of the people I was with went from seeing Coltrane to catching Lenny Bruce at the hungry i, and then Jonathan Winters. So they saw the sixties in one great night. But unfortunately, I was not with the main band of people, because I had completely come apart watching John Coltrane, and I left because I was seeing the music, which was kind of disconcerting. I just couldn't stop seeing it, and that began to get to me. So I went out, and what was outside, of course, just around the corner on Broadway, was Chinatown. I had a tough time with that—I mean, I knew it was Chinatown, but I found it altogether too visual, that being the nature of mescaline.

You do get to a point where you expect, as one of your satisfactions, an experience of the transcendent—at least you acquire a need to connect yourself with something transcendent. The result is, of course, that things never are quite enough after that, so you have to go higher. It's not for nothing that Marx calls religion the opiate of the people. How does that whole quote go? "Religion is the opium of the masses, the heart of a heartless world." I can't remember it precisely.* It's funny how the diagram becomes basically one of salvation: you have to achieve salvific experience. Suddenly the only thing you'll settle for at the end of your evening is a kind of ultimate contact with God. That becomes what you're going for all the time, what you expect from music, say—and in a way, it's not a bad thing to expect from the arts. It's what you get a sense of in Beckett. You find it in all the best things, somehow, that sense of being in touch with the numinous, with something transcendent. In a way, it's vain and foolish and sort of spoils everything for you because you're expecting too much—that kind of spiritual orgasm is what you're always going for. But on the other hand, when you do get it, it wakens that sense.

Finally my attraction for Catholicism remains sentimental. I'm never really able to approach the idea of a serious intellectual commitment to Catholicism or Christianity, although I think it's intriguing how belief has been redefined. The Catholicism of the fifties was an inheritor of that rather mere-

---

*The quotation, from the introduction of *The Critique of the Hegelian Philosophy of Right* (1844) by Karl Marx, reads in full: "Religion is the sigh of the oppressed creature, the feelings of a heartless world, just as it is the spirit of unspiritual conditions. It is the opium of the people."

tricious, pseudo-realist, pseudo-materialist Catholicism of the nineteenth century, when they became absurdly literal with things like the Immaculate Conception. They reified these religious notions and made them mechanistic, real things in a totally fractured way that simply was not going to bear examination. One of the interesting things in Catholicism now, as I perceive it, is the success with which they have come down from that stance and have been able to say, Look, these are entities of which we cannot speak very precisely because we don't understand them, they belong to another dimension. That's a sophisticated attitude toward those things, which has its appeal.

Those of us who left the Church in its unreconstructed phase probably ask ourselves every once in a while, Well, on the new terms, as they've been redefined, can we perhaps accept this now so we can do something sort of neat, like go to church on Sunday and see what that would be like? Or go to church on Christmas, or whatever? But I have never really come to the point of seriously contemplating that.

I certainly find myself being scornful of such former Catholics as I see going up and getting born again for some Southern person in a polyester suit, but apparently there are numbers of former Catholics who have been born again—which, of course, is a very un-Catholic thing. You only do it once in Catholicism. Then there is also charismatic Catholicism, which I have no experience in. When I was living in Honolulu in 1979 and 1980, one of the Catholic churches there used to have joint services with a Pentecostalist church—I mean, this was sort of Holy Rolling. Nuns and seminarians really got off on this. It was a chance to carry on and speak in tongues and the whole number, which seems on the face of it to be the very opposite of everything that Catholicism is all about. I guess it was forbidden fruit for Catholics. They got to sing "The Old Rugged Cross," and they got to talk in tongues and things like that.

Given its way of conducting early-childhood education, you might be excused for thinking that Catholicism is a particularly violent religion. Certainly there is an intimate connection between violence and Catholicism, because Catholicism partakes of all the melodrama of history. If you look at the iconography of Catholicism—just think of the history of European painting from Giotto on—the violence in Catholic iconography is limitless. Just think of all those people carrying around the evidence of their violent deaths, carrying around their various crosses, their grills, their gibbets, the guy walking around with the knife through his head, Peter Martyr. There it is. Obviously, if you think about the iconography and the principal mysteries of the rosary, you have an awful lot of blood, an awful lot of violence. On the other hand, that's the way the world is, too. So it's appropriate, in a way, that Catholicism and its iconography reflect all this, because the world, after all, *is* like that. It is full of violence, and religion would have to incorporate that. It tells you that you have to accept this; it tells you that the world is this way. Catholic pacifism is a fairly new development in modern Catholicism. It was a small minority in the time of Dorothy Day [cofounder of the Catholic Worker movement in the thirties]; it's a larger minority now, apparently.

But you certainly were conditioned to accept all the violence, to accept war as a given, and, of course, to look on death as something vaguely ... death was certainly better than sex. Death was something that could be more comfortably incorporated into Catholicism. There was a way in which I think fifties Catholicism definitely could be said to be pro-death. If it came down to life or death, death was undoubtedly the more virtuous aspect. Dying was an approved Catholic thing to do. You could exist totally within the Catholic culture as a dead person. It was a kind of total resolution of Catholicism. Death was better than fucking, certainly, because it was eminently Catholic. You could be done up with rosaries and tombstones and crosses and holy water. All the accoutrements of death were absolutely orthodox. But sex, on the other hand, was unacceptable, and the Church was not with you. Whereas it was totally with you in death, and you were with it. As a corpse, you could be an ideal Catholic.

War was generally approved of by the Church, partly because it contributed to people dying, which was always a good thing. I don't think that's unfair. There's a level on which dying was really approved of, practically as a virtuous act in and of itself. It was good for religion because it turned people's minds to the ultimate reckoning. But I don't know if that's more true in Catholicism than in any other religion. Certainly it's more true in Catholicism than it is in Unitarianism, but that doesn't make me feel any more warmly toward Unitarianism, which to me is the worship of a potted palm.

The way I see it consciously, speaking of my own work, I address the things that frighten me. Writing is what I do to deal with the world and things generally; that's my response to the implied question of living. So I would say that violence is in my writing because it's in the world. Whether being a Catholic

conditions my interior world, and consequently my perceptions, so that I'm more attuned to violence, I don't know. It's
certainly possible.

In Mexico and Central America you have this bizarre cou-
pling of the machismo sense with the religious impulse and
with the desire for "physical humiliations," as they're called.
This *penitente* syndrome is prevalent among certain Hispanic
Catholics, particularly the so-called Spanish Americans of
New Mexico, and consists of torturing themselves—literally carrying crosses, being scourged—something the official
Church has been trying to suppress all over Mexico, Central
America, and the American Southwest. Those people seem to
have worked toward some kind of synthesis of the sun dance
and the Stations of the Cross. It's what they used to call mor-
tification or self-flagellation, and it flourishes in New Mexico.
It's as though they're inclined to compete with Christ to see
who can take it more.

That is what is going on in the mountaintop scene near the
end of *Children of Light*. That's what Lu Anne is doing: she's
trying to torture herself into some kind of sanity. She's trying
to destroy her own madness by torturing herself, which is what
people sometimes do. She also gives herself the stigmata; that's
in her bag of tricks. That passage refers directly to the Stations of the Cross, and I did call it "The Ascent of Mt. Carmel"
when it was excerpted in the *Paris Review*. I wasn't doing it in
a deliberate, ongoing way. But I invoke it, sure. I'm making a
connection between her personal, self-destructive perversity,
which is partly sexual, and the implied perversity of Catholicism generally, of the Catholic experience, which has within it
a perverse, masochistic element, certainly for women.

One of the things that you see everywhere in Sicily—and this is not part of *Children of Light*, because it's something that I've acquired since, but it makes the point—is Santa Lucia, the great saint in Sicily. There's a shrine to her in the cathedral in Siracusa, and what represents her iconographically in Sicily is principally a goblet and a pair of eyes. She's supposed to have gouged her eyes out rather than get married. This isn't orthodox, because I don't think it can be, but in the popular story she's supposed to have cut her eyes out and sent them in a goblet to the guy who was her suitor, to discourage him, which presumably it did. That makes the point that within Catholic iconography—which, whether it's supposed to be or not, is a large part of the sense of Catholicism itself—there's so much violence, so much suffering and masochism and perversity. And certainly that is one element of Lu Anne's perversity at that point: she's going to transform herself into a martyr. There is in Catholicism this prospect of death as a kind of triumph —after all, martyrs are supposed to get the crown. That's a way of winning: by dying you triumph. In Catholicism, as I've already implied, the easiest and most successful thing you can do is die. We used to joke when I was in high school that the perfect Christian life was to graduate from that place and go to St. John's or Fordham and become an insurance actuary and be buried in Calvary Cemetery. That was the total Christian life.

Some of the same kinds of parallels, incidentally, turn up in *Dog Soldiers* and, of course, in *A Flag for Sunrise*, which has an awful lot of religion in it—just plain, flat-out religion and martyrdom and so forth. Not only is Sister Justin Catholic, but Holliwell is, and I guess Pablo is too. Well, purely pro forma— he's a pagan, a pre-Columbian. But he always thinks everything

that happens to him is there to enlighten him. He thinks he's
on the receiving end of this ever-unfolding process of enlight-
enment. He's always trying to get off, and he thinks life is being
conducted for his edification. If he could only find the right
people who didn't keep turning him around. Poor Pablo, he's
such bad news—that's the secret of life that he never discovers,
that he's just terrible bad news.

Another aspect is the fact that my characters take all those
drugs and drink all that alcohol. I really have to cut it out. They
just go right ahead and do it. It approaches self-parody—I really have to watch it. They're always trying to put something
between them and the thorns of life itself, to live in a world
other than the one they're presented with. In a way, they do
a lot of my drug taking and drinking for me. They do a lot of
things for me so that I don't have to do them, all that dying and
rolling around. In a sense they're trying to find transcendence,
and they have bad habits, and what's the difference?

What takes the place of those things now that I've cut down
on my own indulgence? Supposedly, the mature satisfactions
of life—and as soon as I find out what they are, then that's
what I'll be into next, I'm sure. Any day now.

I think growing up Catholic, taking it seriously, compels you
to live on a great many levels. It's not totally dead to believe in
a whole lot of unlikely, preposterous things. It enriches your
sense of humor if there are so many unlikely things that you
are trying to juggle in your spiritual life at a tender age. At
a certain point, there's something touching and gallant and
funny about the situation of being a kid and having to deal
with eternity and all these absurd and monstrous concepts. I

think there's an inherent comic aspect to all that which is inescapable. That probably is the cause of the specifically Catholic sense of humor. You could certainly find enough material within Catholicism to keep you performing for years and years and years.

When I once said, "In a sense I'm a theologian, and so far as I know, the only one," I meant that in terms of American writers. There is just more religion and more religious questioning in my work. I probably deal more with religion—there is more overt Catholicism in the stuff that I write about than in most writers' work that I am aware of, except Mary Gordon. I felt at various times that I was taking seriously questions that for most educated people were no longer serious questions, and I ascribed that to my Catholic background. I mean specifically the question of whether or not there is a God, or whether or not you can talk about life and its most important elements in religious terms, the question of the absence of God—Heidegger's postulating God as an absence—all these things are, for the most part, not taken too seriously by educated people. I talk to my editor, for example, or most of the people I know, and they aren't concerned with religious questions, not in quite the same way that I am. They might ask the same questions, but not in the same terms that I ask them. That's what led me to make that statement.

I'm concerned with the idea of there not being a God as a kind of dynamic absence that is a constant challenge. Now, if it never meant anything to you, then obviously it isn't a challenge, it's just the way it is. As a result of having been a Catholic, I'm acutely aware of the difference between a world in which there's a God and a world in which there isn't. For people who either have not taken religion seriously or have not been exposed to religion, the question of whether or not there's a God is an obviated question, a trivial or silly question. It's not a silly question for me. I don't see how anybody who took seriously their Catholic upbringing can be comfortable as an atheist—you'd have to doubt that, too.

The question of why there seem to be so few Catholic painters and visual artists may have a different answer. There is a strong element of people with immigrant backgrounds, first- or second-generation working class, among Catholics, and working-class people as a rule are not oriented toward the plastic or visual arts. Catholic education doesn't go out of its way to look for visual artists; you don't feel reinforced in your pursuit of the arts. Where I went to school, the whole of artistic endeavor in human history was something you tried to cram into the college preparation course when you prepared for the Regents scholarship test. They just fed you all this information that you were supposed to memorize, without actually exposing you to the contaminating influences of the art itself. Basically they were saying, Here's a whole lot of stuff that the Gentiles believe and various shibboleths and names that you ought to know because they'll be on the test that the Jews will give us. It was all totally external from life, from the course of our being prepared for our careers with Hartford Accident and Indemnity and for Calvary Cemetery.

The intellectual world that underlies contemporary secular humanism, the intellectual substructure supporting our friends and contemporaries who don't worry about God and so forth, has really been exhausted. Logical positivism has really been exhausted. It's been taken as far as it can go—now, in terms of philosophy and even science, we've come up against the exhaustion of that as a reference point. We have now got to deal with these questions again; they will reintroduce themselves. We're coming into another period of uncertainty. We're coming to the end of a world order, the middle-class world order of the nineteenth century. The empires and that optimistic, materialist, relatively comfortable world are breaking apart. Of course, all generations think they're living at the end of a cycle. But certainly it's happening that the empires are breaking down, that the European domination of the world is coming to an end.

As a result of all this, I do think that these questions are presenting themselves to be dealt with, and they will do so increasingly in this country and other countries. We see the rise of the born-again evangelists—they're answering a need. They're taking advantage—some of them, I think, quite cynically—of a need in ordinary people who feel lost and disoriented. Secular positivism is not giving them anything, and they're lonely and lost and unhappy, and so they want to engage in that orgy of emotionalism and be born again. They're looking for the childhood that they lost and the certainties that they lost with that. It's probably happening less in Catholicism than in Protestantism, where the new evangelism is speaking to a need, and in Judaism, where there's a kind of neo-Hasidism and a return to orthodoxy that's visibly going on. Catholicism alone is still struggling toward a secular consciousness. It's still discovering the folk Mass—it's discovering the sixties. The Church can handle them twenty years later. It's kind of like my old school can handle me thirty years later. They just couldn't deal with me at the time.

—In *Once a Catholic*, 1987

CAPTURE

In this teeming world, each of us is condemned to a fundamental solitude. We live much of our lives in the isolation of the self. A primal mystery separates one human being from another, and in the end we can only imagine our way across this gulf. The earliest and most important lessons we learn concern how to make ourselves at home in a world whose most significant quality is the presence of other people.

What is human in the world is what is most familiar, yet human nature and human motivation and action remain the things we argue and ponder most and by which we are most often bewildered. Our moral systems tell us to identify ourselves with our neighbors, but we quickly recognize others as an ambiguous presence, sometimes even as a threat to life and safety rather than a source of fellowship and support. Human nature, it is finally agreed, is very enigmatic. "Know thyself," we say, the implication being that this helps. We say, "The heart has its reasons."

In our struggle to resolve the perplexities of identity, selfhood, otherness, we are forever contemplating ourselves physically. Hamlet stares into the eyeless skull of Yorick, looking for the meaning of his own impending death. Broken kings call for a looking glass. Readers of modern history turn to the photographic sections that now accompany most books and stare into the impassive faces of victims, failed dreamers, and mass murderers. What are the readers looking for there? What's going to be in a picture? This gauleiter has a cruel mouth or else he looks surprisingly benign. That general has a haunted look. A diplomat smiles super-serviceably. Most of the photographs displayed are banal commercial shots intended to depersonalize and hence conventionalize their subjects within a limited repertory of acceptable poses: brave soldier, man of affairs, happy bride.

The human image has had profound associations since the beginning of time. It was widely held that it reflected the image of the gods. In the Hebrew tradition the belief that the divine likeness had been stamped upon man made human life sacred. All images were forbidden to be reproduced as a guard against idolatry, but the prohibition against rendering the human form was designed to prevent this holiest of images from being debased. The Lord was mighty beyond measure. The earth was his footstool. He was not to be "captured."

The idea of portraiture as "capture" is not gratuitous. An aversion to being photographed is not confined to tribal people outside Western culture. It is an instinctive reaction of many people walking our city streets, not all of whom are on the lam. All the socialization in the world cannot remove completely the partly threatening nature of the Other. The possession or contemplation of another person's image really does provide us with a degree of power over that person: it is the power that our insight can bring to bear, our opportunity to try to understand the personality depicted. What we understand is always a little less threatening, a dread presence is more manageable, if we have the chance to penetrate its mystery. So our fascination with portraits can be seen as yet another way of confronting the old problem of Otherness.

The compulsion to portray, like so many other impulses that are humanistic and life-affirming, may thus be shown to have some root in the ground of primordial combat. And it is strange how much art has something about it that is vaguely suggestive of conflict—the very word "art" and words associated with it can be quickly construed into synonyms for guile, deception, and trickery. Illusion is understandably suspect, and art is nothing if not illusion: it involves pretending, substituting a likeness for the thing itself.

Art might also be defined as the reduction of the things of life to the comprehensible. As an expression of the human soul, it forever obsesses over the human problem of Self and Other. Even at its most transcendental—during the ages of faith in the West—it never ceased its relentless examination of the human condition. The great religious paintings of Christianity were as much concerned with the mysteries of human salvation as with those of divinity for its own sake. The contemplation of a crucifixion scene isn't likely to remove us psychically from the plane of human suffering, human cruelty, and human self-sacrifice. It will spiritualize those things, help us to share them, invite us to believe that the very universe involves itself in them, but such a work of art will still have as its ultimate subject the destiny of human souls.

One of the things we will always require of art is an element of recognition. To succeed in its purpose, a painting, a photograph, a poem, or a piece of music must elicit from the observer a certain complicity. As an example of this principle, let's examine an extremely modest, not to say vulgar, art form: the joke. Jokes aren't often sublime, but it's usually quite easy to tell whether they're any good or not. If they're good, they're funny and we laugh at them. Otherwise they're not, and we don't.

Why is a good joke funny? Why should it produce that curious simian spasm called laughter? What makes it work? A good joke calls forth from us a certain recognition of the conditions of our existence. The implicit punch line to every joke is: That's how it is! All jokes work the same way, on the principle of recognition. And all art works the same way.

From the oldest jazz records available to the frostiest postmodernist jazz on the digital discs of today, if the performance was recorded live and the audience is on the track, the same one-word response keeps resounding, greeting a solo or an ingenious piece of collective improvisation: "Yeah." That's how it is. That's life, trouble, good times, or love. Recognition is everything.

To say so much is to say that all art has truth as its object. That part of art which takes humanity as its subject will be bound to pursue truths about the nature of humankind and to compel recognition of these truths. It will not be enough to state the obvious. The observer, reader, listener must be led to the necessary recognition of truth through the mediation of the work, and led, moreover, to discover it for himself or herself, as something fresh and new, as an insight. If Narcissus had been able to look at himself every day for a month, instead of only once in a pool, he might have found himself with a lot to think about. He might have saved himself with a few second thoughts.

Definitions of truth vary. During the long history of art, artists' attempts to depict, describe, define humankind have been guided by different philosophies. In some periods the individual mattered less than in others. The classical world's way of approaching the truth about humanity was to render the ideal; the ideal human form was *truer* than the bodies people walked around with because it was the "original" beside which ordinary bodies could be seen to display flaws. To the classical world perfection was truth, and truth was available to mortals only through art.

Two thousand years later, imperial court painters like Jacques-Louis David might render the unprepossessing Bonaparte as a physically beautiful, dynamic youth. David's flattery also had philosophical support, because it could be held that the "true" Napoleon was not the small, sallow man in the unadorned uniform but the radiant, godlike genius whom it was the painter's business to discern.

Regardless of philosophy, the enterprise was the same: to display to humankind an element of truth about its nature. This was to be done by rendering the artificial impression of a human presence, to make people seeing only paint or stone or mere words believe that they were experiencing a person.

Certain artists have always excelled at this, and it is interesting, although difficult, to consider why. It has to do, I think, with a certain way of looking at the world. The artist who deals in recapitulating what is human has to be a good listener and a good watcher. He must command the facility to identify and examine all the elements, large and small—all the contradictions and passions that together make up the most ordinary person. In a way, he must deny the existence of such a thing as an ordinary person. He must understand that clichés do not exist in nature, not even in human nature, but only in art. No matter how embittered he may be, he must finally be in sympathy with humankind.

All this, of course, is the easy part. His skill as an observer has now to be equaled by his skill in execution. Knowing the dynamics of an arm in motion and the revelations in a complacent glance, he has to get them down. Just as he understands that a human personality is made up of many disparate elements, he must understand that portrayals are also composed in multiples. There are all the questions to be resolved and all the decisions to be made. What to put in? What to leave out?

The portraitist must also know his enemies. He has to relentlessly fight conventionalization, that eternal enemy of portraiture, the breeder of kitsch and lies. Even if he works in a country where the conventionalization of human nature is demanded by the authorities, he must fight against it secretly or transcend it.

Above all, he must know the difference between sympathy for his subject and sentimentality. Sentimentality kills in art; it destroys everything dignified and honorable about humanity. It insults and degrades sentiment.

The artist who represents the human must realize that only vigilance and discipline will keep him away from things like conventionalization and sentimentality. Modestly, he must also realize the tremendous importance of the work he does and the service he provides.

The humanist artist is indeed a hunter, out to capture. Like a tribesman snatching a salmon from a creek, he needs to be quick and deft, able to lay hands on a moment. Taking hold of it, he lifts it up against the sky. It is beautiful, all colors, sinuous, virtually perfect. We recognize the beauty of it and the hunter's skill.

There is nothing like the capture of a human moment. Going to some of the oldest literature still available, consider Genesis 4:9, where God accuses Cain.

"Where is Abel, thy brother?" the Lord demands.

"And he said: I know not. Am I my brother's keeper?"

The moment of this discourse stays with us. Its authenticity reaches us across time and myth and all of human history. Cain's voice—sullen, sarcastic, and bitter—is a voice that compels us to recognition. We recognize a lonely, self-pitying, guilty adolescent faced with the consequences of a bloody big mistake. Through the verisimilitude of Cain's voice we are put in mind of all such adolescents. Beyond that we are made to recognize ourselves: we, the tribe of actual and potential Cains.

Among all the tricks of art there is none greater than the mediation of human identity, the illusion of life being lived in time. All those captured moments become part of our personal history. All great portrayals combine theater and meditation; around them hang the richest silences in the world. They place before our insight a wealth of recognitions. Peasants, gentlemen and ladies, doges, and Grand Inquisitors are there for us, commanded to perform the drama of their personalities.

At the core of human portraiture lies a great irony. Looking at Titian's portrait of Aretino, we learn so much about the man. At the same time we are learning how little we can ever know about anyone. In the greatest art, questions and answers are suspended units, connected but never meant to be resolved, in an ongoing process like that chase on the Grecian urn. Titian tells us more about human nature than we can absorb and leaves us the more questioning. The sixteenth-century Florentine painter Bronzino's *Portrait of a Young Man* seems to be explaining its subject while in a sense mocking both him and us. Who does the young man, smooth and arrogant, think he is? What does he know about anything? And we who examine Bronzino's picture, what do we think we are looking at? What assurance can we bring to bear to match the youth's hauteur? The painting seems to suggest that we and this insolent young courtier somehow deserve each other.

In Albrecht Dürer's self-portrait the process of the artist capturing life is itself depicted. Dürer doesn't actually show himself painting, but he faces the world beyond his picture like a man looking into a mirror. He is a young, confident artist; a sly, observing aspect to his features makes the work appear to lack the gravity of the aging Rembrandt's self-portrait. At the same time there is a suggestion of wonder, and even timidity, as though he could not continue this bold confrontation with himself or face his own steady gaze for very long. It appears he has decided to be pleased with himself, but his expression is questioning. He has reversed the game and rendered Self as Other. Before him lie all the arcana of humanity. Like Rembrandt's self-portrait, the Dürer painting might well bear the inscription that, centuries later, Paul Gauguin was to write on one of his own examinations of the human condition: "Who are we? Where do we come from? Where are we going?"

At the end we get the mystery back. What can people know

about people? How much is out there to see? After all the haunted canvases of the great painters, and all the living prose of the great writers and poets, after the Titians, the Botticellis, the Dickenses and the Shakespeares, after Balzac, Brady, and Vermeer, the most significant element of humanity remains what is unknowable.

Art will forever remain, as André Malraux said it was, the voice of silence. It is what we oppose to the silence around us. It is the order that we dare to impose on things, finding ourselves, as we do, just *out here* — out here in this vast, apparently indifferent chain of phenomenology.

As dreams are to the waking mind, art is to human history. It is something vital and irreplaceable. Humanity must always be the principal subject of art. Our selves are the units through which the conscious universe perceives itself.

—In *Legacy of Light,* 1987

ON MALCOLM LOWRY

Two thousand nine is the centennial year of Malcolm Lowry, the British novelist and poet, whose extraordinary novel *Under the Volcano* appeared in 1947. Lowry's first version of it was a loosely constructed story about Britons who witness a violent crime in Mexico. Over ten years, much of it spent in a series of shanties on a beach in British Columbia, Lowry worked it into one of the great novels of the twentieth century. For many readers it ranks with the best work of Joyce, Conrad, and Hemingway. Without question Lowry was one of the writers whose work possessed the elegance and insight to define its time. In fact, the work of artists like Lowry does more than represent the era in which it was composed. When we call their work "defining," we recognize that to a degree it is the era, a historical act within it, an aspect of its consciousness and conscience.

Under the Volcano was rejected by twelve different publishers before being accepted by Reynal & Hitchcock in New York and Jonathan Cape in London. It was Malcolm Lowry's second published novel and the last he lived to see in print. All of

Lowry's writing had an element of the surreal, furthered by its psychological intensity and maybe by Lowry's regular intoxication. It was autobiographical at the same time, and his life was adventurous. While still a schoolboy he shipped as an ordinary seaman to the Far East, an upper-middle-class youth from a world quite different from that of his shipmates. Before entering Cambridge University he went to sea again, as a stoker aboard a Norwegian freighter. So long as his youthful energy lasted, he was an avid traveler. Later, as alcoholism overtook him, he might better be described as a wanderer.

Lowry was born in 1909 in Cheshire, the son of a well-off cotton broker. He began taking his own writing seriously in boarding school. From adolescence, it seems, Lowry had the duties of a writer thrust upon him. In 1929, before most people thought of writing as something in which someone might take instruction, he went to Cambridge, Massachusetts, to study with Conrad Aiken, the American poet and novelist. It might not have worked; one good writer does not always have much to say to another. Lowry went because he had read Aiken's *Blue Voyage* and been struck with admiration for it. Sometimes it does work, though, and Lowry's instinct was sound. He spent the summer with the Aikens and they became lifelong friends. In 1933 he published *Ultramarine*, his first novel—lyrical, a bit rich, and influenced by Aiken, but giving promise of an extraordinary career. It would be twenty-four years before he published another.

At Cambridge his writing had impressed his fellow undergraduates as well as his teachers. He developed an interest in music and became an accomplished jazz guitarist. During his university years he discovered cinema, and he knew movies backwards and forwards. His work showed it—in the witty references to film titles and in his storytelling method. The influence was an enhancement in Lowry's case. If his fortunes had been a little different, he might have ended up in Hollywood like any number of other literary Englishmen of the period. His second wife, Margerie Bonner, was an aspiring film actress, and she collaborated with him in writing an uncommissioned, finally unfinished screenplay for F. Scott Fitzgerald's *Tender Is the Night.* It's a bit of a mystery what led him to try this. His own work might have told him that it was impossible.

No less a director than John Huston established, in his 1984 film of *Under the Volcano,* that a collaboration between himself, Chekhov, and Shakespeare had not the remotest chance of rendering into moving pictures such a dense skein of gorgeous language, with its echoes, unconscious and conscious rhymes, considered dissonances, double and triple associations. Nor could it present Lowry's high and low references to just about every level of expression in English or the psychological intensity of the longing, the silent struggle with despair, it depicts. As the pros say in the picture business, How do you photograph that?

When people talk about Lowry, the first thing they talk about is his second novel. The next thing they mention is his alcoholism. Sometimes it's the other way around. We can speculate that in a not uncommon irony it was his hunger for experience, for life more abundant, that drove him to addiction. It's no surprise that experience failed him. Let's say his own experience did not speak well for the writing life. It taught him about suffering. He got to see a lot of the world, and he got to see the inside of a couple of dipso wards—the next institution he passed time in after graduating from Cambridge University, in 1932, was Bellevue Hospital, in New York, in 1936, and this was not his last time in a hospital drying out. He was destined to endure the humiliations of the addict.

Not long after hitting the street again, he began a novel, never published,* never really finished, with the disturbing and beautifully resonant title *Lunar Caustic*. Lowry used some of it in *Under the Volcano*. It says something about the level of his confidence—away from the writing table—that he believed Charles Jackson's *The Lost Weekend* (not a bad book at all) had obviated his work and wrote that author to say so.

Writers with problems like Lowry's sometimes produce work that is narcissistic and entirely self-referential. In *Under the Volcano* Lowry used the grim experiences he had gone through to express his love for the world. He applied his considerable learning and generosity of spirit to a hundred things beyond his own despair, even if the experience of despair informs it. The book addresses a universe containing far more than himself, and the characters are much more than aspects of Lowry, though of course they are that also. It is full of politics. There are many references to the Spanish Civil War and the rise of fascism, which plays a considerable part in the story. There are his characters' reflections on world war, his own rejection of communism, and the acceptance of a truth embodied in a phrase that occurs again and again in the novel: "No se puede vivir sin amor." One cannot live without love.

---

*Stone is mistaken on this point: there was a 1963 edition of *Lunar Caustic*, published by Jonathan Cape, which was also included with another work of Lowry's in a 1979 Penguin Modern Classics volume. —*Ed.*

As Auden wrote, "Time loves language." It forgives much in exchange, he says. So we pardon Lowry his unhappy life. The alcohol was bad luck. He believed that the experience of life was a labyrinth at the heart of which identity dwelled, and he lost himself in his own darkness.

—Not previously published, 2009

Coda

When I was fifteen years old, Thomas Wolfe was my idol. He was my apostle. Yes, I remember, "O lost, and by the wind grieved, ghost, come back again." It used to be one of my comic recitations.

When I became a man, I learned that Wolfe was to be put off as a childish thing. He was so orotund and portentous. In fact, I no longer have the heart to laugh so coldly at his incantatory verses. Not quite, not altogether. I think I mention somewhere that my mother sent Jack Kerouac's *On the Road* to me when I was in the service. As it happens, it was my mother, years before, who insisted that I read *Look Homeward, Angel.* A concurrence there, certainly. Bless her scattered mad Irish bones, she lived by the books. I remember from infancy strange words she spoke. ASOKA. TURGENEV. When we last met, we two, she was a crazy retired New York schoolteacher, on and off the sauce. God forgive me, I pretty much put her aside as well. Selfish things some of us do. She brought me up to think I was so terrific I didn't have time for her.

Wolfe wrote, "Man was born to live, to suffer, and to die . . .

There is no denying this in the final end. But we must . . . deny it all along the way." I will let Wolfe take the rap for that, with its obviousness and preachiness. Except amen. Sometimes we have to pause to hear the obvious.

The following is a portion of folk wisdom, and like all of that, it may have none or the flimsiest truth. They say that among the suffering ill, the Jews, on the one hand, complain incessantly. The Irish, on the other, deny feeling any pain at all.

This has nothing, understand, to do with who's tougher. Because, Christ, I think we all know by now how tough we all are, which is plenty and not enough. The reason for the difference, they say, is this: The Jews believe they can make things better, and with effort, reason, and argument can change the world. Even a little pointless agitation can't hurt. The Irish think they know that nothing under the rain will change, from this time until the last. So they deny their pain, lest it be increased on them by perverse strangers. When at last, trained to be each his own and her own stranger, they act on pain scalded in silence, they can do heartless, spiteful things.

I presume to say these things, having acquired a variety of genetic material out of the dark past. So I appropriate to myself a variety of inappropriate opinions. As a reasonably obscure writer with a small, loyal band of readers on whose love I have lived, as I see it, I wish I had done more. I live in hope, as may surprise some. It isn't despair so much that interests me. I know the line about Thomashefsky's deathbed: Dying is easy, comedy is hard. Let me say that I interpret the actor's joke as artistic metaphor. Before death I have nothing to offer but dread reverence. But the practice of hope, of life against death, of edges and surviving, were what I wanted to write about.

Except that we are all, against our will, adventurers. It was not so much the adventurer's edge — though who, coming after Hemingway, could resist trying themselves against that? But I've spent considerably more time trying to stay awake in quiet rooms than spying on birds, let alone lions. When you have read this through you will have a sense of how drug-ridden, boozy, and wasted a lot of this life has been. When I thought of beginning this coda about Wolfe's reference to suffering, it was of drugs and alcohol I was thinking.

The edges I pursued were of the mind and heart, because I believed they were where insight resided. Insight was my God when I felt deserted. I fell in love with the word in William James or somewhere, with the thing itself in Joyce or somewhere. It was survival, I thought.

Death is hardying. No going back. I happened on the quote from Wolfe in a Sunday supplement, because it's been a long time since I learned about life from Eugene and Ben in Altamont, Catawba. As I write it here, I wish I could tell you, all my beloved readers, the meaning of life. It is to my beloved readers over the years, whom I loved from afar and whose love kept me going, that I am speaking now. So many of you never let me down, whereas: I did you at times. Forgive me, but hold it against my account.

I'm a pretty sensible person in a lot of ways, very much as so many of you are sensible . . . And yet.

I would have given you the meaning of life if I could. My friend and colleague Kesey certainly tried, the MOL, wrapped. Two deluded American writers at the end of the worst century in human history (pray God), with no sense of their place, no artistic modesty. It was as it should be.

I gave you everything I found out, as elegantly, concisely, and clearly as I could present it. You will know that. I pray we are better off. And speaking of prayer, I claim not to be sliding into megalomania. (Is that how it's approached, a slippery slope?) Neither do I end this coda as a farewell. It may be that. It's not meant to be.

What I hope for is that I may keep pursuing, go on loving you, having you go on loving me. I have some tales and want you all around, and more of you.

Meaning of life? As Chico Marx once remarked, "There ain't no Sanity Clause." Perhaps it was rash of me to describe the fisher of Leviathan as a GIANT INVISIBLE BABYLONIAN PAPERWEIGHT. I propose to go on serving, to serve better. God must, in appallingly stranger mercy, understand that he is the one joke by which we live and that he, agent or principal, is at the center of it.

—Not previously published, circa 2013

Credits

appeared in the March 1, 1983, issue of *Esquire;* "The Holy War" first appeared in the October 25, 2001, issue of *Rolling Stone,* "Disruption" first appeared in the August 31, 2013, edition of *Vanity Fair;* "Keeping the Future at Bay" first appeared in the November 1988 issue of *Harper's Magazine;* "East-West Relation" first appeared in the November 1989 issue of *Harper's Magazine;* "A Higher Horror of the Whiteness" first appeared in the December 1986 issue of *Harper's Magazine;* "The Morning After" first appeared in the November 1986 issue of *Harper's Magazine;* "Havana Then and Now" first appeared in the March 1992 issue of *Harper's Magazine;* "Jerusalem Has No Past" first appeared in the May 3, 1998, issue of the *New York Times Magazine;* "Changing Tides" first appeared in the April 24, 1988, issue of the *New York Times Magazine;* "Under the Tongue of the Ocean" first appeared in the June 6, 1999, issue of the *New York Times Magazine;* "Does America Still Exist?" first appeared in the March 1984 edition of *Harper's Magazine;* "The Reason for Stories" first appeared in the June 1986 edition of *Harper's Magazine;* "What Fiction Is For" first appeared in *Bohemian Club Library Notes,* no. 78; "The Man Who Turned On the Here" first appeared in *One Lord, One Faith, One Cornbread,* edited by Fred and Ed McClanahan, published 1973 by Anchor Books; "The Way the World Is" first appeared in *Once a Catholic,* edited by Peter Occhiogrosso, published 1987 by Houghton Mifflin Harcourt; "In Silence" first appeared in *Why I Write,* edited by Will Blythe, published 1999 by Hachette.